FAITH

FAITH

Louis Jacobs

BASIC BOOKS, INC.

Publishers • New York

For Ivor and Tirza

Contents

v

CONTENTS

Preface

M ANY books have been written in English on the meaning, nature and life of faith and the problems to which these give rise. It is difficult to assess the extent to which we are today committed to religious belief but there is an obvious interest in religion and in basic religious issues. This book considers belief in God from the Jewish point of view.

The vast majority of contemporary volumes on belief in God are written either from a Christian standpoint or as a direct reaction to it. Where the author's background is Christian, naturally the categories used are derived from the Christian tradition. There is rarely a hint that Jewish thinkers throughout the ages have been no less passionately concerned, as sincerely dedicated, as daringly speculative, as their Christian counterparts. On the Jewish side today there is an unfortunate suspicion of theological thinking, which is only gradually allowing serious reflection on the significance of Judaism as a religion.

No Jewish writer on faith can afford to ignore the many extremely able and valuable discussions of faith by non-Jews, or apologise for considering them. The God in whom Jews believe is King of the Universe. The great themes of faith are universal, the concern of all Theists. Nevertheless, the Christian concept of God, insofar as one can speak of a concept of God, is at variance with the Jewish. The insights provided by distinguished Jewish thinkers are vital for the Jew and may frequently also be of help to non-Jewish Theists. Maimonides, as Aquinas, is God-intoxicated and it is unforgivable to imply that Israel, which brought God to mankind, has nothing more to offer on the fundamental principle of Theistic faith.

PART I

Introductory

Chapter 1

The Nature of Faith

IN the *Jewish Chronicle* of Dec. 11th, 1964, it is reported that an American Rabbi declared himself to be an atheist but of the 'sophisticated' theoretical kind. 'Personal Comment' of the same issue, remarked that by continuing to serve as a Rabbi the American evidently believed in organised religion even though he did not believe in God. This is a good illustration of the way in which the term 'belief' can be used in two different ways. When it is said of the Rabbi that he did not believe in God, the meaning is that he did not believe *that* God exists. But when it is said that he believed in organised religion, the meaning can hardly be that he believed organised religion exists, since this is self-evident. The meaning is that he had confidence in organised religion, that he saw value in it, even without God. He believed *in* it.

Or consider these two affirmations: 'I believe in ghosts'; 'I believe in the policy of the Labour Party'. The first is an affirmation that there are ghosts, that these are real beings who can appear to the living, not mere subjects of chilling tales or part of folklore and superstition. There is no suggestion of the trustworthiness or reliability of ghosts. The second affirmation is one of trust and confidence. Even the most rabid opponent of Socialism would not deny that the Labour Party has a policy, even though he will think it a pretty poor one. Belief in the policy of the Labour Party expresses faith that the policy is beneficial to the country, that it will prove itself in practice, that it will work. The first proposition is a 'belief *that* . . .', the second a 'belief *in* . . .'.

A 'belief *in* . . .' proposition always presupposes a 'belief *that . . .'* proposition. I cannot believe in the trustworthiness of my friend, for instance, unless I first believe that he and his trustworthiness are real and have been united in the past. My belief in him implies that he will be equally reliable in the future. 'Belief *that . . .'* on the other hand, need not involve any kind of 'belief *in*'. Hamlet's belief that he had seen his father's ghost was not in itself sufficient ground for trusting the ghost's tragic tale and advice.

'Belief *that . . .'* is chiefly a matter of the intellect. The man who believes in ghosts does so because the arguments for their existence convince him. Even if his belief is not based on a careful weighing of the evidence, even if it is the result of a 'hunch', his mind is satisfied that the 'hunch' is correct. Emotional factors are not, of course, absent. He may wish to believe in ghosts. The conviction that there are ghosts may, for some reason, be emotionally more satisfying than the conviction that they do not exist. But the affirmation is more mental than emotional or moral.

On the other hand, 'belief *in . . .'* is primarily a matter of the moral will. The man who believes in his friend (or in himself) does so not so much because he has weighed dispassionately all the evidence for trustworthiness but because it seems right to him to place his trust in that which is worthy of his trust as he sees it. Moreover, the very attitude of trust in one's friend may itself summon forth a response on the part of the friend and so be responsible for the vindication of trust. 'Belief *that . . .'* involves the appropriation of a truth. 'Belief *in . . .'* involves the determination to act on the truth one has seen. It follows that there can be no command to 'believe *that . . .'* But 'belief *in . . .'* can be commanded. We can meaningfully be ordered to be loyal to the truth we have seen just as we can be commanded to obey any other moral imperative.

When the famous Jewish mediaeval philosopher, Moses Maimonides (1135-1204), understood the first of the Ten Commandments as a command to believe that there is a God he was severely criticised on the ground that such a command is logically absurd. If belief is present no command is necessary. If it is absent there is no one to do the commanding. But, apart from this, there cannot be a command to believe that there is a God because 'belief *that* . . .' cannot be commanded.[1]

The truth of the matter is that not only is there no command in the Bible to believe in God but the Hebrew word for 'faith' (*emunah*) always refers, in the Bible, to 'belief *in* . . .', never to 'belief *that* . . .'. When the word is used to denote belief in God it is always in the sense of belief in God's power to help, of confidence and trust in Him, of reliance on His word. In order to appreciate this it is necessary to grasp the reality that, however we understand the phenomenon, the Biblical writers had no doubts of God's existence. His was an all-pervading Presence. He was part of their lives. He had guided their ancestors, and He was guiding them now. He was as real to them as their families and friends. His voice could be heard in the storm and wind, His footprints seen in human history. But trusting in Him, relying on His guidance, obeying the moral demands He made on man, this was a very different thing. The Biblical authors recognised that there is an element of perversity in human nature which all too frequently prevents man from acting on the truth he has seen. There was no tension for the Biblical writers around the belief *that* there is a God. Neither they nor those to whom their words were addressed ever conceived of denying His existence. In those far-off days theoretical atheism was unknown. But there was a good deal of tension around belief and trust *in* God. Indeed, all the spiritual drama of the Bible, all its moral pain and anguish as well as its grandeur and challenge, stem from the creative tensions inseparable from man's inner struggle to live by that which he knows to be true but finds hard to follow.

The Hebrew word *emunah*, denoting trust, confidence in, reliance on someone or something, is connected etymologically with the word *amen* (Amen) and the word for 'truth', *emeth*. The meaning behind all three words is one of affirmation, steadfastness and perseverance. A good illustration of the Biblical usage is Exodus 14:31: *'And Israel saw the great*

---

[1] See Maimonides' *'Sepher Ha-Mitzwoth'*, *Mitzwath Aseh*, I, Part II, pp. 3-4 and commentaries. Some of the commentators defend Maimonides by suggesting that he means that the command is not to believe but to keep the belief alive in Israel. On the whole question of the two kinds of belief see the stimulating discussion by H. H. Price: 'Belief "In" and Belief "That",' in 'Religious Studies', Vol. 1, No. 1.

work which the Lord did upon the Egyptians, and the people feared the Lord; and they believed in the Lord, and in His servant Moses.' Belief here *(wa-yaaminu)* cannot possibly mean 'belief *that . . .'.* According to the narrative, even before their deliverance at the shores of the Red Sea the Israelites did not doubt the *existence* of Moses. They knew Moses was leading them but they lacked confidence in his leadership, and were uncertain that he was the deliverer God had promised. When Israel walked safely through the waters which drowned their foes their doubts were silenced. They now believed *in* Moses. And by the same token the verse on their belief in God refers to the Israelites' reliance on God as their Redeemer from bondage. They had come to trust in Him.

Similarly, Scripture says of Abraham, when he trusts in God's promise to give him a son and multiply his seed, *'And he believed (we-heemin) in the Lord; and He counted it to him for righteousness'* (Gen 15: 6). Abraham's attitude of trust had a moral quality. It was an act of righteousness. This attitude of trust in what is worthy of it is implied by the Psalmist when he proclaims of God's commandments: *'Teach me good discernment and knowledge; for I have believed (heemanti) in Thy commandments'* (Ps. 119: 66).

It is worth noting that the idea of trust implied in the word *emunah* refers in the Bible to the relationship between two human beings as well as to that between God and man, as in the verse: *'And Achish believed (wa-yaamen) David'* (1 Sam. 2: 12). It follows from the Biblical usage that the author of the book of Proverbs is thinking more of an over-enthusiastic mis-application of trust than of credulity, in the verse: *'The simpleton believeth (yaamin) every word'* (Prov. 14: 15). The simpleton of Proverbs is not so much the prey of superstition as the natural victim of the confidence trickster.

Furthermore, the word *emunah* is used of God in the Bible. It is obviously grotesque to speak of God as 'believing'; but to speak of Him as trustworthy is valid. Man is justified in plac-ing his confidence in God because He can be relied upon. Thus the Psalmist says: *'To declare Thy lovingkindness in the morning, And Thy faithfulness (we-emunathka) in the night seasons'* (Ps. 92: 3). In life's morning, when all is bright, man's attention is focused on God's mercy. In the darkness of

6

night, when mercy is obscured, man yet relies on God's faithfulness. In the same spirit the Psalmist says of God: *'All his work is done in faithfulness'* (*be-emunah*) (Ps. 33:4). And the Deuteronomist speaks of Him as *'A God of faithfulness* (*emunah*) *and without iniquity'* (Deut. 32:4).[2]

It would never have occurred to the Biblical writers to attempt to prove God's existence. They were aware of Him as experienced reality. This, no doubt, seems strange to moderns. How could the ancients have had so powerful a conviction that God *is* that it was never questioned as it is today. But this fact is clear beyond doubt to anyone who takes the trouble to read the Bible carefully. The unbeliever will explain this away in naturalistic terms; that in a pre-scientific age the world is inevitably thought of as peopled with spirits or (at a more advanced stage) with a Great Spirit. The believer will not necessarily reject such explanations entirely but will view this very phenomenon as part of God's self-revelation. Thus, for him, the awareness of God's constant Presence by the Biblical authors is not a mere subjective feeling but a reflection of ultimate reality.

The post-Biblical Jews, during the period of the return and down through the Rabbinic period, were the heirs to Biblical thinking in this matter. In the vast Rabbinic literature, too, God is so real and His presence so vividly experienced (Max Kadushin has coined the expression 'normal mysticism' for this phenomenon) that the Rabbis never seem to have been moved to try to prove God's existence. As for the Biblical authors so for the Rabbis *emunah* is 'belief *in* . . .', never 'belief *that* . . .'. George Foot Moore, after surveying the references to faith in early Rabbinic literature, rightly says: 'In conclusion it may not be superfluous to remark that the words for faith in the literature and thought of this age are not used in the concrete sense of creed, beliefs entertained—or to be entertained—about God.'[3]

Many illustrations can be given of the Rabbinic use of the

---

[2] *Cf.* the following Biblical passages: Ex. 4:1, 5, 8-9; 19:9; Num. 20:12; Deut. 9:23; 28:66; II Sam. 20:19; II Kings 12:16; 17:14; 22:7; Is. 11:5; 43:10; Hos. 2:22; Hab. 2:4; Ps. 33:4; 78:22, 23; 106:24; 119:30; II Chron. 20:20 and the article 'Faith' in Kittel's 'Dictionary of the New Testament' by Rudolf Bultmann and A. Weiser.

[3] 'Judaism', Vol. II, p. 238.

word *emunah* for belief and confidence in God or in some person, idea or object. To mention just a few of these, on judgment day, said a Rabbi (*Sabb* 31a), among the questions that will be put to man is: 'Did you conduct your business affairs faithfully?' (*be-emunah*) i.e. reliably, honestly, in a trustworthy fashion. Another Rabbi remarked that God enjoins Israel to spend lavishly on food, wine and good things for the festivals: *'Have faith in Me (heeminu li) and I will pay your debts'* (*Betz.* 15b). In a somewhat cryptic passage (*Taan.* 8a) it is said: 'If this is the case with one who trusts (*maamin*) in the weasel and the well how much more so if one trusts (*maamin*) in the Holy One, blessed be He!' The tradition recorded by the standard commentators is that the reference here is to an ancient love story in which a young man plighted his troth to a maiden, calling upon a weasel and a well to be his witnesses. These avenged her when he failed to honour his promise (the weasel bit him and he fell into the well).

The Talmud (*Hull.* 57b) refers to a certain teacher who is described as an 'experimenter' because he preferred to test things by experience instead of taking them on trust. When he came to the verse: *'Go to the ant, thou sluggard; consider her ways and be wise: which having no chief, overseer or ruler, provideth her bread in the summer'* (Prov. 6: 6-8), this ancient scientist resolved to try to discover empirically whether it is true that the ants have no king. He spread his coat over an anthill so as to cause a shadow. When one of the ants emerged he marked it for the purpose of subsequent identification. The ant returned, evidently to inform the other ants that the sun had gone down. The ants came out to see what had happened but by this time the Rabbi had removed his cloak, whereupon the other ants set upon the marked ant and killed it for misleading them. This provided the Rabbi with the proof he needed that Solomon was right to say that the ants have no ruler. For if the ants have a king surely he would have been consulted before the execution was carried out. Another Rabbi, however, objected to the conclusiveness of the test. The king may have been with the ants, he argued, and may have been consulted, or they may have received the king's permission previously to act in this way when the need arose, or the action may have taken place during an interregnum. Consequently, the empirical test fails to prove the case and one must rely on the 'trustworthiness (*hemanutha*) of Solomon', the traditional author of the book of Proverbs. It might seem at first glance that the reference in this quaint passage is to a 'belief *that* . . .', and this would contradict our argument that this type of belief is never referred to by the term *emunah* in Rabbinic literature. But a careful examination of the passage shows that the concern here is not whether ants have a king but whether Solomon is to be trusted when he declares that ants have a king. The 'experimenter' (Heb. *askan bi-debharim*, lit., 'one who busies himself with facts' instead of resting content with the theories provided by the tradition) wanted to discover the truth for himself. The implied criticism by the other Rabbi is that such a procedure casts reflections on Solomon's reliability. Since in any event no empirical test is conclusive, he says, the only thing to do is to rely on Solomon's trustworthiness. Such reliance, well-founded from the point of view of the Rabbis, is obviously a 'belief *in* . . .'. It is as if the Rabbi is saying (it is irrelevant that this is not our point of view): Solomon's wisdom as recorded in Scripture has never let us down, why not rely on it here?

As in the Bible, the term *emunah* is used in the Rabbinic literature of God. One interpretation of the verse (Deut. 32:4) '*A God of faithfulness*' (*emunah*) is a 'trusting God', a God who has faith in His creation: 'He believed in the world (*she-heemin ha-olam*) and so He created it' (*Siphre ad loc.*).

For us, 'weak in faith' generally has a cognitive connotation. The man 'weak in faith' cannot quite make up his mind that there is a God, and he alternates between belief and unbelief. But the expression, occurring frequently in the Rabbinic literature, 'lacking in faith' (*mehusar emunah*) or 'those little in faith' (*mi-ketane amanah*) (corresponding to 'ye of little faith' in Matthew 6:30) denotes weakness in the attitude of trust. For instance, R. Eliezer the Great said: 'Whoever has bread in his basket and yet says: "What shall I eat tomorrow," belongs to the ranks of those small in faith' (*Sot.* 48b). His trust in God is weak. Since God has today provided him with food he should not lack confidence in God's power to provide for the future. Noah was 'weak in faith' because until the last moment he doubted God's word that the deluge would come. (Gen. R. 32.)[4]

In all this we are far from suggesting that the Rabbis were unconscious of beliefs of the 'belief *that* . . .' kind. But for these they did not use the word *emunah*, 'faith', but words suggesting knowledge or truth, e.g. God's *Torah* is true. As we shall see, the mediaeval contrast between *emunah* ('faith') and *kephirah* ('denial') in a cognitive sense arose as a result of a completely new meaning given to faith. In the Middle Ages faith came to mean 'belief *that* . . .' rather than 'belief *in* . . .'. During the Rabbinic period terms from the root *kaphar* were, indeed, used as the opposite of 'faith' but of faith in the 'belief *in* . . .' sense. The *kopher* was the opposite of the *maamin*. The latter placed his trust in God, the former was lacking entirely in such trust. On the whole (without it being stated in the sources in quite this systematic way) the Rabbinic analysis of 'faith' recognised three stages in the matter of trust in God: one who had perfect trust in God was a *maamin*, a man of faith. The man whose trust was weak and casual was 'small in faith'. The man who had no trust in God was a *kopher*, a 'denier', not so much in the sense of theoretical rejection as of practical failure to live as if this were the truth. The *kopher* may have entertained an abstract belief that there is a God but his belief had no effect on his life, he lived as if he had no God. The following examples will help to make this clearer.

A homily on God's nearness to the poor says that God is quite different from a human being who acknowledges his rich relations but denies (*kopher*) his poor ones (*Jes. Ber.* IX, 1); denial clearly does not refer to a disbelief in the existence of the poor relations but to a refusal to help or even to accept them. In another passage (*Sabb.* 116a) the saying of R. Tarphon is quoted that if he were fleeing for his life he would prefer to seek sanctuary and protection in a heathen temple than in the home of Jewish sectarians, since the heathen do not recognise God and deny (*kopherim*) Him whereas the

[4] *Cf.* the following passages: *Mekhilta, Beshallah*, to Ex. 14:15; *Ber.* 24b; 29a; *Pes.* 118b; *Meg.* 6a; *Hag*, 8a; 14a; *Sot.* 46b; *B.M.* 49a; *B.B.* 8a; 75a; *Makk.* 24a; *Tam.* 28a; *Ex. R.* 22; *Yalkut, Hosea* 519; Psalms 674.

sectarians deny (*kopherim*) while recognising Him, which is worse. Clearly in this passage 'belief *that* . . .' is referred to, by speaking of the *recognition* of God. It is possible, such is the implication, to recognise God (to acknowledge that there is a God) and yet to deny Him, (be disloyal to His will).

However, when using the term *kephirah* ('denial') for a rejection of certain basic principles of Judaism other than belief in God the Rabbis sometimes refer rather to the cognitive aspects of disbelief than to the moral and volitional.[5] There is nothing surprising about this. For the Rabbis belief that God existed was so real as to be utterly beyond doubt. For then the drama of faith was acted out in the sphere of 'belief *in* . . .' Moreover theoretical atheism was virtually unknown among Jews in Rabbinic times. But one who lacked faith in some basic principle of Judaism (other than belief in God) may have failed either because he refused to act on a truth he acknowledged or because he acknowledged no such truth. With regard to belief in God, however, theoretical atheism, even by unbelievers in other principles of Judaism, appears to have been as unknown to the Rabbis as to the Biblical authors. For example, the references in the Rabbinic literature to one who 'denies the root principle'[6] (*kopher ba-ikkar*) seem to be not to one who denies that God exists but to one who denies that God is concerned with the deeds of men, or to one who wishes to dissociate himself entirely from the Jewish Community.

A great change came about in the Middle Ages. Faced with the challenge of Greek and Arabic philosophy (including philosophical denials of God's existence), Zoroastrianism and its offshoots, Christianity and Islam, and, from within, the rejection by the Karaites of the Rabbinic tradition, the traditional Jewish teachers were obliged to cultivate a more systematic approach to the whole question of Jewish beliefs. Not that all the challenges were new. Zoroastrianism for instance produces echoes in the later parts of the Bible and

[5] E.g. 'The sectarians deny the resurrection of the dead' (*R.H.* 17a); 'Whoever denies idolatry is called a Jew' (*Meg.* 13a); 'Job denied the resurrection of the dead' (*B.B.* 16a); 'The nations of the world do not deny that God created the world' (*Midrash* Psalms, 19). The term *kopher* is also used of a man who denies that he owes money (*B.M.* 3a).

[6] *Siphra, Behukothai,* 26; *Sanh.* 38b; *B.B.* 16a; Eccl. R.7.

polemics against it and the Christian faith occur periodically in the Rabbinic literature. In an indirect way the Rabbis faced, too, the implications of Greek thought. Two things were, however, new. First, the combination of vigorous and deeply disturbing challenges demanded a more detailed and a more comprehensive defence. Secondly, the systematic nature of the rival philosophies demanded a systematic refutation. A systematic Jewish philosophy or theology which owed much to Islamic patterns was consequently developed. A systematic discussion of the belief in God's existence as a rational philosophical viewpoint became the urgent demand.

In this period 'belief *in* . . .' yields increasingly to 'belief *that* . . .' as the chief concern of Jewish thinkers. The process receives its culmination in the *Ani Maamin* ('I Believe') formulation of the articles of the Jewish faith. This, modelled almost certainly on Islamic catechisms, first appeared in 1517 and became incorporated into many liturgies.

> 'I believe with perfect faith *that*
> the Creator, blessed be His name, is
> the Author and Guide of everything that
> has been created, and *that* He alone has
> made, does make, and will make all things.'

It would be wrong to maintain that the 'belief *in* . . .' was entirely overlooked during the mediaeval period although it did tend to become relegated to moralistic rather than philosophic literature.[7] New problems, such as the relationship between faith and reason, become more urgent. For 'faith' (*emunah*) has now become identified with the belief *that* there is a God. The tensions of faith were shifted from the moral and the volitional to the cognitive. The new tendency is perfectly obvious in all the great works of Jewish apologetics produced in this period. These were written chiefly to further 'belief *that* . . .' and to provide a rational demonstration of the truth of Judaism. Their authors appear

[7] In Bahya Ibn Pakudah's 'Duties of the Heart', for instance, the first 'Gate' deals with the philosophical understanding of the existence of God and His unity while trust in God is considered in the moralistic part of the book ('*Shaar Ha-Bittahon*').

to have held that if this great work is carried to a successful conclusion the 'belief *in* . . .' could safely be left to take care of itself. When the citadel itself is attacked its defenders cannot be too concerned with the polite conduct appropriate to a more peaceful state. Volitional response gave way more and more to intellectual attempts at proving the truth though, needless to say, this had a moral fervour of its own.

Faith is no longer chiefly a matter of trust and confidence, and disbelief a matter of lack of confidence. For faith now becomes assent to certain propositions; disbelief a rejection of certain propositions. The relationship between faith and reason had been no problem for the Biblical authors and their Rabbinic heirs. For them faith meant trust in God and had little to do with cognition. Reason could neither support nor reject except insofar as it is reasonable to act on the truth one has seen. It was otherwise during the Middle Ages. Faith having become chiefly a matter of accepting certain propositions as true, had to come to grips with reason. For reason has a good deal to say about truth and falsehood and there were some whose reason compelled them to accept a different set of propositions. Even after valiant attempts had been made to demonstrate that faith was supported by reason there arose the new problem of why, in that case, was it necessary for the truth to be revealed by God in a special revelation.

More and more in this period *bittahon* ('trust'), used in both Bible and Talmud as a synonym for *emunah* ('faith'), came to be used on its own to denote the trusting aspect of faith,[8] with *emunah* reserved for the new meaning of 'belief *that* . . .'. By a new meaning we do not suggest that a completely fresh interpretation was given consciously to the older term. 'Belief *that* . . .' had, of course, been implied in the older use of the term. It is impossible to have an attitude of trust towards a non-existent being. But what had formerly been only implicit now became explicit. Faith was now the intellectual perception of truth in propositional form.

[8] Bahya, *op. cit.*, Bahya Ibn Asher: '*Kad Ha-Kemah*', *s.v. emunah* and *bittahon*; pseudo-Nahmanides: '*Sepher Ha-Emunah We-Ha-Bittahon*' in 'Collected Writings of Nahmanides' ed. B. Chavel, Vol. II, pp. 341f. Max Kadushin: 'The Rabbinic Mind', pp. 42-43, has argued convincingly that in the Rabbinic literature *emunah* means general trust in God, not necessarily implying trust for personal security, whereas *bittahon* is more personal.

The mediaeval thinkers were not aware that there had been a change in attitude. The whole concept of historical development, of ideas changing from age to age in response to environmental factors, was foreign to them. They saw nothing anachronistic in using Biblical and Rabbinic references to *emunah* to convey those ideas they themselves read into the term and, so far as we can judge, they believed their meaning was the original one.

Maimonides' statement of the fundamental principle of the Jewish faith is indicative of the new approach. 'The first precept. This is the command which He commanded us to believe in Deity (*be-haamanuth ha-elohuth*). This means that we must believe (*shenaamin*) that there is a Supreme Cause who is the Maker of all things.'[9] Elsewhere Maimonides writes:[10] 'The foundation of foundations and the pillar of the sciences is to know that there is a Primal Being and it is He who brings all things into existence.' Whereas in the Bible and for the Rabbis belief in God is different from knowledge of God,[11] for Maimonides belief and knowledge refer to the same thing and are both a matter of cognition. To believe in God is to know that there is a God. It also follows both from Maimonides' observations here and in other works that man should try to arrive at the truth that God exists by means of his reasoning powers. In the 'Guide for the Perplexed' Maimonides states that for the masses the only way to faith is through tradition whereas the more advanced thinker has a duty to attain the truth by the use of his unaided reason.[12] Bahya Ibn Pakudah, in 'Duties of the Heart', similarly holds that it is man's duty to reason for himself that God exists.[13] Other mediaeval thinkers, notably Judah Ha-Levi,[14] consider belief based on tradition to be superior to belief attained through reason. Belief based on tradition can never be refuted whereas belief based on reason can be contradicted by reason and is

[9] 'Sepher Ha-Mitzwoth', Mitzwath Aseh, I.

[10] Yad, 'Yesode Ha-Torah', I, 1.

[11] The Biblical 'knowledge of God' includes the adequate relationship with Him through moral conduct, through 'walking in His ways'. See Jer. 2 : 8; 9 : 23; Prov. 3 : 6; I Chron. 28 : 9.

[12] 'Guide', I, 33.

[13] 'Duties of the Heart', 'Shaar Ha-Yihud', Chapter 3.

[14] 'Kuzari', I, 25; V. 21.

consequently never secure against refutation. R. Aaron Ha-Levi of Barcelona, the author of '*Sepher Ha-Hinnukh*', adopts a midway position. Belief through tradition is wholly admirable and should not be treated with contempt but the highest order of belief is that reinforced by reason.[15] There is an interesting description of faith in this work: 'The meaning of faith is that man should fix it firmly in his heart that the truth is so and that it is quite impossible for it to be otherwise. If he is questioned on the subject he will reply always that this is his heart's belief, and that he is prepared to be killed rather than acknowledge the opposite. By saying this he actualises the potential and in this way the heart of faith is reinforced and becomes firmly fixed. I mean by this that the words of his mouth fulfil the resolve of his heart. Once he has the merit of ascending in the degrees of science so that his heart understands and his eyes see by incontrovertible proof that his belief is true and that it is impossible for it to be otherwise, he has fulfilled the precept of faith in the highest possible way.'

We shall later examine in greater detail these views of the mediaeval thinkers on faith versus tradition. It is sufficient here to note that even those thinkers who prefer to base faith on tradition are thinking of faith in its new, mediaeval connotation of 'belief *that* . . .'. The mediaeval debate is not concerned with the nature of faith but with the way to its attainment. For the Biblical authors' and the Rabbis' belief that God existed was taken for granted. It was a conviction apparently based on intuitive awareness or direct apprehension. It was part of their very lives and there was no need for them to 'attain' it. Tradition was as irrelevant to it as reason (at any rate on the conscious level, though subconsciously tradition played its part). They did not hold their belief because their fathers held it and did not normally seek to substantiate belief by an appeal to tradition. From this point of view the frequent mediaeval appeals to tradition are themselves untraditional!

Partly as a result of the weakening of the traditional proofs of God's existence by the critiques of Hume and Kant, and partly as a result of the new emphasis by religious existentialists on the need for involvement (all of which we shall consider later), many modern religious thinkers have been moved

[15] No. 25, pp. 76-77.

to work out an approach to faith which, in a sense, recaptures the Biblical view of faith as 'belief *in* . . .'. Without anticipating our later fuller discussion of religious existentialism, it suffices here to call attention to the fresh insight that, on any dynamic view of faith, it is impossible to separate 'belief *that* . . .' from 'belief *in* . . .'. It is now seen that far more is involved in the act of faith and trust than a mere formal assent to the proposition that there is a God, followed by a resolve to trust in Him. The two attitudes of assent and trust cannot be set out in neat chronological sequence but are bound up one with the other. The God arrived at simply as the conclusion of an argument is not the God of vital religion. The mediaeval thinkers were themselves deeply religious men and even though they give the impression of arguing objectively for God's existence, as they would for any other proposition, they were already, in actual fact, committed to the religious life. Logically an attitude of trust in God follows on the belief that He exists but, in practice, belief that there is a God and trust in Him are both part of that complex situation called encountering God. At least, this is how many religious existentialists see the man of faith's situation and there is some validity in their attitude. The man who reaches out in faith and trust because he is aware of his insufficiency and finiteness is helped by awareness to validate the argument for God's existence. Freud would say that this is no more than wishful thinking: because I feel that I need a God I invent one. (A later chapter is devoted to the consideration of Freud's views.) But Freud prejudges the issue on non-psychoanalytical grounds. He assumes that there is no God. The believer sees his very attitude of trust, his very hunger for the divine, so often felt only faintly and sporadically, as part of the validation of the argument. His hunger implies for him that it is capable of satisfaction because reality is so constituted that it can afford him that satisfaction.

Religious existentialism and the whole present-day emphasis on 'belief *in* . . .' is, in a sense, a return to Biblical categories of thinking. Yet it is not a complete return. The past cannot so simply be effaced. The significant difference between the Biblical and modern approach in this matter (both different from the mediaeval) is that for the Biblical authors the question whether God really existed was never really posed as a live question. It was perfectly evident to them that He existed. As we have repeatedly tried to show, they would never have thought of doubting that the Being with whom they had such an intimate personal relationship existed. He was more real to them than the material world they experienced with their senses. The modern attitude seeks to return to the Biblical insight but it is a conscious return, a return in which it is acknowledged that for some men at least there is a query against God's existence.

The matter can be summed up as follows. There have been three stages in the history of faith: (1) The Biblical (and the Rabbinic) period in which 'belief *in* . . .' formed the centre of faith's tensions, with 'belief *that* . . .' taken for granted. (2) The mediaeval period which witnessed a shift in emphasis from 'belief *in* . . .' to 'belief *that* . . .'. At this time it is 'belief *in* . . .' which is allowed to take care of itself. Faith has become much more cognitive than volitional. (3) The modern period which witnesses a partial return to the first period's standpoint. 'Belief *in* . . .' and 'belief *that* . . .' are now seen as two sides of the same coin. 'Belief *in* . . .', or the attitude behind it, is seen as an essential ingredient in the life of faith. All that has so far been said is not, of course, an argument for faith or a defence of it. Our concern in this chapter has been only to describe the nature of faith as understood in different periods of Jewish thinking.

We might try to express these propositions in diagrammatic form.[16] Let belief that God exists be represented by a circle, and trust in God by a straight line. In the Biblical-Rabbinic period and in the mediaeval period the circle and the straight line were drawn distinct from one another. They represented two different areas of life. In the Biblical-Rabbinic period the circle was left alone, as it were. It was taken for granted and questioned by none. All the attention was focused on the straight line. In the Middle Ages the emphasis is shifted to the circle. In this period it is felt that if only the circle be firmly drawn the straight line will take care of itself. In the modern period the straight line is *inside* the circle. Neither straight line nor circle can be approached one without the other.

[16] See diagram on page 18.

But the diagram is still misleading in that it represents both circle and straight line as in the same dimension. In reality 'belief *in* . . .' is qualitatively different from 'belief *that* . . .', in a different dimension as it were. 'Belief *that* . . .' is cognitive, intellectual, propositional. 'Belief *in* . . .' moral, volitional, a response of the whole personality. The statement: 'I love X' is of a different order from the statement: 'There is a table in the room.' If it were possible on paper, a far better illustration would be to represent 'belief *in* . . .' not as a straight line flat on the page beside the circle but as a dagger cutting through the page.

(the wavy lines denote the tensions of faith, the particular emphasis)

(A) **Biblical-Rabbinic view**

(B) **Mediaeval view**

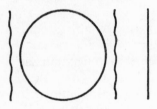

(C) **Modern view**

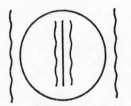

Chapter 2

The Meaning of Faith

I N the previous chapter we examined the two meanings of faith, 'belief *that* . . .' and 'belief *in* . . .', the first cognitive, the second volitional. Both ideas (belief that there is a God and trust in Him) imply that it is meaningful in the logical sense to speak of God. Many modern philosophers, particularly in Great Britain and the United States, while acknowledging that the concept of faith is logically meaningful, question whether the concept of faith's object, God, is logically meaningful. Does it make sense to speak of God? For these philosophers the question is not whether God's existence is true or false but whether the whole God concept has any meaning. Are we talking nonsense when we say that we believe in God? No modern discussion of faith can afford to neglect the careful consideration of this question. It has been pointed out that this, the latest challenge to religious belief, is more serious than the earlier challenges of atheism and agnosticism. The atheist denies that there is a God, the agnostic holds that we can never be sure that God exists. But if the whole concept lacks meaning it is as nonsensical to deny God's existence, or to be unsure of it, as to affirm it.

The new challenge came, in the first instance, from the ranks of the famous 'Vienna Circle' and was elaborated on by the Logical Positivists. Their views were made known in English by Professor A. J. Ayer in his 'Language, Truth and Logic'. Although the more extreme position has been abandoned, there is still much discussion around the meaning of religious language.[1]

[1] See A. J. Ayer: 'Language, Truth and Logic', 2nd ed., Gollancz, London, 1946; John Wisdom: 'Gods' in 'Philosophy and Psycho-Analysis', Blackwell, Oxford, 1953; F. Copleston: 'Contemporary Philosophy, Studies of Logical Positivism and Existentialism', Burns and Oates, London, 1956; Anthony Flew

The difficulty arises as a result of considerations as to what a logically meaningful statement involves. It is argued that statements are of two kinds. The first is analytical. Analytical statements, such as two and two make four, are meaningful but tautologous. Four is simply another way of saying two and two. Such statements do not purport to tell us anything about the external world. The second, the non-analytical, seeks to provide us with information about the world. Examples of this are: 'It will rain tomorrow'; 'There is a table in this room'; 'I can swim to the other side of the river'; 'There are intelligent beings on Mars'. The argument proceeds to demonstrate that this kind of statement is only logically meaningful if we know what would have to happen for it to be either true or false, which facts would count in its favour and which against it, how we would proceed to test its truth. This does not mean that we must be able to prove whether the statement is true or false, only that we must be able to see a possible way of testing it.

In our present state of technological advancement, for instance, we cannot actually carry out the test which would establish the truth or otherwise of the statement: 'There are intelligent beings on Mars'. But we can see even now how one *could* proceed to test it. Men would travel to Mars and would then either discover intelligent beings there, in which case the statement would be true, or, after careful searching, they would fail to discover any beings other than themselves, in

and Alasdair MacIntyre, ed.: 'New Essays in Philosophical Theology', SCM Press, London, 1955; Basil Mitchell, ed.: 'Faith and Logic', George Allen & Unwin, London, 1957; Ian Ramsey: 'Religious Language', SCM Press, London, 1957; E. L. Mascall: 'Words and Images', Longmans, Green, London, 1957; T. R. Miles: 'Religion and the Scientific Outlook', George Allen & Unwin, London, 1959; John Hick: 'Philosophy of Religion', Prentice-Hall, N.J., 1963 and ed.: 'The Existence of God', Macmillan, London and New York, 1964; Hugo Meynell: 'Sense, Nonsense and Christianity', Sheed and Ward, London and New York, 1964. There is an excellent survey of the field in Frederick Ferre: 'Language, Logic and God', Eyre and Spottiswoode, London, 1962. There is a comprehensive bibliography and notes on the whole question in: Paul Edwards and Arthur Pap, ed.: 'A Modern Introduction to Philosophy', The Free Press, Glencoe, Illinois, 1957, pp. 619-621 and a full bibliography in: F. B. Dilley: 'Metaphysics and Religious Language', Columbia University Press, New York and London, 1964. An important symposium is: Sidney Hook ed.; 'Religious Experience and Truth', Oliver and Boyd, Edinburgh, 1962.

which case the statement would be false. Consequently, even now, though we cannot say whether the statement is true or false, it is not meaningless.

But a statement which is so vague that it is impossible to see how it can be either verified or falsified is meaningless. The reason we cannot conceive how it can be tested is that, in reality, nothing is being presented for the test. The famous 'verification principle' does not claim that a statement incapable of verification (or falsification) is meaningless *because* of this but rather that since it cannot be verified (or falsified) it is too wide and too imprecise to have any meaning. If we said, for instance, 'There are grongs on Mars', before we could begin to discuss whether the statement is true or false we would have to know what 'grongs' are. A definition of 'grongs' is first called for and that definition must be sufficiently clear for us to be able to see what would count as evidence for their existence, what against their existence. A definition which left us as puzzled as we were in the beginning would be no definition at all. It would be no more than the substitution of an equally meaningless term, and since the operative word has no meaning the sentence as a whole is meaningless even though, at first glance, it looks like a proper sentence.

Jewish legend has it that Elijah the prophet appears to holy men to teach them the *Torah*. If then a man claims that he saw Elijah and if, by Elijah, he means the actual person who lived in the days of Ahab, and Elijah actually spoke to him with a physical voice, the claim is not meaningless, though probably false. Even though it is possible that a witness (because he lacked the requisite degree of sanctity and spiritual sensitivity) might not have seen the prophet, yet the claimant can test its truth. If he really saw and heard the prophet the claim is true, otherwise it is false. The statement is, consequently, meaningful for others, too, although they are not able to put the claim to the test. But if the claimant went on to say that by Elijah he does not mean a manifestation of the prophet capable of being seen with the physical eye and heard with the physical ear but a state of mind or soul which is 'called' the appearance of Elijah, before we could even begin to consider whether or not he is telling the truth we would have to know of what state of mind or soul he is speaking, of

21

how it differs from other states, of how *he himself* tested his experience. If his definition of 'seeing' Elijah was so vague as to cover almost any experience (or even a particular experience but one which could be explained quite adequately without having recourse to Elijah) we would conclude not that he is lying but talking nonsense, not necessarily in claiming to have an experience but in describing it as an appearance of Elijah.

This leads to the challenge of linguistic analysis to belief in God. What does the man who says 'I believe in God' mean? What does he mean by 'God'? The naïve believer may explain that by 'God' he means a colossal, superhuman being, sitting 'up there' on a throne surrounded by angels. Such a believer may admit that while man is on earth he cannot actually see God with his physical eyes but when he dies and goes to Heaven he will then see God. He will not attempt to explain the difficulty of seeing God with no physical eyes. A belief of this kind, no doubt entertained by few people, will be thought incredibly anthropomorphic but it is not logically meaningless. Just as the statement: 'There are intelligent beings on Mars' is logically meaningful because we know how it could be verified, so, too, the belief of the unsophisticated is meaningful. He knows perfectly well how his belief is to be verified; after death he will go 'up there' and see for himself.

It is more difficult for the sophisticated believer, who thinks of God in spiritual terms and as All-good and Omnipotent, to explain what he means by God.[2] All his statements about God will be qualified for fear of humanising his God-concept. When he says, for example, that God is good he will emphasise that he is using human language, since this is the only language he has, but that the term 'good' with its human associations cannot really be used of God who is beyond all human comprehension. Even to describe God as good or powerful, he will say, is to suggest a point of comparison between God and humans of whom these terms are used in our language.

[2] Howard W. Hintz ('Religious Experience and Truth', *op. cit.*, pp. 254-260) takes Paul Tillich to task for lack of clarity in definition and goes so far as to conclude that the beliefs of Billy Graham are more philosophically and logically tenable than those of Tillich, K. Nielson, in the same symposium, p. 278, remarks that when Tillich equates belief in God with 'ultimate concern' he makes the atheist, who also has 'ultimate concern', into a Theist. Nielson calls this 'conversion by re-definition'.

Furthermore, he will argue, although the fact of evil in the universe appears to contradict God's goodness, it is not really a contradiction. Many theologians even suggest that to say that God exists is a statement which requires considerable qualification since existence is a term applicable to humans and other creatures but inadmissible, because of its limiting connotation, when used of Ground of Being.

But, then, the argument proceeds, these constant qualifications of theological statements tend to make them so vague as to become meaningless. Statements compatible with everything in the universe are not real statements at all suffering 'the death of a thousand qualifications'. The theologians who make them do not seem able to state which facts would verify the statements and, more significantly, what would have to happen for the statements to be falsified. And a statement incapable of either falsification or verification though it may appear a proper statement is really only a jumble of words. The demand, it should be noted, is not for the proof or refutation of theological statements as they may not be forthcoming. But unless it can be shown what would constitute proof or refutation if it were forthcoming, the question of meaning is posed.

Anthony Flew, in the essay in which he coins the phrase 'the death of a thousand qualifications' writes: [3]

'Now it often seems to people who are not religious as if there were no conceivable events or series or events the occurrence of which would be admitted by sophisticated religious people to be a sufficient reason for conceding "There wasn't a God after all" or "God does not love us then". Someone tells us that God loves us as a father loves his children. We are reassured. But then we see a child dying of inoperable cancer of the throat. His earthly father is driven frantic in his efforts to help, but his Heavenly Father reveals no obvious signs of concern. Some qualification is made—God's love is "not merely a human love" or it is "an inscrutable love" perhaps—and we realize that such sufferings are quite compatible with the truth of the assertion that "God loves us as a father (but, of course . . .)"'.

[3] 'New Essays in Philosophical Theology', *op. cit.*, pp. 98-99.

23

We are reassured again. But then perhaps we ask: what is this assurance of God's (appropriately qualified) love worth, what is this apparent guarantee really a guarantee against? Just what would have to happen not merely (morally and wrongly) to tempt but also (logically and rightly) to entitle us to say "God does not love us" or even "God does not exist"? I therefore put to the succeeding symposiasts the simple central questions, "What would have to occur or to have occurred to constitute for you a disproof of the love of, or the existence of, God?"'

Defenders of theological language against this kind of critique have adopted two different attitudes. One group acknowledges the justice of the critique and maintains indeed, that religious language is logically meaningless. It is nonsense but certain kinds of 'nonsense' have value too. The other group denies the validity of the critique. This book, based as it is on traditional Jewish Theism, rejects the approach of the first group, but their views must be discussed before we turn to those of the second group.

Prominent among those who accept the view that religious language is non-cognitive is R. B. Braithwaite in his famous essay: 'An Empiricist's View of the Nature of Religious Belief'.[4] In Braithwaite's view, religious statements are not factually significant but they do possess ethical value. They have no meaning as statements about the facts of the universe but are a way of expressing one's intention to act in a certain way. On this view, when a man says that he believes in God he is really affirming that he intends to act in the way generally associated with belief in God (even though the actual statement: 'I believe in God' is logically meaningless). The statement is a 'nonsense' statement but one with much pragmatic value. Each religion has what Braithwaite calls its 'stories', the Old Testament and the Talmud for the Jew, the New Testament for the Christian, the Buddhist Scriptures for the Buddhist. Although these stories have no real reference to the facts of the universe they provide the context in which the adherents of the particular religion see their ethical duties.

[4] A critique of Braithwaite's position is found in Mascall: 'Words and Images', op. cit., pp. 49-62.

24

A study of human nature shows that man is capable of being inspired even by fictitious stories: Braithwaite gives the illustration of Bunyan's 'Pilgrim's Progress' recognised as a work of fiction and yet a powerful spur to the ethical life.

Moreover, according to Braithwaite, ethical statements, too, are subject to the same critique as religious statements. How would one go about verifying or falsifying the statement: 'It is wrong to steal'? What would have to happen to demonstrate the falsity of the statement: 'It is wrong to steal'? Even if no thief were caught the person making the statement would still hold fast to the view that it is wrong to steal, whereas those who opposed the statement would remain unconvinced even if every thief were caught. How, then, do the two differ except in matters of feeling? Thus, for Braithwaite, when a man says that it is wrong to steal this is really a declaration that he does not intend to steal. And when someone says: 'God has commanded us not to steal' he expresses his intention not to steal against the background of, and inspired by, the stories of his own religious tradition.

The main objection to Braithwaite's explanation of religious (and ethical) language is that religious believers do think that their beliefs are cognitive and more than a mere declaration that they intend to behave in a certain way. Even if Braithwaite were correct that 'belief in God' does no more than provide the 'story', it is clear that the religious believer does not himself see it in this way and is convinced that his beliefs do have factual content. Braithwaite is really maintaining that religious language should continue to be used even though we are now forced to admit that the language has no factual content. It is possible that many believers would agree with Braithwaite that if, indeed, there were no factual content to their belief they should still continue to use the language because of its value as a spur to conduct. But the majority of believers surely do not admit that they are in such desperate plight because of the modern analysis of religious language. It is certain that the vast majority of believers in the past did believe that their language was factually significant, and surely most believers today will prefer to resist the attack in some other way rather than allow their language to be deprived of its factual significance. This is to say nothing of that other objection which has been brought against Braithwaite. People do sometimes say: 'It is wrong to steal but I intend to do so.' But, on Braithwaite's view, this is a contradiction since, according to his analysis, the statement: 'It is wrong to steal' *means* 'I do not intend to steal'. Braithwaite might, however, counter this by saying that, in fact, when people speak in this way they are contradicting themselves without being aware of it.

Another exponent of the non-cognitive nature of religious language is R. M. Hare.[5] Hare contributes a new term to the discussion. People frequently have their own way of looking at things irrespective of the facts. Hare calls this a 'blick'. He gives the illustration of an undergraduate who is convinced that all dons are engaged in a conspiracy to kill him. Despite evidence presented to him of the inoffensiveness of dons he persists in his 'blick' that they intend murder. On this view religious statements are not assertions nor do they profess to give information regarding any facts about the universe. But they are in the nature of a 'blick' about life, and religious language is consequently significant in describing the 'blick' of religious people.

But here the same objection holds as to Braithwaite's view. Religious people have meant and do mean their religious statements as assertions and not merely as 'blicks'. Furthermore, Hare refers to a 'right' and 'wrong' 'blick', the undergraduate has a wrong 'blick' about dons, religious people believe that their 'blick' is the right one. But one cannot speak of 'right' and 'wrong' in this context without reintroducing the cognitive aspect of religious and moral language which Hare seeks to avoid.

We must turn, therefore, to the second group of thinkers who defend religious language as factually significant. There are a number of cogent arguments here and there is no reason why these should not be complementary. Basil Mitchell[6] argues, surely correctly, that it is simply not true to say, as for instance Flew does, that nothing *counts* for the believer

[5] 'New Essays in Philosophical Theology', *op. cit.*, pp. 99-103.
[6] *Ibid.*, pp. 103-105.

against God's goodness. If the believer's position was that nothing *counted* against the belief in God's goodness or His very existence then, indeed, a very good case could be made out for the contention that his beliefs are factually insignificant. But the truth is that while the believer does recognise that the existence of evil provides an argument against God's goodness or His existence, as a man of faith, committed to belief that God is good and that He exists, he refuses to renounce his belief, convinced that in a way he cannot at present understand how the fact of evil can be reconciled with the goodness of God.

Mitchell gives an illustration worthy of the great Jewish masters of the religious parable:

'In time of war in an occupied country, a member of the resistance meets one night a stranger who deeply impresses him. They spend the night together in conversation. The Stranger tells the partisan that he himself is on the side of the resistance—indeed that he is in command of it, and urges the partisan to have faith in him no matter what happens. The partisan is utterly convinced at that meeting of the Stranger's sincerity and constancy and undertakes to trust him.

'They never meet in conditions of intimacy again. But sometimes the Stranger is seen helping the members of the resistance, and the partisan is grateful and says to his friends, "He is on our side."

'Sometimes he is seen in the uniform of the police handing over patriots to the occupying power. On these occasions his friends murmur against him: but the partisan still says, "He is on our side." He still believes that, in spite of appearances, the Stranger did not deceive him. Sometimes he asks the Stranger for help and receives it. He is then thankful. Sometimes he asks and does not receive it. Then he says, "The Stranger knows best." Sometimes his friends, in exasperation, say, "Well, what *would* he have to do for you to admit that you were wrong and that he is not on our side?" But the partisan refuses to answer. He will not consent to put the Stranger to the test. And sometimes his friends complain, "Well, if that's what you mean by his being on our side, the sooner he goes over to the other side the better." '

It is *in spite of* appearances that the partisan believes in the Stranger, not because he disregards the appearances. It would only be meaningless if the believer said that God is good but in a sense in which He can tolerate evil, good in a sense different from the one we usually understand the term to mean. This would indeed be nonsense for there is no sense to the word 'good' other than the sense we understand when we use the word. The believer says rather that somehow the existence of evil is compatible with God's goodness but it is still evil and against God's will. The non-believer may declare that such belief is false. He cannot declare that it is meaningless.

It would be mistaken to object to Mitchell's illustration on the grounds that it deals with 'belief *in* . . .' not 'belief *that* . . .'. Both the partisan and his friends agree that there is a Stranger. They debate only whether he is for or against them. And here one can argue that the partisan has acquired faith and confidence in the Stranger despite appearances. But Mitchell's argument is not to prove that God is good or that He exists but that believers in His goodness and His existence are not talking nonsense. In his reply to Flew, who deals with the question of the meaning of God's goodness, Mitchell gives his illustration to show that this belief is logically meaningful. To illustrate the other question regarding God's existence one would have to vary the parable slightly so that the friends try to persuade the partisan that his claim to have met the Stranger was an illusion, that there was no Stranger at all in reality. In the new illustration, the friends would seek to support their case by referring to the success of the enemy which, if the Stranger really existed, he would have prevented. In either event the real point of the illustration is that a believer does not feel obliged to deny that there are facts which seem to count against his argument and this prevents the case being rejected on grounds of its meaninglessness.

Flew makes this rejoinder to Mitchell's defence,[7] acknow-

---

[7] *Ibid.*, pp. 106-107.

ledging that although the theologian accepts that the existence of evil counts against his belief and that he seeks for an explanation, ultimately he will be obliged to resort to qualification. For, Flew says, the Stranger in the parable even if on the side of the resistance, may not always be in a position to help whereas God is omnipotent and if He is good He should not tolerate evil. Flew thinks that ultimately the defender of a Theistic viewpoint will be bound to *qualify* the concept of God's goodness and once this happens the whole concept becomes meaningless. But the problem of evil, difficult and terrible though it is for the Theist, has received many attempted solutions which have seemed to believers to point the way, at least, towards explanation without involving the 'death of a thousand qualifications.'

In fact, the main traditional attempted solutions to the problem of evil seek to qualify the omnipotence rather than the goodness of God.[8] Traditional Theists have rarely denied that evil is real or that God is unqualifiedly good. Valid solutions seek to understand the meaning of 'omnipotence' in this context. The most favoured solution to the problem of evil is that for man to be able to choose the good freely there must be evil as well as good in the universe, otherwise there would be no free choice. Now, if this is correct, one cannot legitimately ask why God, who is Omnipotent, should not permit freedom of choice in a universe in which there is no evil. For the idea of freedom of choice between good and evil in a universe in which there is no evil is nonsense and it is meaningless to suggest that God's Omnipotence can make sense out of nonsense. This kind of qualification is not open to the objection to which repeated qualifications of God's goodness would be open. For in the one case if the word 'goodness' is so qualified as to deprive it of its meaning it ceases to have any meaning when applied to God. You are then applying a meaningless term to God. But the qualification of the term 'omnipotence' does not involve (as does the qualification of 'goodness') an appeal to a special use of language when speaking of God. It seeks rather to demonstrate that the word omni-

[8] See *infra*, pp. 115f.

potence, whenever it is used, cannot meaningfully be made to embrace a contradiction. Here it is not the qualifying Theist who is talking nonsense but the objector who demands that no qualification be made.

Another attempt at defending religious language as cognitive and religious statements as assertions accepts the verification principle but invokes what has been called 'eschatological verification[9]'. The account of God and His relationship to man involves, in Judaism, Christianity and Islam, the belief that the soul of man is immortal and that the soul of the good man will enjoy God's goodness for ever. Now if this belief is true it will be verified by the good man after the death of his body. If the belief is false this can never be determined since if there is neither God nor After-life no man will ever be in a position to put it to the test. But the mere fact that we can see even now how the belief is capable of being verified is sufficient to give it meaning.

On the deeper level, this raises questions as to how man, after the death of his physical body, will be able to verify the belief. All three religions speak of the soul 'seeing' God and by this is not meant, of course, sight through the physical organs but knowledge of such a kind as to make all doubt utterly impossible. It is the contention of all three religions that this absolute certainty of God's existence, so vivid as to be called 'seeing', is not given to man in this life, since here on earth, where he has to strive for the good, it would have the effect of neutralising his freedom of choice. Tension in the life of faith is essential if man is to be provided with the means of freely responding to God and freely acknowledging Him in his life. But once the free choice of God and His goodness has been made in this life it is the possession of the soul which has made the choice for all eternity and that soul is able to 'see' God.

[9] See I. M. Crombie in 'New Essays in Philosophical Theology', pp. 109-130 and the same author's essay in 'Faith and Logic', *op. cit.*, pp. 31f. In the latter essay (p. 32) Crombie rightly points out that it is no answer to the verification principle to attempt to side-step the whole question, as some believers do, by drawing the distinction between 'belief *that* God exists' and 'belief *in* God' (as above) since one cannot believe *in* God unless one *first* believes *that* God exists. As we have suggested in the previous chapter, 'first' is not quite the right term here but the point is well taken.

John Hick,[10] developing this line of speculation, gives the illustration of two men walking along a road. One of them believes that the road leads nowhere, the other that it leads to the celestial city. While they are actually on the road all the circumstantial proof of the celestial city produced by the believer is rejected by his unbelieving friend. But when they turn the last corner of the road and reach the city, the belief of the one is confirmed and the doubts of the other nullified. Naturally, their respective beliefs influence the attitude of mind in which they undertake the journey and also their conduct during its course. Although both travel along the same road it is these differences which save their respective beliefs from being logically meaningless.

Paul Ziff, in an article entitled 'About God',[11] argues for the logical meaningfulness of religious language. Ziff remarks that the conditions governing the term 'God' are those of being omnipotent, omniscient, eternal, creator of the world, a non-spatiotemporal being, a Spirit, the cause of itself, and so forth. These conditions can be understood and therefore the question whether God exists is an intelligible question. It is true that I may not know how to establish whether these conditions can be satisfied but *understanding a condition does not depend on knowing how it can be satisfied*. Ziff gives the illustration of someone agreeing to do something on the condition that the last man on earth will approve of it. There is no difficulty in understanding the condition and yet I have no idea how to establish that such a condition is satisfied.

Paul Edwards in 'Some Notes on Anthropomorphic Theology'[12] takes issue with Ziff's contention that understanding the conditions is sufficient to dispose of the problem. I can, for instance, (he says), have 'some understanding' of the statement 'the Absolute is lazy' (simply because it is in English and

[10] 'The Existence of God', *op. cit.*, pp. 253-274; 'Philosophy of Religion', *op. cit.*, pp. 94-106. An elaboration of the 'eschatalogical verification' idea is to point out that it is incorrect to say that belief in God makes no difference (which can be tested) for it makes at least more probable that the proposition that I shall survive bodily death is true, see A. C. Ewing: 'Meaninglessness' in 'Mind', 1937, reprinted in 'A Modern Introduction to Philosophy', *op. cit.*, pp. 576-585.

[11] 'Religious Experience and Truth', *op. cit.*, pp. 195-202.

[12] *Ibid.*, pp. 241-250.

I can understand the words in a way in which a Chinaman cannot) but it is still meaningless. Edwards does, however, admit that what he called belief in an 'infinite anthropomorphic God' is not meaningless but it is, he claims, false to the facts, i.e. of evil in the universe. This is the argument we have already encountered, that if belief in God and His goodness is not qualified it is contradicted by the fact of evil in the universe and if the belief is qualified, so as to remove the difficulty, what remains is meaningless. But, once again, we must be reminded that Theists have grappled with the burning problem of evil and as Edwards, indeed, acknowledges in his essay, terrible though it is, it is irrelevant to the question of meaning. We have seen that the qualification of the term 'omnipotence' throws light on the problem of evil without reducing belief to meaninglessness.

A different approach is that of Markus Barth: 'On God's Existence'.[13] Barth argues that the traces, if not proof, of God's existence are the Jews (Barth, as a Christian, adds Jesus, the church) and possibly the Bible, i.e. those phenomena in the world of spirit and matter, space and time, that cannot be observed, understood and explained except by reference to a god different from other deities. This is a variant of the 'argument from tradition' used by mediaeval Jewish teachers[14] with the difference that for them the question was one of truth and falsehood whereas for Barth in this context it is one of meaning.

For these reasons the believer refuses to accept the view that his belief is logically meaningless. It makes sense on the logical level and on the moral plane it is the most meaningful thing in his life. But this does not mean to say that he claims to understand the nature of God. His contention is that it is logically meaningful to speak of a Supreme Being whose nature is far beyond all human comprehension and hence beyond meaning. From this point of view, linguistic analysis of religious language, with its severe demand for precision, ought to be welcomed by the religious thinker. He too, is bound to acknowledge an area in which all talk of God is

[13] *Ibid.*, pp. 220-223.
[14] See *infra*, pp. 98f.

meaningless. In this respect he will view linguistic analysis as an ally and not a foe.

During the Middle Ages the *via negativa* was a widely held approach to God and its insights can be utilised by the modern believer. Maimonides (following earlier thinkers under the influence of Neo-Platonism) taught that one can only legitimately say what God is *not*, never what He *is*.[15] This is known in the history of Jewish thought as the doctrine of negative attributes. When it is said, on this view, that God is good the meaning is that He is not evil and so forth. The whole point of negative description is that it introduces the qualification that when we speak of God we must not seek to describe Him in the limiting terms appropriate to human language, the only language we have. This does not result in the 'death of a thousand qualifications' because concepts like 'good' are not emptied of all their meaning. We are not using a word like 'good' and giving it any meaning we choose (and hence no meaning at all). The word has content, in a negative sense, since a Being who is described as 'good' is, at least, one who is not evil. We safeguard the meaning of our terms by referring to their negative aspects and yet we rightly recoil from seeking to describe the essence of the divine nature. By refraining from the positive affirmation we declare not that God is non-existent or not-good but that He is more than what we mean by existent and good.

In some of the writings of the *Kabbalah* (the Jewish system of mystical thought) this idea receives further elaboration, again following Neo-Platonic concepts. God as He is in Himself is called in this system *En Soph* ('That which is without limit'). God can only be known and spoken of if the reference is not to His nature as it is in Itself but in manifestation in the universe. This goes much further even than Maimonides' doctrine of negative attributes. Maimonides does admit the legitimacy of negative attributes used of the Deity. We can say something about God even if it is only to say what He is not. But for some of the Kabbalists even this is limitation. *En Soph* cannot be spoken of at all. *En Soph* is only hinted at, not mentioned in the Bible. The God of the Bible is God in manifestation. True to this conception, the *Zohar*, the

[15] 'Guide', I, Chapters 51-60.

classical work of Kabbalism, hardly ever speaks of *En Soph* and when it does it is only to say that one cannot speak of *En Soph*.[16]

The famous Kabbalist Moses Cordovero (1522-1570) could hardly have been more emphatic on this score: [17] 'When your mind conceives of God do not permit yourself to imagine that there really is a God as depicted by you. For if you do this you will have a finite, corporeal conception, God forfend. Instead, your mind should dwell only on the affirmation of God's existence and then it should recoil. To do more than this is to allow the imagination to reflect on God as He is in Himself and such reflection is bound to result in imaginative limitation and corporeality. Therefore, put reins on your

[16] See I. Tishbi: '*Mishnath Ha-Zohar*', Vol. I, pp. 75f.; *Zohar*, I, 22b; III, 225a. The *via negativa* is found, among ancient non-Jewish sources, in Pseudo-Dionysius, see A. C. Bouquet: 'Sacred Books of the East', Part III, 7 (iv), pp. 218-220. *Cf.* Jer. Talmud *Ber.*, IX, 1 and *Midrash* Psalms, 19: 'R. Abin said: When Jacob of the village of Neboria was in Tyre, he interpreted: "Praise is silence for Thee, O God" (Ps. 65:2) to mean that silence is the ultimate praise of God. (So Jastrow, taking *samma* in the sense of *siyyum*. But *Rashi*, *Meg.* 18a *s.v. samma*, takes the word to mean 'medicine': 'Silence is the best medicine'. Levy, *Wörterbuch*, understands *samma* as derived from the Greek *soma*, 'body', and translates it as 'Hauptsache' i.e. 'The main thing is silence'). It can be compared to a priceless jewel; however high you appraise it, still you undervalue it'. See the comment to this of R. Joseph Karo to *Tur*, '*Orah Hayyim*', 113, in the name of R. Jonah of Gerona, that it does not apply to a rehearsal of Biblical verses praising God, also, in the name of R. Aaron Ha-Levi of Barcelona, that it does not apply to a rehearsal of God's wondrous deeds and miracles. In the parallel passage in the Babylonian Talmud (Meg. 18a) the exposition is given in the name of R. Judah a man of Kephar Gibboaya or of Kephar Gibbor Hayyil (but in some versions Kephar Neboria, as in the Jer. Talmud) and at the end of the passage this occurs: 'When R. Dimi came, he said: "In the West they say: A word is worth a *sela*, silence two" (or, in some versions, "A word is worth a *sela*, silence has the value of a precious stone").'

[17] '*Elimah Rabbathi*', I, 10, p. 4b. It should be noted that the Jewish mystics do nevertheless permit the use of human language in speaking of the divine. Thomas McPherson: 'Religion as the Inexpressible' (in 'New Essays in Philosophical Theology', *op. cit.*, pp. 131f) argues that the Theist should admit that *all* his language is nonsense and that he should remain silent and worship in silence. McPherson quotes in support Otto's contention that the really important elements in religion are those aspects of faith which cannot be conceptualised. But, as Ferré ('Language, Logic and God', *op. cit.*, pp. 36-37) argues, in that case what becomes of prayer? Furthermore, on this view there could be no such thing as religious 'truths' since, in the absence of language, these could never be formulated. The mystic's case is different, says Ferré, 'since his high ecstasy is forged in discipline, contemplation and study.'

intellect and do not allow it too great a freedom but assert God's existence and deny the possibility of comprehending Him. The mind should run to and fro—running to affirm God's existence and recoiling from any limitations induced by the imagination, since man's imagination pursues his intellect.'

In the same tradition, Rabbi Schneor Zalman of Liady (1747-1813)[18] states that of God as He is in Himself one cannot even say that it is impossible for any creature, high or low, to grasp His wisdom, for this would imply that God's wisdom belongs to matters which can be 'grasped' but that *we* cannot grasp it. This is akin to saying of a particularly subtle theory that it cannot be 'felt' (i.e. with the physical hand), the verb being inapplicable because the sense of touch is irrelevant to an idea. Similarly, God's wisdom is incomprehensible to man not because it is too deep for him but because it is of an entirely different order. To use of God's wisdom words like 'grasp' even metaphorically is like using, literally, terms drawn from sense experience in speaking of ideas. In that case why is God called 'wise'? (i.e. what meaning is there in the attribution of wisdom to God; if what is referred to is totally other, what significance is there in calling it 'wisdom'?). Rabbi Schneor Zalman replies that God is the source of wisdom, that all wisdom stems from Him.

This means that when we say of God that He exists or is good or powerful or wise we are saying that His true nature is beyond all human comprehension. But impossible though it is for us to conceive of that nature and meaningless though it therefore is to speak of it at all, we do know that it is a nature compatible only with goodness, wisdom and power and totally incompatible with evil, folly and weakness.

We can summarise the discussion by stating that the Theist holds that the function of religious language is not to describe God's nature but only to provide man with a vocabulary of worship, to enable him to speak of God in manifestation. The following two passages in the Talmud are relevant to this line of thought.

1. 'Someone in the presence of Rabbi Hanina said in his prayer: "God the Great, the Valiant, the Terrible, the Mighty,

[18] *'Tanya', Shaar Ha-Yihud We-Ha-Emunah*, Chapter 9, p. 172.

the Strong, the Tremendous, the Powerful". Rabbi Hanina said to him: "Have you finished all the praises of your Master? Even as regards the first three epithets used by you we could not have uttered them if Moses our Master had not pronounced them in the Law (Deut. 10: 17) and the Men of the Great Synagogue had not subsequently come and established their use in prayer (Men of the Great Synagogue were considered to be the authors of that part of the liturgy in which these praises occur). And you come and say all this. What does this resemble? It is as if a mortal king who had millions of gold pieces were praised for possessing silver pieces. Would this not be an offence to him?" ' (*Ber.* 33b).

Maimonides[19] has the following comment on the passage: 'Consider in the first place his reluctance and unwillingness to multiply the affirmative attributes. Consider also that he has stated clearly that if we were left only to our intellects we should never have mentioned these attributes or stated a thing appertaining to them. Yet the necessity to address men in such terms as would make them achieve some representation—in accordance with the dictum of the Sages: *The Torah speaks in the language of man* (*Yeb.* 71a; *B.M.* 31b)—obliged resort to predicting of God their own perfections when speaking to them. It must then be our purpose to draw a line at using these expressions and not apply them to Him except only in reading the *Torah*. However, as the Men of the Great Synagogue, who were prophets, appeared in their turn and inserted the mention of these attributes in prayer, it is our purpose to pronounce only these attributes when saying our prayers. . . . Accordingly, we should not have mentioned these attributes at all but for the first necessary obligation; and but for the second necessity, we should not have taken them out of their context and should not have had recourse to them in our prayers. . . . Hereupon I shall return to completing the indications concerning the dictum of Rabbi Hanina and to giving it correct interpretation. He does not say, for example: *What does this resemble? It is as if a mortal king who had millions of gold pieces were praised for possessing one hundred pieces.* For this example would have indicated that the perfections of Him, may He be exalted, while

[19] 'Guide', I, 59, translation of S. Pines.

more perfect than the perfections ascribed to Him, still belong to the same species as the latter. As we have demonstrated this is not so. But the wisdom manifest in this parable lies in his saying: *gold pieces and were praised for possessing silver pieces*. He says this in order to indicate that in God, may He be exalted, there is nothing belonging to the same species as the attributes regarded by us as perfections, but that all these attributes are deficiencies with regard to God, just as he made clear in this parable when he said: *Would this not be an offence to him?*'

2. 'Rabbi Joshua b. Levi said: Why were they called Men of the Great Synagogue? Because they restored the crown of the divine attributes to its ancient completeness. Moses had come and said: "The Great God, the Valiant, and the Terrible" (Deut. 10 : 17). Then Jeremiah came and said: Aliens are destroying His Temple. Where are, then, His terrible deeds? Hence he omitted (Jer. 32 : 17f) "the Terrible". Daniel came and said: Aliens are enslaving His sons. Where are His valiant deeds? Hence he omitted (Dan. 9 : 4f) "the Valiant". But they (the Men of the Great Synagogue) came and said: On the contrary! Therein lies His valiant deeds that He suppresses His wrath, that He extends His long-suffering to the wicked. Therein lies His terrible powers: For but for the fear of Him how could one nation persist among the nations! But how could the earlier teachers (Jeremiah and Daniel) abolish something established by Moses? Rabbi Eleazer said: Since they knew that the Holy One, blessed be He, insists on truth, they would not ascribe false things to Him' (i.e. it was not true in their experience even though it was true from God's point of view, as it were). (*Yom.* 69b). In the parallel passage in the Jerusalem Talmud (*Ber.* VII, 3) the conclusion is: 'But have mortal men the power to impose such limits (as did Jeremiah and Daniel)? Rabbi Isaac b. Eleazer said: The prophets know that their God is true and they do not flatter Him.'

In both these passages it is implied that the really significant thing is man's experience and the psychological need to speak of God in terms of that experience. It is further implied that by using a prayer language hallowed by tradition, rather than our own composition, we provide ourselves with the constant reminder that whatever we say of God is of God as He is manifested in human history and experience and that we are not trying to say anything meaningful about God's true nature.

The balance here is extremely difficult to maintain and theologians have all too frequently spoken as if their human formulations really did describe adequately the divine nature as it is in itself. It is precisely here that a severe scrutiny of religious language is of the utmost help as a corrective. The famous concluding sentence of Wittgenstein's 'Tractatus Logico-Philosophicus' is both a spur to clarity in religious thinking and a proper attitude of religious humility: *'Whereof one cannot speak, thereon one must be silent.'*

PART II

Ways to Faith

Chapter 3

The Way of Reason

MANY of the great mediaeval thinkers were not only convinced that it was possible to discover for oneself by means of reason that there is a God but that it is one's duty to do so. If one had the requisite intellectual ability and yet failed to exercise the mind so that it arrived at a belief in God one was guilty of a breach of duty.[1] From the mediaeval writings on the subject it appears that the use of reason to discover the truth about God was admirable on three counts. (a) To prove by reason that there is a God is to render this belief immune from subsequent doubt. (b) The use of reason to discover God had the effect of refining one's conception of God. (c) Reason itself was elevated as a result of the quest.

(a) *To prove by reason that there is a God is to render this belief immune from subsequent doubt.* It should be noted that the majority of mediaeval Jewish thinkers, rightly or wrongly, never doubted the capacity of man's God-given reason to arrive unaided at belief in God. The evidence appeared to them to be so utterly convincing that it seemed stupid to refuse to avail oneself of the certainty it afforded.

---

[1] The main discussions in mediaeval Jewish philosophy of the role of reason in the life of faith are to be found in the following works: Saadiah Gaon (892-942): *'Emunoth We-Deoth'*, ('Beliefs and Opinions') (*cf.* Henry Malter: 'Saadiah Gaon His Life and Works', pp. 174-260); Bahya Ibn Pakudah (Eleventh cent.): *'Hobhoth Ha-Lebhabhoth'* ('Duties of the Heart'), Part 1, *Shaar Ha-Yihud* (*cf.* S. B. Urbach: 'Pillars of Jewish Thought' pp. 94-135); Moses Maimonides (1135-1204): *'Moreh Nebhukhim'* ('Guide for the Perplexed'); Abraham Ibn David (1110-1180): *'Emunah Ramah'* ('Elevated Faith'); Gersonides (1288-1344): *'Milhamoth Ha-Shem'* ('Wars of the Lord'); Hasdai Crescas (1340-1416): *'Or Adonai'* ('Light of the Lord'). Attaching far less importance to human reasoning are: Judah Ha-Levi (11th-12th cent.): *'Kuzari'* (I, 63; III, 19); Joseph Albo (*c.* 1380-*c.* 1444): *'Sepher Ha-Ikkarim'* ('Book of Principles').

They had attained this sense of absolute conviction before they wrote their works, attributing their success in large measure to their rational approach. Naturally, they felt it to be their duty to advocate that others follow the same path. These thinkers were sufficiently realistic to acknowledge that the task, like any other difficult intellectual enterprise, was beyond the scope of good folk with limited minds. But, for those able to attain it, certainty was always to be preferred to uncertainty on the most significant truth of all. The idea, which appears here and there later, that it might be more meritorious to opt for faith in the absence of certainty rather than have certainty given, simply did not occur to them. The basic truth that God *is* had to be reached by man before he could even begin to proceed on the road of religion and it was his duty to make the truth his own by the surest method of all. Bahya Ibn Pakudah was expressing the general attitude among the thinkers of this period when he compared the believer through tradition to the blind being led by the blind, the believer through reason to the man whose eyes have been opened.[2]

(b) *The use of reason to discover God had the effect of refining one's conception of God.* It should not be imagined that all the efforts of the mediaeval thinkers were exhausted by the bare proof of God's existence. Indeed, among the Jewish thinkers, this occupied only a small portion of their work. Their main aim was to understand, through reasoning, the true nature of God, even if their conclusion was that God's nature cannot be grasped by the human mind. This, too, they felt, was an insight of significance, to know how little one could legitimately know about God and how mistaken are crude notions of the divine. Beyond the question of bare belief was the deeper question of what was believed in. It is no accident that in mediaeval Jewish thought belief in God's existence is generally discussed in the context of God's unity. In the interests of a pure monotheism the mediaeval thinkers sought to demonstrate that all corporeality, all limitation, all plurality must be negated of God. Theirs was a mighty attempt to equate the 'God of Abraham, Isaac and Jacob' with the

[2] *'Shaar Ha-Yihud'*, Chapter 2.

'God of the philosophers'. The believer through tradition alone, who had never exercised his mind in contemplation of the full meaning of God's unity, had, they maintained, a gross, even offensive, conception of God's nature. Bahya Ibn Pakudah quotes with approval[3] a 'philosopher', that the only persons who really worshipped God were the prophet, with his intuitive awareness of the Deity, and the philosopher, with his reasoned account of God and His nature. All other men, even when they believed they were worshipping God, were really worshipping something other than God, a mere figment of the imagination.

(c) *Reason itself was elevated as a result of the quest:* It was widely held in the Middle Ages that man's highest pursuit was to exercise his mind in the discovery of the metaphysical truths regarding God and His nature. Many thinkers believed that in such exercise man created, as it were, a new type of soul or, it would be better to say, brought such soul from potentiality to actuality. In their view it was this actualised soul alone (the so-called 'acquired intellect') that is immortal. Thus, over and above the question of the attainment of the truth, significant though this was, the use of human reasoning for the exploration of divine matters had the tremendous advantage of rendering immortal the soul engaged in it.[4]

These three reasons are not stated explicitly in the sources but they are implicit in the whole approach of many of the mediaeval thinkers, Christian, Muslim as well as Jewish. Only the second reason is valid in quite the same way for moderns but all three are not without relevance to the contemporary discussion of the rational approach to religious belief particularly when such an approach is under heavy fire as it is today.

The first reason, that rational investigation produces the greater degree of certainty, has considerably less force since the attacks of Hume and Kant on the traditional arguments for the existence of God and the questioning of whether pure

[3] *'Shaar Ha-Yihud'*, Chapter 2.
[4] See I. Husik: 'A History of Mediaeval Jewish Philosophy', Introduction, pp. xlvi-xlvii.

reason has the power of arriving at truths beyond the world of experience. With the exception of Roman Catholic thinkers many modern theologians accept the Kantian critique and acknowledge that reason alone cannot bring a man to God. Yet reason does have a part to play in the life of faith. Unless we are prepared to surrender blindly to superstition, we must have some means of distinguishing between faith and credulity and the only means we have are our reasoning powers. It is these which enable a man to investigate the claims of faith to see whether they cohere with the rest of his knowledge and experience. Ultimately sound faith is only attained when it makes sense of the whole of existence.

The second reason is as valid for faith today as it was in the Middle Ages. It is undoubtedly true that unless some thought is given to the question of what is meant by 'God' there is danger of crudity in conception.

The third reason strikes no echo as it stands. The whole concept of the 'acquired intellect' is a piece of out-dated ancient Greek philosophy. We are, however, reminded that reasoning about faith can be an edifying experience. No one would claim that the philosophy of religion is itself religion or that one has to be a religious philosopher in order to go to Heaven. Yet to think deeply about those things which, more than any others, concern the man of faith is surely not without spiritual benefit.

While there was determined opposition in some circles in the Middle Ages to any rational inquiry into faith it remains true that some of the greatest figures in the history of Jewish thought at that period were staunch upholders of the rational approach though, historically considered, they were less purely rational than they believed themselves to be. Saadiah Gaon's 'Beliefs and Opinions', for instance, is devoted chiefly, as its title implies, to a consideration of the relationship between faith and reason and is a defence of the role of reason in the life of faith. According to Saadiah[5] knowledge is derived from three sources: (1) sense perception, (2) intuition, (3) inference. For Jews there is the further source of authentic tradition contained in the *Torah*. If, as sometimes happens, knowledge

[5] *Op. cit.*, Introduction, *cf.* Malter, *op. cit.*, pp. 195-196 and note on page 459.

derived from the first three sources appears to contradict knowledge derived from the *Torah*, then it is first necessary to consider whether our senses or intuition have been misled or whether the inference we have drawn is unfounded. But if we are convinced that knowledge derived from the first three sources is not faulty and still it seems to contradict the knowledge derived from the *Torah* then the *Torah* should be interpreted in other than its literal sense (figuratively or allegorically) so that its teaching does not conflict with reason. For Saadiah, the Jew is not called upon to sacrifice his reason in the name of faith. He defends the use of reason in matters of faith on two grounds. First, reason verifies in fact that which is taught theoretically by God's prophets. Secondly, a sound apologetic by which the Jew wards off the attacks on his faith can only be effective if based on reasoned argument.

Another famous protagonist of reason in the life of faith is Gersonides. It should be noted, however, that the mediaeval rationalists were chiefly concerned in their discussions with the secondary beliefs in God's providence, His attributes, miracles, etc. It was with regard to these that faith was apt to come into conflict with reason. On the primary belief that there is a God they say little. This was for them so evident that there was no real conflict with reason. Gersonides, speaking of these secondary beliefs, remarks[6] that his investigations are not intended for the simple believers. These, he says, are content to *believe* and do not seek to *know*. Here belief (*emunah*) is used in the sense of 'belief *that* . . .' but is treated as inferior to actual knowledge, i.e. truth arrived at by the use of reason. He quotes further the familiar distinction beween opinions, arrived at by reason, which do not contradict the *Torah* and opinions which seem to do so. In the latter case the correct procedure is not to deny reason but to re-interpret the *Torah*. The anthropomorphic passages in Scripture, for example, contradict reason if interpreted literally and must consequently be interpreted figuratively. 'For the *Torah* is not a Law which compels us to believe that which is false but it provides us with the best possible means of apprehending the truth'.[7]

[6] *Op cit.*, Introduction, p. 2a.
[7] *Ibid.*, pp. 2b-3a.

There are a number of attempted demonstrations of God's existence. These are frequently referred to as 'proofs' but if they are proofs it is odd that so many should be required. It is far better to speak of them as arguments. A number of arguments, each starting from a different proposition and all arriving at the same conclusion, does tend to produce conviction. None of these arguments possess the demonstrative power of a 'proof' but taken together they lend the strongest support, on grounds of reason alone, to belief in God.

This is how we can meet the objection that a number of invalid proofs cannot become more valid simply because they are added together. An invalid proof has no weight at all and to attempt to add such proofs together is like adding a series of noughts. If valid, one proof suffices. If invalid, no matter how many proofs are adduced, the case has still not been proven. But if we approach these not as proofs but as indications or arguments there can be point in an accumulation of evidence. An archaeologist, for example, may be able to date his finds accurately by discovering absolute proof of the date. He may, for example, discover a coin that bears a recognisable emblem to which a fixed date can be ascribed. This would constitute proof of the date. But if no such proof were available the archaeologist would then proceed to advance a number of arguments for his dating. He would then perhaps point to the strata in which his discoveries were made, to the type of pottery excavated, to literary sources which seemed to tally with his dating. If he found that the arguments from various premises converged to suggest a particular date it would become extremely plausible to suggest that this was in fact the date of his material.

With one exception, the arguments for God's existence are from the world to God, they are a *posteriori*. They reason from our knowledge of the world to the God who brought the world into being. The exception is the *ontological argument* invented by St. Anselm, Archbishop of Canterbury. This is an *a priori* argument. It reasons from the idea of God to God's actual existence. This argument was rejected as invalid by St. Thomas Aquinas. It is not found in any of the Jewish sources.

Anselm defines God as the being than whom no greater (i.e.

more perfect) can be conceived (*quo nihil majus cogitari potest*). This, says Anselm, is the meaning of the name 'God' and whoever uses the term has this in mind. But a being who actually exists is obviously greater (i.e. more perfect) than one who does not. Consequently, if God does not exist then a greater being is conceivable, namely one who does enjoy existence. But, by definition, God is the being than whom no greater can be conceived so that it follows, according to Anselm, that if we can conceive of God at all, and we obviously can, He must exist. The attempted refutation, that because we can imagine a perfect island it is no proof of its existence is countered by Anselm by noting that the argument applies only to God. The point of the argument is that since God is *defined* as the being than whom no greater can be conceived, and this definition is peculiar to God, then God must, by definition, enjoy existence.

Thus the very idea of God implies that He exists. According to Anselm the atheist who declares that he does not believe in God is guilty of self-contradiction. For even in his denial he uses the term 'God' and this must mean that there really is a God. Anselm asks the atheist to think about the meaning of the words he uses. He denies God. But by 'God' he must mean a being than whom no greater can be conceived. Since this must imply that such a being exists, to say that God does not exist is to say the being who exists does not exist.

Much has been written on the *ontological argument*. It has convinced many minds. But the basic objection to it is that while Anselm is right in declaring that when we *think* of God we perforce think of an *existing* being it by no means follows that the being of whom we think actually exists. Despite periodic attempts at reviving the argument it is accepted as valid today by very few thinkers. The variation of it which does enjoy some degree of plausibility, but no more than this, is that which affirms that we can trust our thinking to correspond with reality, else we could place no trust at all on our thinking. But, if this is so, then it should follow that the idea of God present in the human mind and involving as we have seen existence, in thought at least, corresponds to reality. In other words, there must be a God for how is the emergence of

47

the very idea, of a supreme being than whom no greater can be conceived, to be explained?[8]

The two better known and more convincing arguments are the *cosmological* and the *teleological*. The *cosmological argument*, of which there are various forms,[9] is based on the need to find a reason for the cosmos. The universe does not explain itself. Why should there be a universe? Why should there be anything at all? And our minds are so constituted that this is the kind of question that we are always asking. If we start with a particular object and ask why it is here some explanation will be forthcoming. We ask why a particular book is on a shelf. The reply is that someone bought it from the retailers who in turn bought it from the publishers. The publishers produced it by obtaining the manuscript from the author, the paper from the manufacturer, etc. The author had his reasons for writing the book and these, in turn, can be traced still further back. Now each of these explanations is only partial and relative. To say that the owner bought a book from the retailers, and so on, does not really explain why it is on the shelf, since we are moved to seek an explanation for this, too, so that in our search for explanation we go on looking for still further explanations and never reach a final one, which means that we never reach a full explanation at all. The only way out of the difficulty is to say that there is an explanation for all things which requires no further explanation, because it is

[8] Anselm's argument is translated with notes in: 'Selections from the Literature of Theism', ed. A. Caldecott and H. R. Mackintosh pp. 1-9. A new translation and comment on the argument is: 'St. Anselm's *Proslogion*', trans. with an Introduction and Philosophical Commentary by M. J. Charlesworth, Oxford, Clarendon Press, 1965. Selections from philosophers who have discussed the argument are given in: John Hick: 'The Existence of God', pp. 23-70 and bibliographical note p. 299.

[9] St. Thomas Aquinas has five 'ways' of demonstrating God's existence: '*Summa Theologica*', Quaest 11. *An Deus sit?* Art. 3. These are given in translation with notes in: Caldecott and Mackintosh, *op. cit.*, pp. 23-28; 'A Modern Introduction to Philosophy', ed. Paul Edwards and Arthur Pap, pp. 445-542; John Hick, *op. cit.*, pp. 80-86, bibliography p. 300. St. Thomas's fifth way corresponds to the teleological argument. His first four ways are: (a) the argument from motion, (b) the argument from efficient cause, (c) the argument from possibility and necessity, (d) the argument from the gradation to be found in things. These four all belong to the cosmological argument. The most famous treatment of the teleological argument is William Paley's 'Natural Theology', where the well-known analogy of the watch is given. Hick, *op cit.*, pp. 300-302, has a good bibliography on the arguments.

self-explanatory. Belief in God provides us with such an ulti-mate explanation. The ultimate explanation of the cosmos is God, to Whom all existence can be traced. Now it is true that we can have no idea of the nature of God and hence the ex-planation offered does not really enable us to understand how the world came into being. But the alternative, which appar-ently the sceptic is prepared to accept, is not that we do not or cannot know the explanation but that there is *no* explana-tion. This is contrary to all our experience, to the way we use our minds, to the constant quest for meaning and the principle of explanation which the sceptic himself shares.

The point has sometimes been made that it is futile to speak of Theism as a more probable explanation than atheism because in this context probability has no meaning. We can say of two or more possibilities that one is more probable, but if we are thinking of the universe *as a whole* we are not weighing more than one possibility and it is consequently meaningless to talk of probability. But the real force of the cosmological argument is not that it renders the Theistic ac-count more probable but that it calls attention to the fact that the Theistic account is the only one which accepts the principle of explanation. The Theist does, indeed, declare that he can-not understand how the explanation works but he stakes his life on the conviction that there is an explanation. The atheist can only say that he is prepared to live without any explana-tion, which only means that belies himself. He offers and seeks for explanations for the individual phenomena of the universe while accepting that there is no explanation for the universe as a whole. But, it might here be objected, an explanation which does not explain is no explanation at all. Moreover on the Theist's own admission the Theistic account puts forward the idea of God as self-explanatory in a way which cannot be comprehended. Is not the Theist similar to the atheist, com-pelled to live without explanation? The answer to this is that belief in God is belief in Mind as the Ground of the universe. We can see how a mind explains the existence of things, how a mind works creatively. The mind of the author, for instance, is an explanation of how the book on the shelf came to be written. The author conceived the book in his mind and then put it down on paper. On the Theistic view, that part of the ultimate explanation which is beyond our comprehension is the postulate of a Mind which does not depend on anything else for its existence (as the mind of the author of the book does). But if there is a God it is reasonable to assume that His nature would be incomprehensible to a finite mind. The Theistic affirmation of Mind at the heart of things is an affirmation that there is an explanation at the heart of things, that things can be explained.

The *teleological argument* goes further in claiming that Mind is evident, not alone in the sheer existence of anything, but also in the purposive way in which particular things function together. It calls attention to the order and regularity in the universe, to the way in which things, without minds or purpose, seem to adapt themselves to a purposive arrangement. The book on the shelf was composed by an author. He used his mind to put his ideas in a certain sequence so that his work might be read and understood by other intelligent beings. Because the author has a mind he is able to find the words which enable him to communicate with other minds. Now, during the long climb from the amoeba to people capable of writing and reading books, mind must have entered the process somewhere. But how can mindless matter have produced mind unless Mind was there from the beginning directing the whole process? The mind there from the beginning cannot have been human mind for human mind is precisely what emerged. It can only be that the planning Mind there from the beginning was a Mind independent of matter and this only makes sense on the Theistic account.

Both the cosmological and the teleological arguments were used by the great mediaeval Jewish thinkers. But H. A. Wolfson, in an important article: 'Notes on Proofs of the Existence of God in Jewish Philosophy',[10] observes that on the whole their preference is for the cosmological argument. They do not use the argument from design as an independent argument for God's existence but either as a reinforcement of the cosmological argument or as evidence of divine goodness, unity and intelligence. The formulation of some of the more important Jewish thinkers on this question will here be given but before doing this it might be helpful to con-

[10] 'Hebrew Union College Annual', Vol. I, 1924, pp. 575-596.

sider the earlier formulations in the classical Jewish sources.

From what has been said earlier regarding the non-systematic nature of Biblical and Rabbinic thinking and that the existence of God was self-evident for the scholars of this period, we cannot expect to find in the Bible or in Rabbinic literature any formal proof of God's existence. There are, nevertheless, a number of passages in which the arguments appear in rudimentary form.

That it is God who brings order out of chaos and that the order in the universe cannot be understood without an ordering Mind is implied in the sublime account of creation in the opening chapter of Genesis as well as in Psalm 8. In Psalm 19 the heavens which 'declare the glory of the Lord' are compared to the laws of the *Torah*. It is not too fanciful to see implied here that there are 'laws' which the heavenly bodies obey, that the regular order of nature is by divine fiat. Similarly in Deutero-Isaiah there occurs the verse: *'Lift up your eyes on high, And see: who hath created these? He that bringeth out their hosts by number, He calleth them all by name; By the greatness of His might, and for that He is strong in power, Not one faileth'* (Is. 40: 26). True, the prophet is not arguing for God's existence but for evidence of His power. Yet many men have been moved to follow his advice and, gazing at the starry heaven at night, have been compelled to declare, who made these if not God? Moreover, a careful study of the verse demonstrates that the prophet sees God's power reflected not alone in the sheer tremendous existence of the heavenly bodies but in their regularity, in the orderly way in which they move in their courses, in the planning of the divine Mind which apportions each to its place. It is the teleological as well as the cosmological argument which is implied. In the same chapter there occurs the verse:

> *'Who hath measured the waters in the hollow of his hand,*
> *And meted out the heaven with the span,*
> *And comprehended the dust of the earth in a measure,*
> *And weighed the mountains in scales,*
> *And the hills in a balance?'* (Is. 40: 12).

Here, too, the thought of the prophet is concerned primarily with God's power as evidenced in creation. The hills and the mountains, the heavens and the waters, are all encompassed in God's smallest measures. But in the very reference to measuring and weighing there is implied the notion of a design or plan. So, too, the Psalmist says: *'He that planted the ear, shall He not hear? He that formed the eye shall He not see?'* (Ps. 94:9). Could eyes and ears have emerged without purposive Mind?

In Rabbinic literature, too, the references to God's power to do that which is utterly beyond all human capacity are sometimes examples of the teleological argument in rudimentary form. Thus, in one passage (*Ber.* 10a) it is said that the capacity of human beings falls short of the capacity of God. A human being can sketch a figure on a wall but he cannot invest it with a 'breath and spirit, bowels and intestines'. But God 'shapes one form in the midst of another' (i.e. the embryo in the mother) and 'invests it with breath and spirit, bowels and intestines'. Hannah's prayer in which she said: 'there is no rock (*tzur*) like our God' (I Sam. 2:2) is made to read 'there is no artist (*tzayyar*) like our God'. A painting or sculpture implies the artist who fashioned it. The existence of living creatures implies the great Artist who fashioned them. In the same vein a mediaeval Jewish teacher, Abba Mari b. Moses of Lunel (b.c. 1250) remarks[11] that there is no need for man 'to make ladders to heaven' (i.e. to reflect on the cosmos as a whole) in order to recognise that there is a God. He can discover this through reflection on the marvellous structure of his own body, which shows evidence of plan and purpose. With homiletical license this author quotes the verse: 'All my *bones* shall say, Lord, who is like unto Thee' (Ps. 35:10). In a late *Midrash*[12] it is said that if all the human beings in the world came together for the purpose they would be unable to create out of nothing a living creature even of a size less than a lentil seed.

Earlier, Philo of Alexandria, influenced by Greek thought, has more direct formulations of the teleological argument.

---

[11] *'Minhath Kenaoth'*, Chapter 7, pp. 8-9.
[12] *'Tanna De-Bhe Elijahu'*, 7.

Thus, Philo[13] argues from the existence of the human mind to the Mind of the universe. Anticipating the Rabbinic illustration of God as the Great Artist, Philo writes: [14] 'Who can look upon statues or paintings without thinking at once of a sculptor or painter? Who can see clothes or ships or houses without getting the idea of a weaver or a shipwright and a housebuilder? And when one enters a well-ordered city in which the arrangements for civil life are very admirably managed, what else will he suppose but that this city is directed by good rulers? So then he who comes to the truly Great City, this world, and beholds hills and plains teeming with animals and plants, spring-fed or winter torrents, streaming along, the seas with their expanses, the air with its happily tempered phases, the yearly seasons passing into each other, and the other heavenly bodies fixed or planetary and the whole firmament revolving in rhythmic order, must he not naturally or rather necessarily gain the conception of the Maker and Father and Ruler also? For none of the works of human act is self-made, and the highest art and knowledge is shown in the universe, so that surely it has been wrought by one of excellent knowledge and absolute perfection. In this we have the conception of the existence of God.'

As we have seen, it is the cosmological argument that is particularly popular with the mediaeval Jewish thinkers, although occasionally supplemented by the teleological argument. Saadiah Gaon's version of the argument is as follows.[15] The world, he says, is not eternal. It must have had a beginning in time. Among the proofs Saadiah advances for the view that the world is not eternal is that all things in heaven and earth are composite. But these different parts must have been joined at some time, that is to say, composite things must have had a time of composition. From this it follows that the world had a beginning in time. Furthermore, time itself must be a creation for if time were eternal it would be infinite. For Saadiah this is impossible since, on his view, that which is infinite can never be arrested, as it were. We could never

---

[13] 'De Migratione Abrahami', 33-35, Loeb Classical Library, Vol. IV, 1949, pp. 239-249.
[14] 'De Specialibus Legibus', I, 6, Loeb Classical Library, VII, 1950, p. 119.
[15] 'Beliefs and Opinions', op. cit., Part I, Chapters 1-2, pp. 40-50.

grasp it at any given moment. It could never be held in the finite. Since there obviously is time and we can experience the time sequence here and now it must follow that time is not eternal but a creation.

Having established by means of this and other proofs that the world was created in time, Saadiah then points out the absurdity in the notion of a thing creating itself. It could not have created itself before it existed because it did not then exist that it might engage in creation. It could not have created itself after it came into existence because it would already be in existence. Since it is absurd to say that the world created itself and since it has been shown that the world is created (and not eternal) it must follow that it was created by something other than itself. This something other than the world which created the world is God.

Saadiah's cosmological argument thus depends on the belief that the world is created. If we were to allow that the world is eternal there would be no proof of God's existence from the existence of the world. For if the world is eternal, if it was always there, the possibilities are not exhausted between creation by God and the world's creation by itself. The world would then not have been created at all but would have existed from all eternity and if this were so there would be no proof of God. But Saadiah holds that he has proved adequately that the world was created. This, he argues, is not only attested to by Scripture, which speaks repeatedly of God as Creator of the world, but is the only doctrine which satisfies reason.

Bahya Ibn Pakudah in his 'Duties of the Heart'[16] has a similar proof of God's existence. With Saadiah, Bahya holds that the world was created in time and his proofs for this follow the same lines. Bahya, however, considers the possibility that even if the world had a beginning in time it might not have followed that it was *created*. It might have come into being by chance. To this Bahya replies that there is clear evidence of purposiveness in the universe and this rules out the possibility of chance. Bahya is thus led to the teleological argument for which he gives a famous illustration: If we read, says Bahya, a beautifully written passage which makes sense

[16] *'Shaar Ha-Yihud'*, Chapter 4-6.

we ridicule the suggestion that it was simply the result of the inkpot spilling onto the sheet to form letters and words by accident. We conclude from the manuscript that it had an author and by the same token we must conclude that the world had an Author.

Maimonides' proofs for God's existence[17] are extremely complicated and cannot be stated here in adequate detail. They are based on the doctrines of Aristotle and his Arabic commentators. Unlike Saadiah, Maimonides holds his proofs to be independent of the doctrine of creation though, in fact, he does believe in *creatio ex nihilo*. But, he argues, even if the world were eternal there would still be proof from it of the existence of God. Maimonides' proofs are cosmological, going back to Aristotle and later used by Aquinas of the unmoved Mover. Nothing can move unless it has a mover which sets it in motion. But that mover, too, must have had a mover to set it in motion. We are led on to the unmoved Mover and this is God.

The teleological argument appears in Judah Ha-Levi's '*Kuzari*'[18] not as a direct proof for the existence of God but as a reminder to man of God's wisdom and his moral duty of weighing his deeds since God in His wisdom is aware of all that man does. 'The religious person never acts, speaks or thinks without believing that he is observed by eyes which see and take note, which reward and punish and call to account for everything objectionable in word and deed . . . he remembers that all his limbs are placed with consummate wisdom, in proper order and proportion. He sees how they obey his will, though he know not which part of them should move. If, for example, he wishes to rise, he finds that his limbs have, like obedient helpers, raised his body, although he does not even know these limbs. It is the same when he wishes to sit, walk, or assumes any position. . . . One must not consider the work of creation in the light of an artisan's craft. When the latter, e.g., has built a mill, he departs, whilst the mill does the work for which it was constructed. The Creator, however, creates limbs and endows them continually with their faculties. Let us imagine His solicitude and guidance

17 'Guide', Part II, Introduction and Chapter 1.
18 III, 11; V, 20.

removed only for one instant, and the whole world would suffer.'

Judah Ha-Levi is one of the few Jewish theologians of the Middle Ages to face the existence of evil and faultiness in creation as apparently contradicting the whole idea of a planned universe and a divine ordering of things. He offers no solution except to point out that since reason can clearly detect the guiding Hand from the evidence of purpose in the universe, faith must step in when the way is obscure. Ha-Levi refers specifically in this context to the problem of animal suffering: 'See how wonderfully conceived is the nature of the creatures, how many marvellous gifts they possess which show forth the intention of an all-wise Creator, and the will of an omniscient all-powerful Being. He has endowed the small and the great with all necessary internal and external senses and limbs. He gave them organs corresponding to their instincts. He gave the hare and the stag the means of flight required by their timid nature; endowed the lion with ferocity and the instruments for robbing and tearing. He who considers the formation, use and relation of the limbs to the animal instinct, sees wisdom in them and so perfect an arrangement that no doubt of uncertainty can remain in his soul concerning the justice of the Creator. When an evil thought suggests that there is injustice in the circumstance that the hare falls a prey to the lion or the wolf, and the fly to the spider, reason steps in warning him as follows: How can I charge the all-Wise with injustice when I am convinced of His justice, and that injustice is quite out of the question? If the lion's pursuit of the hare and the spider of the fly were mere accidents, I should have to assert the necessity of accident. I see, however, that this wise and just Manager of the world equipped the lion with the means for hunting, with ferocity, strength, teeth and claws; that He furnished the spider with cunning and taught it to weave a net which it constructs without having learnt to do so; how He equipped it with the instruments required, and appointed the fly as its food just as many fishes serve other fishes for food. Can I say aught but that this is the fruit of a wisdom which I am unable to grasp, and that I must submit to Him who is called: "The Rock whose doing is perfect" (Deut. 32:4).'

Like other Jewish thinkers Levi b. Gershon (Gersonides) is particularly impressed with the wonder of life and its mystery as the strongest evidence for the existence of the divine Creator. His teleological argument[19] proceeds from the purposiveness evident in the birth of animals and humans. Since this is a regular feature of the universe it cannot be due to chance, for chance may produce an occasional perfection but not one so constant and widespread. We are obliged to conclude that there is purposiveness in the universe. Now this purposiveness as evidenced by birth cannot reside in the animal sperm but must be due to the influence of an Intelligence apart from it. This is the 'Active Intellect' which belongs to the divine Mind.

Hasdai Crescas[20] has this version of the cosmological argument. Since every cause has an effect it follows that any particular effect is only possible, not necessary. That is to say, the effect only exists because it was caused and if the cause were absent the effect, too, would be absent. The effect depends for its existence on its cause and cannot therefore be said to enjoy necessary existence. It is possible for it to exist or not to exist, just as it is possible for its cause either to exist or not to exist. But the cause, too, follows this pattern. The cause itself is an effect with its own cause and so on. But this would mean that all things are only possible and yet there is existence, the universe does exist. For existence to be necessary, not merely possible, there must be a causeless Cause and this is God.

One of the clearest formulations, based on one of Maimonides' proofs, of the cosmological argument is that of Joseph Albo in his *'Sepher Ha-Ikkarim'*.[21] Albo claims that his proof is implied in the creation narrative at the beginning of Genesis. In the narrative all things in heaven and earth are created but at different times. All creation was only potential and becomes actual during the 'six days of creation'. Now the experience of our senses shows us that things constantly pass from potentiality to actuality. But the cause of this change from potentiality to actuality cannot reside in the things them-

[19] *'Milhamoth Ha-Shem'*, *op. cit.*, Book V, Chapters 4-6.
[20] *'Or Adonai'*, *op. cit.*, Book I, Part 3, Chapter 2.
[21] Book II, Chapters 4-5.

selves for if that were so they would have become actual without even being potential. There must therefore be an actualising cause which was never merely potential. This abstract cause which causes all things to pass from potentiality to actuality is God.

Naturally the formulation of the two arguments by the mediaeval thinkers uses the vocabulary of that age and reflects the notions current in mediaeval philosophy. We would not today normally use terms like 'Active Intellect' or discuss the divine creative activity as a matter of actualising the potential or build a theory on the distinction between necessary and possible existence. Yet the basic formulation of the arguments is there and includes, on occasion, certain ideas to which the attention of those who consider the arguments today is bound to be drawn.

Judah Ha-Levi, for instance, grapples with evidence of faulty design and says all that can be said even today on this question if the teleological argument is to be used at all. The teleological argument does not seek to explain in detail how the divine Mind actually operates in the universe but to point to the evidence that there is a divine Mind. The question really amounts to this. Does the evidence of faulty design destroy the teleological argument entirely? But how then does one explain the evidence of purposiveness in the universe? That there is evidence of purposiveness is sufficient to convince Ha-Levi that there is a divine Mind. When the equally strong evidence of faulty design is produced he does not fall back simply on faith, with an attitude of accepting the evidence when it favours him, and rejecting it when it does not. He is saying rather that, although admittedly we have to fall back eventually on the idea of an inscrutable divine Mind, nevertheless if that Mind is divine its full workings would necessarily be inscrutable to the mind of finite man.

In Albo's discussion[22] a question to be raised centuries later by John Stuart Mill is faced. If God is omnipotent why should He have needed to 'design' at all? Why could He not have created the universe all at once as it were? Does not the very notion of a planning or designing Mind suggest a Mind limited or controlled by forces outside it? Albo replies that the whole

[22] Book II, Chapter 4.

idea of a design must not be understood from God's point of view. God could have created spontaneously a perfect universe but such a universe without purposiveness (or rather with purpose already realised from the beginning) would have no meaning for man. The design and the purpose must be evident for man's sake not for God's so that man can struggle for the attainment of the good in obedience to God's will.[23] 'We have already explained,' says Albo, 'in the First Book that the *Torah* begins with the story of creation to prove the existence of the Maker. The account of the way in which the things passed from potentiality to actuality proves the existence of an agent who brought them into actuality. And the fact that they passed into actuality at different times, namely in the six days of creation, shows that the agent is one who acts with intention and will, and does things at different times as His wisdom dictates, though they could have come into being at the same time. The reason they were produced at different times is to indicate intention and will. For these are at the basis of the *Torah* as a whole and of the reward and punishment mentioned therein, as we said before. And the Rabbis say also, "The world could have been created with one word. And the reason there is ten is in order to exact punishment from the wicked . . . and to give reward to the righteous" (*Abhot* 5:1).'

Gersonides' idea that the purposive element cannot reside in the animal sperm itself but in something outside it, namely in purposive Mind, is important for the consideration of how Darwin's theory of natural selection affects the argument from design. There is no doubt that after Darwin any glib attempts to show purposiveness in particular characteristics of animals is suspect but the evolutionary process as a whole still requires to be explained. And just as Gersonides remarks that the purposive element cannot reside in the animal sperm itself, it cannot reside in the 'Life Force' if that is invoked in order to avoid a purely mechanistic view. A blind force cannot be purposive.

The more serious objections to the teleological and cosmological arguments were made by Hume and Kant. No one can today satisfy himself as to whether the arguments have any

[23] See *infra*, pp. 120f.

validity at all unless he has read and digested the formidable critique of them in Hume's 'Dialogues Concerning Natural Religion'[24] and Kant's 'Critique of Pure Reason'[25]. Hume brilliantly points to the flaws in the teleological argument, stressing particularly that if there is evidence of adaptation in the universe there is also evidence of non-adaptation, while Kant questions completely the validity of any argument which starts with the cosmos in order to arrive at that which transcends it. Many thinkers, including believers, have been convinced by Hume and Kant and therefore reject entirely the whole idea of a valid, demonstrative proof of God's existence. If God is believed in it is on other grounds. It is our thesis that the demonstrative nature of the arguments has certainly been killed by Hume and Kant but that the arguments are, as has been suggested, still valuable as *pointers* to the truth.

The above is a bare and no doubt inadequate statement of the two arguments for the existence of God, the *cosmological* and the *teleological*. There is a vast literature on these arguments. Each has received many refinements and been subjected to much criticism. If they were entirely convincing in themselves one would have to conclude that all atheists are intellectually stupid for failing to grasp the arguments. Our experience of atheists shows that this is far from the truth. But ultimately it seems to remain true that unless we accept the Theistic account we are obliged to surrender both the explanation of how mind emerged from the mindless and of why there is anything at all. A tough minded atheist would no doubt admit that there is no explanation for these things, but then his own mind functions in such a way as to suggest that there is meaning to the demand for explanation and that he believes mind to be reliable in a way in which it could not possibly be if it were emergent matter.

Two further arguments are frequently used to supplement the others. These are the *moral argument* and the *argument from religious experience*. Basically, these arguments are, like the others, an attempt to invoke the Theistic account as the

[24] Ed. Norman Kemp Smith, Edinburgh, 1935.
[25] The relevant passages are printed in full with notes and a bibliography in Caldecott and Mackintosh, *op. cit.*, pp. 183f.

only possible means of explanation, with the implication that on the atheistic view the search for explanation must be abandoned.

The moral argument is based on the need to account for man's moral sense, for his conviction that he *ought* to do certain things and *ought not* to do others. An atheist of strong moral principle, Bertrand Russell for example, agrees with the Theist, that Hitler was an evil man. He will condemn the concentration camps, the tortures, the mass annihilations by the Nazis. Moreover, he will not rest content with equating his condemnation of these horrors merely with feelings of strong personal disgust. He will not say that the foul deeds of the Nazis were simply unpleasant to their victims and to Russell himself, though pleasant or at least desirable for the murderers. He will no doubt say that Hitler and his henchmen were evil men who pursued evil and that it was wrong of them to have done so. They *ought not* to have done so. Now on the Theistic account this makes sense. God is the source of goodness. Goodness is written into the very structure of the universe and he who pursues evil offends against the very source of life. But this implies that there are standards of good and evil apart from man, standards to which man *ought* to conform even if he personally finds it profitable or pleasant to act otherwise. On the atheistic view there can be no standards 'out there' in the universe apart from the man because apart from man there is only soulless, mindless matter.

To argue in this vein is not to suggest that the atheist cannot be morally good. On the contrary it is precisely because many atheists live moral lives and pursue goodness and truth courageously and heroically that the argument has force. For the atheist, too, behaves as if his moral standards were far more than personal preferences. He acts as if these standards are grounded in a reality other than and far greater than himself. And unless this Ground is God it is difficult to see what else it can be.

The *argument from religious experience* is based on the incontrovertible fact that men everywhere and at every stage of civilisation have claimed an experience of a reality not themselves, met in wonderment and awe as immeasurably superior and majestic. This experience, different in kind from other experiences,[26] is, on the Theistic account, an experience of God. This does not necessarily mean that all who have had it have seen it as an experience of God. But if there is no God how is this unique kind of experience to be explained? It is fallacious to argue that the mere fact of men having the experience is in itself a validation of the Theistic position. The experience may be real enough to those who have it and yet be explained in a purely naturalistic fashion. But it is difficult to see what form such naturalistic explanation can take without suggesting as delusion man's total urge to worship and his conviction that in worship he is in touch with a reality other than and greater than himself. This may be so. Men, even millions of men, can all be mistaken and yet if man is mistaken, if he is deluded, on these elevated matters does not this place a huge question mark against all man's interpretation of experience? Furthermore, the mystics and men of religion belonging to quite different faiths have been remarkably in agreement in trying, albeit inadequately, to describe their experience. This agreement is all the more pronounced when it is realised that their vocabulary is taken quite obviously from the particular religious tradition to which they belong. Over and above the particularistic colouring, dependent on the mystic's own group, temperament and background, there seems to be a real core of universal experience. The Theist affirms that this is an experience of God.

Naturally, although the Theist sees the basic experience of religious men as an experience of the one God he will not recognise equally every manifestation of it. Idolatry is still idolatry. But what the Theist can and will claim is that idolatrous worship can itself be an experience of the divine though apprehended in an entirely unsatisfactory form. Ibn Gabirol and others have not hesitated to suggest that even the idolator is really worshipping the true God without knowing it.

Taking all the arguments together we are led to complete conviction or, in any event, to very good *reasons* for believing in God, apart from the other considerations to be discussed later in this book. Thus, on the atheistic view, the existence of the universe is a sheer unexplained brute fact, the pur-

[26] See *infra*, pp. 81.

posiveness in nature is only apparent, moral standards inhere only in man and yet men obey them even when they seem detrimental to their own interests, and the religious experience of mankind is a vast delusion. But once it is acknowledged that God is, despite the terrible problem of evil, there is an explanation. The idea of God as the most conceivably perfect being is in the mind because there really is such a Being (the *ontological argument*); the world is because God is (the *cosmological argument*); there is evidence of design in the universe because there really is a designing Mind (the *teleological argument*); moral standards inhere in God (the *moral argument*); and man has religious experiences because his nature is such that he can approach his Maker (the *argument from religious experience*). All this makes Theism the most *reasonable* way of explaining the world, indeed, the only way of accepting the principle of explanation itself.

And yet there are atheists. Why do they remain unconvinced by the traditional arguments? Whenever men differ on matters appertaining to how life should be lived their final position is arrived at by something more than an examination of the bare pros and cons. The atheist may wish to live in a universe in which he is accountable to no one but himself, he may even enjoy the feeling of stoical resignation in the face of a hostile universe which man cannot altogether control. He may find an exquisite fascination in the despair which he sees as man's unalterable lot. To some minds it is oddly comforting that human existence is bleak and human life transitory, that nothing matters ultimately. It would, however, be extremely rash and unwarranted for the Theist to accuse the atheist of a flight from reason, for the accusation can apply to himself equally. The Theist, too, may be governed in his decision by motives which have very little to do with a careful weighing of the evidence for and against his position. He, too, may be indulging in wishful thinking when he affirms that there is a God. He may opt for Theism because this best satisfies his infantile need for a father figure, as the Freudians would have it, or because it satisfies the requirements of his social and economic concerns, as the Marxists would have it. For all the Theist knows to the contrary God may have His own purpose, in the world He has created, for the honest atheist. The really important point here is that man may arrive at the truth even though his motives are less than worthy, just as he may miss the truth even when his motives are worthy. Many an atheist is so because of a mistaken attitude which sees God as man's enemy, curbing his attempts at self-realisation and creativity. But to see God in this way is a travesty of any refined form of Theism. From the Jewish point of view God did not create man for abasement and unworthy grovelling at His feet but, in the words of the Rabbis, to be His partner in the work of creation.

Chapter 4

The Leap of Faith

THE mediaeval rationalistic approach to faith, discussed in the previous chapter, has been heavily assailed by more recent thinkers, particularly religious existentialists. The traditional proofs of God's existence have been subjected to serious criticism from Hume and Kant onwards. But even if the traditional proofs were capable of producing complete intellectual assent it has become increasingly obvious that something far more is involved in faith than mere assent to a proposition. Alexander Altmann has said:[1] 'The mediaeval discussion of faith was primarily concerned with the claims to truth of Revelation and Reason respectively. It investigated the validity of Faith against the authority of Reason, but left the nature of the act of faith as such more or less unexplored. Wherever faith is defined by the mediaeval schools the emphasis is placed on the intellectual element in the act of faith. In the extreme case (in Islamic and Jewish *Kalam*) faith is identified with the sense of certitude accompanying scientific knowledge. *'I'tikad* and *'emunah* are interpreted as "scientific conviction" (Aristotle's *pistis*). No worse misreading of the true nature of religious faith is imaginable. The strange fact has to be recognised that an age so strong in faith completely failed to account for the character of its religious experience, except for the mystics in whom faith merged too clearly into revelatory experience to be mistaken for rational knowledge.'

Because this is so no one today can consider the question of faith without facing the existentialist challenge. The religious existentialists interpret faith as the response of man's

---

[1] 'The Modern Analysis of Faith' in 'Addresses given at the Ninth Conference of Anglo-Jewish Preachers—May 14th-17th', London, 1951, pp. 33-38.

entire being, not reason alone. That there are fresh and significant insights in religious existentialism should be freely admitted. It must also be realised that frequently the rejection of the exclusive role of reason in the quest for faith unfortunately results in the complete abandonment of reason in that quest. It is one thing to underscore the inadequacies of a shallow rationalism. It is quite another to embrace the kind of irrationalism in religion which appears to be deep only because it is obscure.

Although William James's thinking on religion is not generally considered to be sufficiently personalistic and individualistic for inclusion among the existentialists, his famous essay 'The Will to Believe'[2] is without doubt the most articulate statement of the position that man has a right to believe even though the merely logical intellect may not have been coerced.

James's essay was delivered originally as an address to the Philosophical Clubs of Yale and Brown Universities. James is fully aware that his thesis is strikingly unconventional and likely to meet with resistance by people trained to test theories who refuse to believe anything on insufficient evidence. James observes[3] that when we are called upon to choose between two alternative theories our option is genuine if it fulfils three conditions. It must be living, forced and momentous. A momentous option is one in which there is no second chance, i.e. unlike a scientific hypothesis which can be discarded after a period of testing without results. A forced option is one in which there is no middle way, i.e. unlike the choice of carrying an umbrella outdoors. One can avoid the choice by staying at home. A live option is one in which both views have at least some appeal to the person making the choice. As an example of a 'dead' option James gives: Choose whether to believe in the claims of the Mahdi. In the Western world no one has the slightest attraction or desire to believe in the Mahdi. To decide for or against Theistic belief fulfils all three conditions. It is live since for most of us both sides are living choices. It is forced because agnosticism is itself a choice against a living

[2] Published originally by Longmans, Green, New York, 1897 and republished freq.
[3] Part I.

66

relationship with God. And it is momentous because the whole quality of one's life is affected by the choice.

James was one of the first to call attention to the forced nature of the decision for or against God. His point here is that faith involves a living relationship with God. The true believer is not content with simply stating that God exists in the same way as he would affirm that the moon is a quarter of a million miles distant from earth. He lives a God-directed life. God is in his thoughts and his actions. The agnostic holds that we can never know if there is a God and he claims to suspend belief. But by leaving the question open he leaves open, too, the question of whether man can have the relationship with God that is of the essence of faith. If there is no God there is no one with whom to have this relationship. This means surely that in opting for agnosticism he is opting against the relationship with God. The very fact that he is uncertain whether there is a God means that even if there is he can never have this relationship with Him which belongs to the essence of faith. For it must be obvious that while agnosticism regards God's existence as an open question, by so doing it rules out the whole possibility of relationship. It is surely psychologically impossible to have a warm association with a being whose existence one doubts. Thus it is unreal to read man's situation as a choice between atheism and belief in God with agnosticism as the middle way. Agnosticism is itself a choice against the relationship with God. The real choice is between a relationship with God and the lack of it.

What is the role of the will in belief? James refers[4] to Pascal's famous wager. A game is in progress, Pascal argues in James's interpretation, between you and the nature of things, and the day of judgment will decide a win or a loss. What are the chances? If you stake your life that God is, the gain, if He is, is eternal bliss. If He is not and you have staked your life on belief that He is what have you lost? The loss is merely finite whereas the gain is infinite. It is surely most reasonable to stake finite loss against the possibility of infinite gain. On the surface, says James, this is objectionable. We do not believe by volition. 'If we were the Deity we should probably take pleasure in cutting off such a calculating believer from

[4] Part II, Pascal's wager is found in his 'Pensées', No. 233.

his eternal reward.' Pascal's wager seems to lack the 'inner soul of faith's reality'. Surely Pascal himself must have been attracted to belief by something more than a cold calculation of the odds. James quotes Clifford: 'It is wrong always, everywhere, and for everyone, to believe anything on insufficient evidence.'

All this is true, replies James,[5] and yet we are mistaken if we imagine that when we banish all sentiment, wish and will, it is intellectual insight which remains or that pure reason then finalises our opinions. There is passion in our every choice. Our belief in truth, for instance, is a passionate affirmation of desire. Our non-intellectual nature does influence our convictions. And therefore Pascal is in this sense correct to say that however we choose in this matter of faith there is the necessity for a decisive choice and it is our will by which we decide.

Thus James states his thesis:[6] *'Our passional nature not only lawfully may, but must, decide an option between propositions, whenever it is a genuine option that cannot be decided on intellectual grounds; for to say, under such circumstances, "Do not decide but leave the question open", is itself a passionate decision—just like deciding yes or no—and is attended with the same risk of losing the truth.'*

It is important to realise that James's argument is based on the view that the question of God's existence cannot be decided on intellectual grounds. The arguments for and against are not conclusive. Since, then, belief of this kind 'cannot be decided on intellectual grounds' and since it is a 'genuine option' our passional nature must step in to decide. James's thesis regarding the 'will to believe' is based on his pragmatism.

James cannot agree with Clifford that rather than risk embracing error it is better to chance never attaining truth since we must remember that these feelings of our duty regarding truth and error are only expressions of our passional life.[7] Clifford's argument, remarks James, is like that of a general urging his soldiers never to fight rather than risk a single wound. The most momentous questions of human existence— for example moral questions—cannot wait for sensible proof

[5] Part III. [6] Part IV. [7] Part VII.

before we decide. Are our moral preferences true or false? Pure intellect cannot decide. Unless your heart *wants* a world of moral reality your mind cannot make you believe in one.[8] Thus James arrives at the conclusion that we have a right to will to believe.

The most serious objection to James's thesis is that the believer holds his belief to be true, whereas if James's thesis were taken as it stands it would allow him to believe anything he wished to believe. The objection has often been made as to (for example) why one should not believe in the Mahdi, if, according to the Mahdi, so much depends on belief in him. James retorts that this is not a 'live' option but why is it not if one wishes to discover and live by the truth? There are a number of ideas in James that we shall meet again in our discussion of religious existentialism but the basic fault with James's view is that it lacks the certainty which belief provides and which the religious existentialist passionately seeks.

Søren Kierkegaard (1813-1855), the founder of religious existentialism, refers to the 'leap of faith', the very cornerstone of existentialism.[9] The uninformed critic of the 'leap of faith' might interpret it to mean that when one is unsure if God exists, he should choose to believe that He does and hope the choice is correct. This is a complete travesty of the philosophy. We may not entirely agree with Kierkegaard but he and his followers are far from superficial.

The rational approach seems to assume that man can be argued into faith, into a belief in God. Demonstrations are provided to prove that God exists and it is taken for granted that unless a man is intellectually obtuse he will follow the argument to its conclusion, becoming a believer. This whole approach tends to treat the embryonic believer as standing outside life in some mysterious way, viewing the human scene

---

[8] Part IX.

[9] See Walter Lowrie: 'Kierkegaard', Oxford University Press, 1938; 'Kierkegaard as Theologian' by Louis Dupré, Sheed and Ward, London, 1964; J. Heywood Thomas: 'Subjectivity and Paradox', Blackwell, Oxford, 1957; David E. Roberts: 'Existentialism and Religious Belief', Galaxy Books, New York, 1959; Ernst Breisach: 'Introduction to Modern Existentialism', Grove Press, New York, 1962; Frederick Copleston, S.J.: 'Contemporary Philosophy', Burns and Oates, London, 1956; John A. Hutchinson: 'Faith, Reason and Existence', New York, Oxford University Press 1956.

with detachment. There he is faced with two propositions, that God is or He is not, and he calmly decides, when he finds the arguments convincing, that the first is true.

It is extremely unlikely that anyone ever approaches the question of faith in this detached way. Man is himself involved intimately in the fundamental questions of human existence. His own personality, his hopes, strivings, ambitions, anxieties and frustrations, are all involved in his decision because all are part of life's structure. It is no phantom that makes the choice but a human being whose whole life depends on this basic decision. The truths which challenge him are subjective rather than objective. If they are true they are true independently of him but they matter so profoundly to his life that they cannot, without delusion, be viewed in a completely detached way. Neither the Theist nor the atheist is reasoned into conviction. It is more a matter of man being obliged freely to choose the way he believes to be true.

Man is in the position of having to decide whether God is and is to be worshipped, or is not so that there is no Object of worship. He cannot make this momentous decision on the basis of reason alone, though reason can help him. The arguments which convince the Theist are unacceptable to·the atheist and between two men of equal intellectual ability the differences can hardly be based on the arguments alone. But the atheist cannot take refuge in the thought that since the case for God is unproven he can rest secure in unbelief. For if God is and cannot be reached by unaided reason but only by the total response of man's whole personality (if He is a Person to be met, as the Theist holds) then the atheist, by refusing to opt for God, is himself deciding to lead his life on grounds other than the rational. It is as if a person with few opportunities for meeting the opposite sex solemnly decides by the use of his reason that the poets are talking nonsense when they speak of falling in love. The only course for the believer is to leap into faith to discover that his faith is vindicated.

The term 'subjective', used by the religious existentialists when referring to 'subjective truth', does not mean without reference to the question of truth. They are certainly not saying that the statement 'there is a God' is solely an expression of personal preference. What they are saying is that the traditional attempt to prove God's existence by demonstrations taken from the physical world is 'objective', i.e. apart from man and his needs, whereas in any vital view of faith it is these last which are most relevant. In this sense faith is 'subjective'. It is true for man, it affects his whole way of life, it demands the strongest personal commitment. In terms of our analysis in the first chapter of this book, 'belief *that* . . .' cannot be divorced from 'belief *in* . . .'. The trusting attitude is an essential ingredient in faith, though it must be admitted that all too often religious existentialists give the impression that 'belief in . . .' is all that matters. This is, of course, nonsense. One cannot believe *in* God unless one believes that there is a God in whom to believe.

The religious existentialists argue that when we say that the glory of God is seen in the heavens which 'declare' it we do not, in fact, see God in the heavens unless we already have a concept of God. God is the postulate of the argument, not its conclusion. We do not begin, as it were, from the beginning and eventually arrive at God. If we proceeded in this way it is extremely doubtful if we would ever arrive at this conclusion. We use the argument to see God's glory when we gaze up at the heavens.[10] Kierkegaard is not advocating the 'leap of faith' as something worth taking which he argues upon us. His aim is rather to show that whoever undertakes to demonstrate God's existence has already taken the leap.

There is a further point of great significance. Even if the traditional proofs were entirely valid they would not in themselves be more than a demonstration. They cannot provide the 'passion' of faith. For this the 'leap' is necessary. Indeed, too much concern with demonstrative proof of God's existence suggests the lack of that burning passion which belongs to the real life of faith. Kierkegaard and his followers do not argue that since God's existence cannot be rationally demonstrated His existence is therefore only probable. On the contrary they are fighting this uncertain attitude. The essence of faith is, for them, its passionate certainty and for this to be attained the 'leap' is necessary.

On this view faith is not something one can win once and

[10] J. Heywood Thomas, *op. cit.*, pp. 77-102.

forever. There is tension in the life of faith. Throughout his life man is faced with the burning choice between belief and unbelief. The 'knight of faith', to use Kierkegaard's name, lives as other men, differing only in that he must constantly opt for faith (as the lover is loyal to his beloved even when—especially when—tensions disturb their relationship).

For the existentialists, man's situation can be compared[11] to that of a weary traveller lost in a blizzard on a mountain with many paths before him. He cannot be certain which is the path to safety but he cannot remain static for this is to invite certain death from exposure. All he can do is to choose intuitively one path hoping it is the way that eventually leads to the warmth and security of the valley. There is risk from the moment he takes the very first step along the path he has chosen, but it is one he must take if he is not to perish.

The existentialist insight that we are obliged to choose if we are to live fully is valuable. It is a necessary reminder that we cannot find our way of life simply by constructing philosophical systems which seek to explain everything in heaven and earth but which, in the process, ignore the individual human being. For a philosophy of life to be true it must be 'true for me'. Faith is a prayer we pray with all of our being or remain silent. The life of faith demands our total commitment; the difference between religion and philosophy is that 'religion does something about it'. And, as we have noted earlier, the existentialist suspicion of system is, in part, a return to the Biblical insight that God is to be experienced, not a subject for argument.

The danger, however, is that in the existentialist approach reason tends to become completely silenced. Reason is an inadequate tool for the comprehension of ultimate reality but it is the only tool we have for distinguishing faith from credulity, true religion from superstition, enthusiasm from fanaticism. True, the man stranded in the blizzard is compelled to move unsurely along a blindly chosen path, but if he is wise he will try, so far as he possibly can, to choose the way he has reason to believe will lead him safely to his destination.

[11] This illustration is quoted by William James: 'The Will to Believe' and from Fitz James Stephen.

It would be a counsel of despair to urge him to walk on regardless of the risk.

Kierkegaard owes much to a tendency in Christian thought which advocates the crucifixion of reason in the name of faith. Such tendencies are not unknown in Jewish thought[12] and the opposite tendencies are known in Christianity. It is true, nevertheless, that Kierkegaard lays particular stress on 'the absurd', because other distinguished Christian thinkers in the past have pointed to the central doctrine of Christianity as the supreme example of reason's unreliability in matters of faith. Reason is incapable of grasping that three is one or that God assumes flesh. It is therefore possible to argue as Kierkegaard does that since, in any event, reason cannot take man to the heart of the Christian faith (and, indeed contradicts a basic premise of faith) it has no part at all to play in the life of faith or, at the most, only a very insignificant part.

Reference has often been made in this connection to Tertullian's paradox: 'The Son of God was crucified; I am not ashamed because man must needs be ashamed of it. The Son of God died; it is by all means to be believed, because it is absurd. And He was buried and rose again; it is certain, because it is impossible.'[13] 'Because it is impossible', certainty is secured for faith by removing it entirely from the domain of conceptual thinking; this must be done, for Tertullian, because faith, in any event, affirms that which is 'impossible' for the human mind.

David E. Roberts[14] puts the objection to Kierkegaard from the Christian view. For Judaism the objection is even more cogent: 'It is one thing to show why an object we approach cannot be the sole method for dealing with religious questions, and why, insofar as it excludes passion and faith, it is intrinsically defective. Yet it is quite another thing to conclude, as he seems to do, that the objective approach is inapplicable to religious questions, and that it cannot be combined with passion and faith. Hence, while his negative warning against rationalism can certainly be accepted, Kierkegaard cannot be swallowed whole by anyone who sees the search for objective

---

[12] See *infra*, pp. 201-209.
[13] *'De Carne Christi'*, V, pp. 173-4.
[14] *Op. cit.*, pp. 107-108.

truth in any sphere (including the application of scientific findings and method to the study of religion) as an integral part of his *passionately* affirmed ideal of Christian integrity, (for *Christian* substitute Jewish and the point is valid for Jews).

In its more extreme form the 'commitment' argument runs that *whatever* philosophy man chooses is arbitrary, since reason does not justify itself. Even if one chooses a course of action or a way of life because it seems reasonable one can always ask 'why be reasonable?'. No 'reasonable' reply can be given. Consequently, some religious existentialists argue the rationalist is as arbitrary and unreasonable as the religious person; indeed, he may be less rational in that he does not recognise the irrationality of his rationalism.

This position has, with justice, been vigorously attacked by William Warren Bartley III,[15] in an acute study of the problem. Bartley rightly observes[16] that this kind of appeal only increases the invulnerability of its opponents to criticism. For this position is argued for. Books are written in defence of it and to attack its opposite. But if, in the final analysis, any position is arbitrary there is no point in arguing for one above others. 'Those who gain a refuge of safety for themselves through appeals to the limits of rationality thereby provide a similar refuge for all others whose commitments differ from theirs. Thus, the many criticisms which the Protestant theologians have levelled at rationalism and liberalism become as pointless as those the liberals have directed at theology. Ultimately, the *tu quoque* makes nonsense of the historical development and change of ideas in the face of criticism.' In denying *through argument* the use of reason as a guide the objectors demonstrate in that very process their reliance on reason.

Bartley's own attitude is that of 'comprehensive critical rationalism', i.e. that all of man's beliefs are rational if they can be treated critically, including the rationalist position. Here the mediaeval emphasis, for all its inadequacy, can be of help to us. The great Jewish thinkers of the middle ages believed that theirs was a 'comprehensively critical rationalism'. It should be acknowledged, however, that, at times, their

[15] 'The Retreat to Commitment'.
[16] pp. 96-97.

conclusions were arrived at by non-rational means without their being aware of this. Bartley wittily concludes: 'In the old story, the Pennsylvania Dutchman says to his wife: "Everybody is crazy but me and thee, Hannah, and sometimes I wonder even about thee." Anybody, from the neurotic to Reinhold Niebuhr, can play Pennsylvania Dutchman and ask us to "take the leap of faith"—whether it is a "great leap forward", a great leap backwards, or a somersault on the *status quo*—to his own irrational commitment. That commitment may carry consolations; there are, as Ibsen knew, such things as "saving lies". But if we look before we leap—and when the chasm is very wide, he who hesitates is not necessarily lost—many of us will be unable to crucify our intellects without impaling our integrity.'

We must conclude that, as the existentialists remind us, we fail to understand what faith involves if we see it as simple assent to the proposition that God exists. On the nature of faith religious existentialism is very sound. 'Belief *in*' God, the reaching out in trust, the personal relationship in which our totality is involved, the passionate affirmation of that which is 'true for me', all these are essentials in the life of faith. But one can only 'believe *in*' a being who actually exists. 'Belief *that*' there is a God must justify itself at the bar of reason. This does not mean that before one can honestly believe one must be convinced by the type of demonstration provided by the traditional 'proofs'. There are other ways to faith (discussed elsewhere in this book). But it does mean that however faith is attained it must be a reasonable faith, it must cohere with the rest of our knowledge. When the 'leap of faith' is invoked to ignore reason entirely it is an open invitation to credulity.

No Jewish approach to faith can consider existentialism without taking note of the work of Martin Buber.[17] Buber's writings, too, are not free from the occasional surrender to irrationalism and his difficult style is not helpful to clear thinking in matters of religion. Moreover Buber's emphasis

[17] See Maurice S. Friedman: 'Martin Buber, The Life of Dialogue', Chicago University Press, 1955; Will Herberg: 'Judaism and Modern Man', Farrer, Straus and Young, New York, 1951; Malcolm L. Diamond: 'Martin Buber, Jewish Existentialist', New York, Oxford University Press, 1960; Jacob B. Agus: Modern Philosophies of Judaism', Behrman's New York, 1941.

on the personal appropriation of religious truth frequently excludes the traditional Jewish ideal of submission to God's commands. Nevertheless, Buber does draw his inspiration from Jewish sources. He has always claimed that he speaks at the door of his father's house and he must certainly be considered the most seminal Jewish thinker of the twentieth century.

Buber's particular contribution to the question of faith is his emphasis on the life of dialogue as the means for encountering God. Few contemporary works on religious faith make no references to Buber's 'I-Thou'.[18] Buber's central thesis is that man can have two different relationships to other human beings, to ideas and institutions, even to animals and to inanimate things. In the one relationship man *uses* the world of people and things outside himself, in the other he *meets* them. When man is a user his relationship is that of 'I-It'. When he 'meets' the person or thing his relationship is that of 'I-Thou'. He is then addressing, not using.

There is not only a distinction between the 'It' and the 'Thou'; this is obvious. Buber is saying that the 'I' is different in the two kinds of relationships. The 'I' of the 'I-Thou' is different from the 'I' of the 'I-It'. In the latter instance man is not truly involved. Since he uses the other as an 'It' his 'I' also becomes an 'It', detached from the other. In the 'I-Thou' his 'I' is enriched precisely because it is involved and engaged.

Buber does not, however, reject the 'I-It' relationship. The 'I-It' is, indeed, the only way in which we can obtain scientific knowledge of the material universe. The scientist is more likely to succeed in his investigations if he is not emotionally intoxicated with the subject. Here detachment is called for, a rigorous exclusion of personal predilections and prejudgments in the interests of truth. The less the self intrudes the greater the chance of success because it is not the 'true for me' that is sought. But in personal relationships the 'I-Thou' is imperative, though seldom realised, if life is to be lived at its fullest with engagement. 'The primary word *I-Thou* can only be spoken with the whole being. The primary word *I-It* can never

[18] Buber's classic work is: 'I and Thou', English translation by Ronald Gregor Smith, Scribner's, New York, 1937.

be spoken with the whole being.'[19] We can get to know other human beings, for example, not by dispassionately studying their habits, dress or character (by treating them as things to be used or investigated) but by meeting them as equals and by conversing face to face. Or, to take an example from the impersonal, there is a vast difference between the 'I-It' of someone consciously determined to enjoy music (in which case he does not fully enjoy it since part of him is sufficiently detached to observe himself and therefore not fully engaged) and the 'I-Thou' of someone whom the music moves spontaneously so that it can be said to meet him and, in a sense, even to converse with him.

For Buber, argument about God's existence cannot take man very far on the road of faith. In this relationship God is only thought about and is an 'It' in relation to man's 'I'. In prayer, on the other hand, man speaks to God and God responds. The relationship here is 'I-Thou'. But it is not only, or even chiefly, in prayer that man meets God. God is the eternal *Thou* of the universe including in His being all temporal 'Thous'. Whenever man meets others in the 'I-Thou' he meets God. 'Every particular *Thou* is a glimpse through to the eternal *Thou*; by means of every particular Thou the primary word addresses the eternal *Thou*. Through this mediation of the *Thou* of all beings fulfilment, and non-fulfilment, of relations comes to them: the inborn *Thou* is realised in each relation and consummated in none. It is consummated only in the direct relation with the *Thou* that by its nature cannot become *It*.'[20]

At one period, Buber was very interested in Jewish mysticism, but he eventually rejected the mystical approach in which man's 'I' tends to become nothing before the Infinite. It is, for Buber, man in his human situations who becomes the 'I' capable of meeting the 'Thou'. In one respect, however, Buber does follow the mystical tradition. The mystics distinguish between God as He is in Himself and God as He becomes revealed to others. With the mystics Buber holds that it is impossible for man to know God as He is in Himself. This aspect of Deity is, indeed, irrelevant for Buber. The God of

[19] *Ibid.*, Part I, p. 3.
[20] *Ibid.*, Part III, p. 75.

vital religion is God as He is revealed and, for Buber, the revelation is always through dialogue. Whenever a man meets the other in the true 'I-Thou' relationship he glimpses God, the eternal *Thou*.

It needs further to be said that one of the main aims of existentialist thought is to free the individual from subservience to system. The existentialist mood (a better term than existentialist philosophy, which itself implies system) demands that man engages in a constant quest for individual authenticity. Man finds his freedom in choosing and the choice itself is more significant than what is chosen. Atheistic existentialists like Sartre hold that since there is no God there is no special pattern for man to which he must adapt himself. In Sartre's own words, which reverse the classical formulation, 'existence precedes essence'. There is no essence for man to which his individual existence must be shaped. His existence, the choices he makes and the kind of life he leads, determine his essence. But even the religious existentialists, like Kierkegaard and Buber, are impatient with a system, even the highest, imposed upon man from without. Kierkegaard finds this easier of attainment, easier for man to embrace his naked individuality, because of the strong individualistic tendencies in Christianity. It is no accident that Buber's attitude to the Law is for Jews highly unconventional. Man can, of course, meet God through the Law even for Buber but only in the 'I-Thou' relationship in which the Law 'speaks' to his individual condition. This is far from the traditional Jewish picture of the Law written large into the very structure of the universe.

Traditional Judaism teaches that there is a pattern. It is concerned with answers to the great questions of human existence even though these are not easy or comfortable answers. It teaches that man should choose and what he should choose. It advocates, for example *Imitatio Dei* and describes this with reference to concrete actions: 'Just as He is called merciful be thou merciful. Just as He is called compassionate be thou compassionate.' And there are, too, negative rules. Murder, theft, adultery and fraudulent dealing are wrong. There are limitations from without of man's choice. There are areas into which he must not venture and duties he must fulfil. But man becomes truly human by accepting these limitations since, as

Judaism sees it, the world is so constituted by God. This is not to suggest that a man should seek to evade his responsibility by neurotic submission to an order with which he feels himself at variance. The Jewish prayer book speaks of Israel 'accepting God's sovereignty *willingly*'.[21] For God's truth is infinite and man finds his true fulfilment in its appropriation for himself. Judah Ha-Levi writes:

> '*A slave of slaves is the servant of time;*
> *The servant of the Lord alone is free.*'

To revert to the theme of our analysis in the first chapter of this book, the existentialist mood is much closer to the Biblical insight into the nature of faith than is the rationalistic approach of the mediaeval thinkers. The Hebrew Bible, too, deals with faith in terms of passionate concern and commitment. It recognises the needs of the individual face to face with his God. It stresses that the whole man and not his reason alone must be involved in the life of faith. It is non-systematic and God is both nearer and yet more mysterious than in the too-tidy schemes of the mediaeval thinkers. The mood of existentialism with regard to self-commitment and involvement provides us with the 'belief *in* . . .' so typical, as we have seen, of the Biblical and Rabbinic categories. But the Bible knows, too, of 'belief *that* . . .'. This is affirmed so passionately as to remain unnecessary of precise formulation. The Bible teaches that God does have a plan for man, that there is an 'essence' ordained by God. '*It hath been told thee, O man, what is good, And what the Lord doth require of thee: Only to do justly, and to love mercy, and to walk humbly with thy God*' (Micah 6:8).[22]

---

[21] Singer's Prayer Book, new edition, p. 120.
[22] There are very few discussions of existentialism from the Jewish point of view. One of these is 'Anatomy of Faith' by Milton Steinberg, ed. Arthur A. Cohen, Harcourt, Brace, New York, 1960.

Chapter 5

The Way of Experience

THE existentialist approach to faith, examined in the previous chapter, is opposed to the systematic rationalist approach typical of the Middle Ages but it is not necessarily opposed to reason as such. According to the existentialists reason must not be elevated as the sole means for faith's acquisition. The whole man must be involved. Yet reason has a part to play (except for the more extreme religious existentialists whose approach borders on the irrational and who appear to hold their beliefs without any cause). Existentialism, for all its mistrust of system, is a philosophical approach to life. It makes use of reasoned argument. Its exponents seek to elucidate, explain and convince by an appeal to man's reasoning powers.

A very different approach to faith is to see it as basically non-rational. According to this view religious faith is a special kind of *experience*. The mystical tradition in religion has always emphasised this but in modern times our attention to this aspect of faith is due to Rudolf Otto (1869-1937). In this chapter we shall first examine Otto's specific contribution and then the mystical approach in general. In the way of reason God is to be known in the same way as a proposition is known, through ratiocination. In existentialism God is to be known as a person is known, through encounter. In the way of experience God is to be known as beauty is known, through the use of a special faculty peculiar to itself.

Otto,[1] more than any other thinker, has called attention to religious experience as *sui generis*, not to be understood in terms of any other experience, not even in terms of the rational.

---

[1] 'The Idea of the Holy' by Rudolf Otto. *Cf.* Robert F. Davidson: 'Rudolf Otto's Interpretation of Religion', Princeton University Press, 1947.

Religious experience is non-rational in the sense in which art and music are non-rational. One cannot adequately explain why a painting, a sculpture, a symphony is aesthetically satisfying and the failure is not due to any weakness in the reasoning process but the inevitable result of confusing the aesthetic with the rational. Appreciation of beauty is in a category of its own. One cannot be coerced into having it by a reasoned argument. Religious experience too can only be appreciated on its own terms. Otto seeks to analyse the experience and claims that his is an insight which alone makes sense of all the authentic descriptions of religious experience from the most primitive to the most sublime. Reason has a part to play, of course. Otto, too, has written works to persuade others by means of rational argument that his insight is correct. But the purpose of such reasoning is not to demonstrate rationally the existence of God but rather to show that religious people have *experienced* God and that religious faith is a matter of such experience.

Otto coins the word numinous to describe the object of religious experience, from the Latin *numen*, 'spirit', i.e. the divinity residing in a sacred spot or object. The Biblical account of Jacob's dream (Gen. 28: 10-22) is a powerful illustration of a numinous experience. *'And he was afraid and said: "How full of awe is this place! This is none other than the house of God, and this is the gate of heaven"'* (Gen. 28: 17). Jacob, in the narrative, is not afraid that God may harm him. The cause of his dread is the awareness of the tremendous Presence pervading the place where he had dreamed. Here was strangeness and sublimity, so different from his normal experience that he trembles at the contemplation of the thing in itself. And yet, observes Otto, the man undergoing the numinous experience finds fascination in its object as well as fear. He both recoils from and is mysteriously but irresistibly drawn towards it. Otto's famous definition of the numinous is then: *mysterium tremendum et fascinans*. The Bible speaks of this category as 'the holy'. In the original German edition Otto's best-known book is *'Das Heilige'*, translated into English as: 'The Idea of the Holy'. Its sub-title is 'An Inquiry into the non-rational factor in the idea of the Divine and its relation to the rational'.

It follows from Otto's analysis of religious experience as *sui generis* that it does not of itself belong in the category of the ethical. Theoretically there is no reason why a man gifted with a strong sense of the numinous should have an equally powerful sense of the good, any more than a highly talented artist must necessarily be of good moral character. But in the Biblical accounts of the numinous, such as we find in the writings of the Hebrew prophets, the ethical is combined *with* the numinous to produce 'the holy'. Both must be present in the religious life. Holiness for the Hebrew prophets denotes a combination of the *mysterium tremendum et fascinans* with the ethical.

There have been earlier attempts to describe holiness. Among Jewish thinkers is Nahmanides (1195-c.1270), in his commentary to the Pentateuch. Commenting on the verse: '*Speak unto all the congregation of the children of Israel, and say unto them: Ye shall be holy: for I the Lord your God am holy*' (Lev. 19:2), Nahmanides first observes that the root meaning of *kedushah*—the Hebrew term for 'holiness'—is 'separation'. Consequently, Nahmanides understands the command to be holy as an injunction to separate oneself from that which is legally permitted but nevertheless harmful to the character and to society. For instance, certain foods are forbidden by Scripture, but it is still possible for the man obedient to the dietary laws to be a glutton with permitted food, or to be a drunkard even though he drinks no forbidden wine. Certain sexual unions are forbidden but, in the polygamous society which Scripture assumes, it is still possible, without any infringement of the law, for a man grossly to over-indulge himself sexually. The injunction to lead a holy life is, according to Nahmanides, a command to discipline one's appetites and ambitions beyond the limits imposed by the Law. This, too, is part of the Law, i.e. part of the demand Scripture makes of the Jew, though the extent of separation will depend on individual need and temperament. Unless this injunction is observed man becomes, in Nahmanides' cogent phrase, 'a libertine with the permission of the *Torah*'.

But, if Otto is right, Nahmanides' analysis lacks precision. The command to engage in holy living involves, for Nahmanides, an extension of the ethical so as to cover instances not governed directly by the Law. The call of the holy is a call to a more virtuous life. But, for Otto, although the holy embraces the ethical it is not identical with the ethical. Nahmanides is within the Biblical conception in seeing ethical conduct in the ideal of holiness but, as Otto states, the holy as found in the Bible contains three elements—the numinous, the ethical and the rational.

Otto's analysis is very different from that which sees religious experience as mere feeling. No one would deny that men frequently have emotions generally called religious. But the significant question for faith is whether these are purely subjective or whether an actual object is really apprehended by them. For Otto, apprehension of the numinous ('divination') is awareness of an objective reality. The 'holy' which man experiences is something outside himself. The use of 'outside' in this connection is unavoidable but more than a little misleading, suggesting as it does a spatial situation for the object experienced. On the more primitive level the reality encountered in the numinous experience is thought of as actually located in a particular spot. The history of sacred sites pregnant with deity is a reminder that this is so. On the more sophisticated level, however, the experience is seen as taking place within the soul of man. The object has no spatial situation and yet the experience is not purely subjective. The man who sees pink elephants as a result of alcoholic over-indulgence has a purely subjective experience. The alcohol induces the experience but the elephants exist only in his imagination. Whereas, the man who gets intense aesthetic pleasure from a beautiful picture is moved by something other than himself. He would not normally say that the picture induces the feeling of pleasure but that he responds to the real beauty which is 'there' independent of the observer. If it be asked why the religious experience should be compared to the one rather than the other the answer of the believer is that God, the Object of the numinous experience, really exists. If, on the other hand, there is a denial of God's existence then, indeed, the only explanation for religious experience is to see it as self-induced delusion. One man drinks alcohol and sees pink elephants, the other man fasts and sees God. Hume writes that when a man says God appeared to him in a dream it merely means that he dreamed of God. But on the Theistic premise there really is a God to be 'seen'. Otto does not claim that religious experience is itself a validation that there is a God. But once one believes that God is, the religious experience is seen as an experience of God.

So, either religious experience is explained in a purely naturalistic way or it is understood as an actual experience of the 'living God'. The believer need not deny that the experience could be explained away if he did not, on other grounds, believe in God. It might be said, for instance, that certain childhood events may be the cause of subsequent numinous experiences and it is not difficult to see that they are therefore attended by the sense of fascination. However, this does not seem altogether adequate to explain why men belonging to very different cultural traditions similarly describe the experience in a way which suggests that for them it is a real apprehension of the divine.

There is the further point, to which Otto calls attention, that the experience is not given to everyone and in its most intense form is only accessible to those of special 'holiness'. This suggests that the Object of the numinous experience is 'there' to be reached by those who strive to attain it through the quality of their lives. The spiritual eye must be developed before it can catch even an obscure glimpse of God. At any rate this is the claim of some of the greatest religious teachers. The religious traditions of Judaism and her daughter religions are at one in that it is not given to man to see the full vision in this life.[2]

'There are more things in heaven and earth than are dreamed of in your philosophy.' Otto's contention is not that philosophical systems fail to give an adequate account of the

[2] In recent years a number of attempts have been made both to study and to invoke experiences, hitherto associated with the religious or supernatural, in purely natural ways, see: 'The Doors of Perception' and 'Heaven and Hell' by Aldous Huxley, Penguin Books, 1959 and the critique by R. C. Zaehner: 'Mysticism Sacred and Profane', Oxford, Clarendon Press, 1957; Marghanita Laski: 'Ecstasy', The Cresset Press, London, 1961; 'Religions, Values and Peak-Experiences' by Abraham H. Maslow, Ohio State University Press, Columbus, 1964. Maslow (p. 5) writes: 'If you look up the words "sacred", "divine", "holy", "numen", "sin", "prayer", "ablation", "thanksgiving", "worship", "piety", "salvation", "reverence", the dictionary will often tell you that they refer to a god or to a religion in the supernatural sense. Now what I want to say is that each and all of these words,

numinous but that the numinous as a unique non-rational experience is a thing apart from philosophy. The rational element does, however, enter here, in that reason can help distinguish between the more primitive and the more advanced levels of the experience. The more refined Theist has an experience of the living God. The savage interprets his experience in terms of *mana*, each bush, stream and tree being, for him, alive with its own divinity. But, Otto claims, the experience is basically, in its essence, the same for both. Otto[3] gives the illustration of primitive music: to us it would be mere cacophany yet it is still music and can produce a similar response to our reaction to a Bach fugue.

The comparison of the numinous with art and music is instructive, too, in calling attention to the need for its cultivation. The religious of every age have taught that aids are required for the development of the religious experience. They have built awe-inspiring houses of worship. They have composed and used in their worship prayers and chants evocative of the Infinite. They have encouraged and fostered a sense of the wondrous and mysterious. The 'beauty of holiness' differs chiefly from other forms of beauty precisely in its evocation of the 'Other'. It is an unearthly beauty, partaking more of eternity than of time. Jews appear to have had this in the ancient Temple. To this day, as Otto remarks, the Jewish liturgy is rich in numinous hymns and prayers. But after the destruction of the Temple, Jews rarely stayed long enough in one place or felt sufficiently rooted to have been inspired to build anything comparable to the great mediaeval cathedrals. Admittedly the line between a sense of mystery

and many other "religious" words, have been reported to me by non-theistic people in their effort to describe particular subjective happenings in "non-religious" (in the conventional sense) peak-experiences and illuminations. These words are the only words available to describe certain happenings in the natural world. This vocabulary is the language of a theory which people have had about these subjective happenings, a theory which is no longer necessary.' But this is precisely Otto's point that the experiences demand explanation in terms of an Object met and cannot adequately be explained in subjective terms. There is no reason, from the religious point of view, why 'non-theistic people' should not have an experience of God.

[3] 'The Idea of the Holy', pp. 73-74.

and wonder and mystification for its own sake, between the splendidly awe-inspiring and superstition, is finely drawn but drawn it must be if Jews are to recapture the insight that religion is a matter of man's contact with the Infinite, that it arose in the mystic East and must not allow its spirit to be stifled by Western standards of decorum.

It is said that the idea of the numinous came to Otto when he witnessed a Day of Atonement service in a little Synagogue in North Africa. There he saw the worshippers completely wrapped in large, white prayer-shawls, expressing their sense of God's tremendous majesty during a day on which they allowed no food or drink to enter their bodies. In fact the Day of Atonement (*Yom Kippur*) and the New Year Festival (*Rosh Ha-Shanah*), which falls ten days earlier, are known in the Jewish tradition as 'The Days of Awe'. A prayer recited on these days and attributed to the Babylonian teacher Rab (160-247) contains these words:

'Now, therefore, O Lord our God, impose thine awe upon all thy works, and thy dread upon all that thou hast created, that all works may revere thee and all creatures prostrate themselves before thee, that they may all form a single band to do thy will with a perfect heart: even as we know, O Lord our God, that dominion is thine, strength is in thy hand, and might in thy right hand, and that thy Name is to be revered above all that thou hast created.'

Another hymn of later date, speaking of these 'days of judgment', declares: [5]

'The great trumpet is sounded; the still small voice is heard, the angels are dismayed; fear and trembling seize hold of them as they proclaim, Behold the Day of Judgment! The host of heaven is to be arraigned in judgment for in thine eyes they are not pure.'

When the great mediaeval Jewish masters of the spiritual life speak of the 'higher fear' of God they appear to mean a similar state to Otto's experience of the numinous. The fol-

[4] 'New Year Prayer Book', ed. Routledge, 1955, p. 15, referred to by Otto, *op. cit.*, p. 190.
[5] 'New Year Prayer Book', p. 146.

lowing description, for instance, is found in the *Zohar*: [6]
'There are three types of fear: two have no proper roots,
while the third is the real fear. There is the man who fears the
Holy One, blessed be He, in order that his children may live
and not die, or lest he be punished in his body or his possessions: and so he in constant fear. Evidently this is not the
genuine fear of God. Another man fears the Holy One,
blessed be He, because he is afraid of punishment in the other
world and the tortures of Gehinnom. This is a second type
which is not genuine fear. The genuine type is that which
makes a man fear his Master because He is the mighty ruler,
the rock and foundation of all worlds before whom all existing
things are as nought'. In the first two types to which the *Zohar*
alludes the fear is not of God but of God's punishments.
Genuine fear is the third, when man is aghast at the recognition of the sheer majesty of his Creator.

Similarly, the fifteenth-century theologian, Joseph Albo,
in his *'Sepher Ha-Ikkarim'* ('Book of Principles of the Faith'),
has a chapter on the fear of God which analyses 'fear' in terms
strikingly reminiscent of Otto.[7] Albo defines fear as 'the reced-
ing of the soul and the gathering of all her powers into herself,
when she imagines some fear-inspiring thing'. Fear, says Albo,
may be of two kinds. The first is when the soul imagines an
evil thing, which she fears for the harm it might do. 'Or the
soul may imagine something very great, exalted, elevated
and high, which she fears when she considers her own poverty
and lowliness in comparison with that great thing, though she
has no fear of any harm coming to her from that thing.' One
who serves God from fear of the first kind is called an 'insin-
cere worshipper'. The nobler fear derives from contemplation
of God's sublimity and dignity. 'For if a man reflects and
considers that God sees his open as well as his hidden acts, and
compares his imperfection and poverty of understanding with
the sublimity and dignity of God, he will stand in great awe
before Him and will be ashamed to transgress His commandments and not to do His will, as a person is ashamed to do an
unbecoming thing in the presence of an honourable prince,

[6] I, 11b.
[7] Ed. and trans. I. Husik, Jewish Publication Society of America, Phila
delphia, 1946, Vol. III, Chapter 32, pp. 298-303.

a respected and wise old man, who has a reputation for learning, character and dignity. Though he may not contemplate that any harm will come to him from a violation of his command, nevertheless he will without doubt feel ashamed and abashed and hesitate very much to offend his honour in his presence.'

Otto is careful to note[8] that in the Hebrew prophets (and, for that matter, in subsequent Judaism) the numinous becomes 'the holy' through being rationalised and moralised, that is to say it becomes charged with ethical import. But the numinous itself is not overcome, only its preponderance. 'The numinous is at once the basis upon which and the setting within which the ethical and rational meaning is consummated.' Thus the prophets preach the most powerfully ethical message but they do this in the name of the 'holy' and 'living' God. Otto concludes: 'And all those who later championed against the "God of philosophy", the "living God", and the God of anger and love and the emotions have unwittingly been defending the non-rational core of the Biblical conception of God from all excessive rationalisation. And so far they were right. Where they were wrong and sank into anthropomorphism was in defending, not figurative "anger" and "emotion", but literal anger and emotion, misconceiving the numinous character of the attributes in question and holding them simply to be "natural" attributes, taken absolutely, instead of realising that they can only be admitted as figurative indications of something essentially non-rational by means of symbols drawn from feelings that have analogy to it.'

In discussing faith as experience it is necessary to refer to the mystical approach to religion. In Otto's analysis this aspect of religious experience is noted but is allied with the rational and critical aspects of religion. In the mystical approach the non-rational element is given the fullest prominence. As Otto remarks: [9] 'But essentially mysticism is the stressing to a very high degree, indeed the over-stressing, of the non-rational or super-rational elements in religion; and it is only intelligible when so understood. The various phases and factors of the non-rational may receive varying emphasis, and the type of mysti-

[8] 'The Idea of the Holy', pp. 75-77.
[9] 'The Idea of the Holy', p. 22.

cism will differ according as some or other fall into the background. What we have been analysing, however, is a feature that recurs in all forms of mysticism everywhere, and it is nothing but the "creature-consciousness" stressed to the ultimate and to excess, the expression meaning, if we may repeat the contrast already made, not "feeling of our createdness" but "feeling of our creaturehood", that is the consciousness of the littleness of every creature in the face of that which is above all creatures.'

The essence of the mystical approach is, then, the feeling of 'creaturehood'. The mystic feels that his individual self is as nothing before the 'Other' into which he desires to become absorbed. Mysticism is primarily a matter of *feeling*. It is the supreme example of the non-rational in religion. From the Jewish point of view, however, two things require to be said in qualification. The first is that in Judaism, and to a very large extent it would seem in all Theistic religion, the gulf between the Creator and His creatures is too vast ever to be completely crossed. As Aldous Huxley has said: 'The Western mystic seeks to know God, but the Eastern mystic to be God.' The Jewish mystics do not normally represent the ascent of the soul in the mystical experience in terms of a *union* with God.

The second feature to be noted is that the Jewish mystical system, the *Kabbalah*, is not in itself a matter of feeling. Indeed, the system is speculative, it is a theosophy. But the experience at the heart of it is one of feeling, though with rare exceptions the Jewish mystics are extremely reluctant to discuss their experiences in personal terms and tend to dwell far more on the intricacies of the system. They speak more of the divine than of their own halting attempts to experience the divine. As Scholem rightly observes: [10] 'It is well known that the autobiographies of great mystics, who have tried to give an account of their inner experiences in a direct and personal manner, are the glory of mystical literature. These mystical confessions, for all their abounding contradictions, not only provide some of the most important material for the understanding of mysticism, but many of them are veritable pearls of literature. The Kabbalists, however, are no friends of mystical autobiography. They aim at describing the realm of

[10] 'Major Trends in Jewish Mysticism', pp. 15-16.

Divinity and the other objects of the contemplative life in an impersonal way, by burning, as it were, their ships behind them. They glory in objective description and are deeply averse to letting their own personalities intrude into the picture. The wealth of expression at their disposal is not inferior to that of their autobiographical confrères. It is as though they were hampered by a sense of shame. Documents of an intimate and personal nature are not entirely lacking, but it is characteristic that they are to be found almost wholly in manuscripts which the Kabbalists themselves would hardly have allowed to be printed. It is obvious that the absence of the autobiographical element is a serious obstacle to any psychological understanding of Jewish mysticism as the psychology of mysticism has to rely primarily on the study of such biographical material.'[11]

Because of this phenomenon one has on occasion to go to the non-Kabbalists for mystical testimony on the level of personal experience. We find, for example, Rabbi A. I. Karelitz (1879-1954), known as the *Hazon Ish*, a latter-day thinker of the Lithuanian, non-mystical school, describing beautifully the mystical joy of faith and trust in God:[12]

'No sooner does man's mind have the merit of perceiving the truth regarding God's existence than limitless joy and rapture become his. His soul delights, his imagination co-operates with his reason to see the pleasantness of the Lord. All the pleasures of the flesh melt away and his noble soul becomes clothed in holiness as if it had departed from the murky body to soar in the highest heavens. A new world opens to the man who rises to the heights of these sacred values. For, at times, it is possible for man, even in this world, to become as an angel to enjoy the splendour of holiness. All the pleasures of this world are as nought in comparison with the delight of man's attachment to his Creator, blessed be He. This is one of the secret powers with which

[11] An interesting and very unusual example of Jewish mystical testimony of a personal nature is the 'Tract on Ecstasy' by Dobh Baer of Lübavitch (1773-1827), see my translation with an Introduction and notes, Vallentine, Mitchell, London, 1963.

[12] '*Hazon Ish Al Inyane Emunah, Bittahon We-Od*', pp. 11-12.

the Creator has endowed man's soul. This power testifies that man is bound to the Creator of all things and that he was created to serve his Creator and become bound to Him.'

Not infrequently, one finds in the literature of Jewish piety the description of techniques for arousing feelings of awe, measures intended to increase man's natural sense of the 'fear of God'. A typical example is the discussion by Elijah ben Moses de Vidas (sixteenth century), in his famous mystical devotional work: *'Reshith Hokhmah'*, of 'the things which evoke the inner fear of God'.[13]

De Vidas urges man to dwell on the vastness of the universe and on his utter insignificance in the face of its magnitude, *a fortiori* in the Presence of God who created all this. De Vidas' universe was tiny compared with the immensities revealed by modern astronomy but he invokes to his aid early Jewish speculations (which he considered to be a true picture of reality) on the stupendous size of the worlds above this one and the heavenly hosts which inhabit them. Thus, to quote one example, the distance from the earth to the firmament is a journey of five hundred years, and the thickness of the firmament is a journey of five hundred years, and the distance between one firmament and the other is a journey of five hundred years. Above the seven heavens (the 'firmaments') are the holy living creatures (seen by Ezekiel in his vision of the divine Chariot). The feet of the living creatures is equal to all of them together (all these vast distances combined). The ankles of the living creatures are equal to all of them; the legs of the living creatures are equal to all of them; the knees of the living creatures are equal to all of them; the thighs of the living creatures are equal to all of them; the necks of the living creatures are equal to all of them; the heads of the living creatures are equal to all of them; the horns of the living creatures are equal to all of them. Above them is the throne of glory. The feet of the throne of glory are equal to all of them; the throne of glory is equal to all of them. The King, the Living and Eternal God, High and Exalted, dwelleth above them (*Hag.* 13a).

Possibly some Jewish teachers who relied on this kind of

[13] Venice, 1578, ('*Shaar Ha-Yirah*', Chapter 2).

argument, perhaps de Vidas himself, interpreted all this in spiritual terms, the five hundred years' journey as a journey of the mind in reflection, and the like. It is extremely unlikely that moderns will be impressed by this kind of mythological approach, but they, too, know of the wondrous size of the modern universe and man's insignificance. We now know, for instance, that the mass of the Sun is about 332,000 times the mass of the earth. The nearest star is at a distance of about four light-years. A light-year is the distance that light takes to travel in one year and is about six million million years.[14]

It might be objected that to approach the idea of the fear of God by reference to physical size and magnitude is to be guilty of religious Philistinism. God is spirit and the size of the physical universe is surely irrelevant to any approach to his Being. But man does live in the physical universe and is impressed by size. His sense of awe and wonder is increased by reflection on the vastness of the universe created by God.

A second consideration advanced by de Vidas is that man's sense of awe is aroused by meditation on the wonder of life, the daily miracles we see around us, the marvellous growth in plants, animals and humans. And, we might add, in the achievements of man's brain in science and technology.

A keen analysis of faith from the Jewish mystical point of view is to be found in the lengthy essay on 'Faith in God' by Rabbi Menaham Mendel of Lübavitch (1789-1866).[15] This mystical theologian was the third leader of the *Habad* movement in Hasidism, a movement which stressed the value of contemplation on the theme of God and His relationship to the world. For Rabbi Menaham Mendel 'faith' is distinct from 'knowledge'. Man does not need to invoke faith in order to be convinced that God exists. The heavens declare His glory and the earth is filled with it. That God is immanent in His creation is similarly a matter of knowledge rather than faith. Following earlier teachers, Rabbi Menaham Mendel declares that the evidence for God's immanence can be derived from man's own psychic life. God is 'in' the universe as the soul is 'in' the body. How else explain life and growth in the uni-

---

[14] See Sir Harold Spencer Jones 'Astronomy' in 'The New Outline of Modern Knowledge', pp. 111-133.

[15] *'Derekh Mitzwothekha'*, section on belief in God, pp. 88-118.

verse? Faith is the term we apply to that which cannot be directly apprehended, to that which has to be taken on trust. We do not 'know' that it is so, we 'believe' that it is so. But Rabbi Menahem Mendel will not permit us to aver that the two basic doctrines of Judaism, that there is a God and that He is imminent in the universe, are only to be taken on trust. They can be perceived. They are 'known' not merely 'believed in'.

What then is faith (*emunah*)? We have seen that in the Bible and in the Rabbinic literature *emunah* is 'belief in' God (trust in Him), while for the mediaeval thinkers it denotes *that* there is a God. Rabbi Menahem Mendel introduces a novel idea. Faith, he argues, must apply to that aspect of belief upon which knowledge of a direct kind can never be forthcoming. This is belief in God's complete transcendence of the universe. If man's reason ('knowledge') could bring him to the apprehension of the transcendent it would not be transcendent. Man can have no knowledge of God's nature apart from God's manifestation in the universe. He cannot consequently 'know' that God is transcendent. He can only 'believe it'. He can, however, trust that his belief is true because he relies on the Jewish tradition in which it is taught, that is, revealed by God Himself. Through the sacred literature of Israel the Jew learns the truth regarding God's utter transcendence and, since Scripture is God's revelation to man, it is a truth revealed by God.

Faith means, then, for Rabbi Menahem Mendel, that God is utterly beyond all human knowledge. It is not only impossible to 'know' (by direct apprehension) that God is beyond all human knowledge but it is, strictly speaking, illegitimate to say that one can 'know' that God as He is in Himself is beyond all human knowledge. It has to be accepted as an article of faith. (Knowledge that it is so because it is taught in Scripture is not a conviction attained by direct apprehension and belongs, therefore, not to 'knowledge' but to 'faith'.) 'Faith is belief that God, blessed be He, is raised and elevated infinitely higher than the very category of wisdom.' The recognition that there is a God is called 'seeing'. Just as a man 'sees' that he has a soul (i.e. he knows it directly from his own psychic life) he 'sees' that the larger body we call the world has a Soul. From the microcosm man can discern the Soul of the macrocosm. How, otherwise, can movement and growth be explained? How else would bushes grow or, indeed, be there at all if they were not aflame with God? All this belongs to 'knowledge'. Faith is conviction of the reality of the completely transcendent, of that which is beyond all attempts at comprehension.

It must not be thought, however, Rabbi Menahem Mendel continues, that in speaking of man's recognition of God as 'knowledge' and therefore accessible to the human mind it is implied that it is easy of attainment. Severe intellectual effort is required before the knowledge of God can be realised. For true knowledge involves far more than bare assent to the proposition that God exists. It must be attended by the most powerful conviction that the truth is really so. Thinking about God's existence and even a calm acceptance that this is true is far different from the sure knowledge that God is. The latter, resulting in strong emotional attachment to the truth, can only come through contemplation. Hence the knowledge of God can be enjoined, as in the verse: 'Know the God of thy Father' (I Chron. 28 : 9); the command being to dwell long in meditation until the truth becomes part of man's very self, until mere thought becomes true knowledge. This is why we are commanded not to forget God (Deut. 6: 12) since God is always 'there' to be apprehended were it not that man tends to forget. Failure to attain to the knowledge of God is not failure to comprehend a truth still to be won but an overlooking of a truth already evident for those who have eyes to see.

Knowledge of God in this sense is not knowledge of God's nature, only knowledge that God is. Only God Himself can know His nature. That nature is utterly incomprehensible to man. Here, too, states Rabbi Menahem Mendel, the analogy of the soul in the body is helpful. Man knows beyond any doubt that he has a soul but the soul's nature is hidden from him. That his body is animated by a soul is perfectly evident to him. How this happens and the nature of this animating force is beyond his grasp. Only the prophet in his vision of God can have some faint comprehension of God's nature and it is to this that Scripture alludes when it speaks of God 'appearing' to man (e.g. in Gen. 18:1). In the world to come the prophetic faculty of divining something of God's nature will be granted to all (Is. 40:5; 52:8). But, even in this life, all men are capable of seeing God's glory as manifested in creation, though much contemplation is required if the vision is clearly to be seen. In this sense all men are mystics or, at least, they have the potential mystical nature which can be lit through contemplation. Moreover, even in this life, something not too dissimilar from the knowledge of God's nature can be attained through very deep reflection on the theme that God is in all things. Those who engage in this type of contemplation taste some of the delights reserved for the saints in the Hereafter. It can be compared to the wealthy man who takes pleasure in the thought of his possessions even when he is not actually able to see them.

Rabbi Menahem Mendel's analysis of the stages of spiritual ascent are of a kind rare in Jewish mystical writing for the reasons given earlier. The stages are:

1. The bare thought that there is a God.

2. True knowledge that there is a God, attained through contemplation of God as manifested in the universe and in man's soul.

3. Deeper knowledge of God's complete unity, attained through contemplation, that amid the multiplicity of things there is only God.

4. The knowledge of God's nature, attained only by the prophet in this life and by all men in the Hereafter in some small degree.

5. Faith, that is 'belief', that God transcends all human comprehension.

By its very nature the final stage can never be a matter of knowledge, only of faith.

As we have noted, Rabbi Menahem Mendel was a leader of the intellectual movement of Hasidism. For this school there can be no true mystical awareness without contemplation. The direct apprehension of God is the result of profound meditation. God's glory is ever manifest in creation but the blindfold on the mind, which prevents it seeing that glory, can only be removed by the mind itself. Other mystical schools have preferred to think of mystical experience as direct apprehension by a special non-rational faculty of the soul. *Habad*, too, knows of this but the main emphasis in its thought is on intellectual contemplation as the means to the knowledge of God.

Since knowledge in its truest form involves emotional awareness, Rabbi Menahem Mendel continues, the contemplative will be helped to lead a godly life because his meditations bring truth to him vividly. From his knowledge that God is he is led to the love and fear of God. Furthermore, although for the contemplative faith only concerns God's transcendence, God's immanance is perceived by him directly, for the non-contemplative faith embraces that which is, in reality, a matter of knowledge. Such a man does not *know* that God exists, he only *believes*. But belief, as opposed to knowledge, has an indirectness which prevents it from influencing the emotions and (since man's deeds are inspired by his feelings) it does not have any real or lasting consequences for his actions.

This helps to explain the strange paradox, to which the Rabbis call attention,[16] that the thief asks God for help while breaking into a house he intends to rob. At one and the same time the thief believes in God (for he is no hypocrite when he asks for God's help) and yet flouts God's law by stealing. This is because the thief *believes* in God but does not *know* Him. Hence his recognition that God exists influences neither his feelings nor his actions. Rabbi Menahem Mendel would not, of course, claim that the contemplative will never be guilty of moral turpitude but that insofar as his contemplation succeeds in bringing him truth he will be incapable of disobeying God for as long as the effects of his contemplation endure. When they wane the contemplative becomes as other men, no longer *knowing* God but only *believing* in Him.

Even for a contemplative mystic like Rabbi Menahem Mendel, who advocates strongly the use of the intellect in reflection upon God, God as He is in Himself is utterly beyond all human comprehension. Indeed, the very emphasis in his thought on the possibility of man knowing God's existence by means of the mind, frees the realm of the transcendent to be approached by faith alone. Thus, as in the mystical approach generally, while the Object of contemplation is conceived of

[16] *Ber.* 63a, in the *En Yaakobh* edition.

in personal and rationalistic terms, its nature is elevated far beyond the personal and the rational.

The theistic rationalist, Maimonides, sees no incongruity in speaking of God as Infinite Mind, even though he acknowledges that the divine Mind is so far above the human that the categories of the latter can only be applied to it in a negative sense. We can say that God is not ignorant but any further attempts to pursue the meaning of His knowledge must fail. In God, says Maimonides, the knower, the process of knowing and that which is known are one.[17] But, following his teachers and earlier mystics, Rabbi Menahem Mendel refuses to apply the term 'knowledge' to God even in this restricted sense. However, since human language based on human experience is the only language man has, he is obliged to speak of God as Mind, in spite of this. In reality, however, God is 'the Holy One', a term which means separateness in Hebrew. God is 'Wholly Other'. The only analogy of any help at all is that of the soul in the body. Man only knows that he has a soul. He does not know the soul's true nature. Here Rabbi Menahem Mendel meets Otto in the recognition of the non-rational element in religious experience.

[17] *Yad, Hil. 'Yesode Ha-Torah'*, 11, 10.

Chapter 6

The Way of Tradition

ALTHOUGH many theologians in the Middle Ages may have thought they based their faith on reason alone, it is now widely recognised that they were, subconsciously at least, convinced of God's existence because they were members of a religious community which taught that God had revealed Himself to man. Moreover, this belief was then shared by Judaism and her daughter religions and so firmly held that atheism was an oddity. Most men in the West accepted the established religious tradition of the Western world in which there was unanimity that there had been a revelation from God. For all the attempts of natural theology to prove, without recourse to revelation, that God exists, it is obvious that even an effective intellectual argument could not possibly lead to God as He is thought of in that religious tradition. At the most it could demonstrate that an intelligent Being had brought the world into existence or that the world was dependent on such a Being for its existence. The qualities generally associated with this Being, such as perfect goodness and limitless power, were known through Scripture.

Today it is debated whether a natural theology is possible at all. Some modern religious thinkers (of whom Barth is the most distinguished and influential) argue that man cannot know anything at all about God unless God chooses to reveal Himself to them. They delight in demolishing the traditional arguments for God's existence, attacking them with a relish greater than the atheist's. But even those who still believe that man's unaided reason can bring him to the certainty of God's existence must eventually return to the idea of revelation in order to comprehend the nature of the God their reason tells them exists. Few people would claim that God had revealed

Himself to them personally by direct communication. And even if a personal revelation did take place, it is difficult to see how this could be communicated to others. The reliance therefore on revelation in contemporary thought is ultimately reliance on Scripture, on the Biblical record of God meeting man.

For moderns this raises the very important question of what reliance can be placed on Scripture. This problem is particularly acute since historical investigation of the Bible has shown (to the satisfaction of most of us) that it contains error as well as truth; that the Biblical books were not composed in a vacuum but belong to a background common to ancient Nazi Eastern culture; that, in short, there is a human element in the Bible and that it was given *through* men, not only *to* men. The standard defence, and it is sound, is that in its essentials at least (in its record of the human encountering the divine) the Biblical tradition is reliable. It follows that for the modern believer faith based on revelation is ultimately faith arrived at through tradition.

To find God through tradition is not at all the same thing as to argue that there must be a God because people in the past have believed in Him. People in the past, even millions of them, may have been as wrong in this as in believing the earth flat, or the impossibility of a flying ship (this latter was a frequently adduced illustration in mediaeval literature of the clearly impossible). The appeal of faith to tradition is that men in the past (particularly as evidenced in the Biblical record) have claimed to have met a Being who endowed their lives with moral worth and significance. They have handed down what the encounter meant for them so powerfully that their heirs relive the tremendous meeting and hear God's voice speaking to *them* when, for instance, they read of how He had spoken to Isaiah, Jeremiah and Micah.

This is, in fact, the way in which most of us obtained our concept of God in the first instance. Hardly any of us are moved to reflect on God's existence as if this were a question we had considered entirely for ourselves. Born as we were into a particular Theistic tradition, one which has been severely challenged in modern times, we are obliged, as soon as we begin to reflect on life's meaning, to decide whether the tradition speaks truth or not, whether there is a God or not. If we finally decide that the tradition is true for us this is because it provides the most adequate key to life's meaning, because it answers our own profoundest stirrings of soul. When we opt for God on the basis of tradition we do so because the knowledge found there coheres with the rest of our knowledge. The Person we meet there makes sense of our own lives at their deepest level. We do not argue that the belief is true because it is in the tradition but we come to appreciate that the belief is in the tradition because it is true.

The argument from tradition was used particularly by Jewish thinkers in the Middle Ages. As we have seen, some of these favoured the way of reason. Men like Bahya Ibn Pakudah held that mere reliance on tradition was a very poor substitute for a reasoned demonstration that there is a God. But some of the mediaeval thinkers had a different approach. For them the way of tradition was superior in that it was far less at the mercy of refutation than the way of reason. At least among its worthier representatives this approach was, however, very different from ancestor worship. The appeal to contemporaries was not that they should believe *because* their ancestors had believed before them but because their ancestors had spoken the truth. In reality the appeal to tradition was itself a form of appeal to reason. It seemed completely reasonable to the thinkers who favoured this approach that events attested to by countless witnesses had actually happened and should be relied upon. The only difference between the way of reason and the way of tradition was that in the former reason made a direct assault on the problem while in the latter reason was coerced in indirectly. In the former there was ever present the fear of error while in the latter man's own individual reason was reinforced in its conclusions by the experience of so many others.

In a sense the appeal to tradition is anticipated in the Bible itself, though we must keep in mind the distinction made earlier between the Biblical meaning of faith ('belief *in* . . .') and its later meaning ('belief *that* . . .'). Two passages in Deuteronomy contain an appeal to tradition. 'For ask now of the days past, which were before thee, since the day that God created man upon the earth, and from one end of the heaven unto the other, whether there has been any such thing as this great thing is, or hath been heard like it? Did ever a people hear the voice of God speaking out of the fire, as thou hast heard and live? Or hath God assayed to go and take Him a nation from the midst of another nation, by trials, by signs, and by wonders, and by war, and by a mighty hand, and by an outstretched arm, and by great terrors, according to all that the Lord your God did for you in Egypt before thine eyes' (Deut. 4 : 33-34). 'Remember the days of old, consider the years of many generations: Ask thy father and he will declare unto thee, Thine elders and they will tell thee. When the Most High gave to the nations their inheritance, when he separated the children of men, He set the borders of the peoples according to the number of the children of Israel' (Deut. 32 : 7-8). Similarly the Psalmist says:

'For He established a testimony in Jacob, And appointed a law in Israel, Which He commanded our fathers, That they should make known to their children:

That the generation to come might know them, even the children that should be born; Who should arise and tell them to their children,

That they might put their confidence in God, And forget not the works of God, But keep His commandments'

(Ps. 78 : 5-7).

The great mediaeval thinkers read their history as a reinforcement of the Biblical claim. God had not only performed great deeds on His people's behalf in the remote past but He had kept Israel miraculously alive throughout the ages and inspired their sages, teachers and the ordinary man to keep the tremendous truth alive. Even Maimonides, a staunch rationalist, does not advocate it for all men. Maimonides argues that reason leads to a most refined and sophisticated God-concept but it must be attained gradually. At first the most helpful and spiritually healthy approach is the way of tradition. To attempt to teach the way of reason to the intellectually immature is akin to feeding an infant food too rich for his digestion. The result of such an attempt would be to empty the God-concept of all its meaning and would lead eventually to atheism. This is why, according to Maimonides, the 'secrets of the *Torah*' (which he equates with advanced metaphysics) are reserved for the initiated. For those less advanced the only possible approach is through tradition, through the plain, simple record of God's dealings with Israel as found in the Bible, even though these may be taken with a literalness offensive to the more cultivated taste.[1]

Prominent among the mediaeval advocates of belief through tradition is Judah Ha-Levi. Ha-Levi's *'Kuzari'*[2] is in the form of a dialogue between a Rabbi and the King of the Khazars, a people on the shores of the Black and Caspian Seas who converted to Judaism. The Khazar King, in the book, first consults a Philosopher on the question of faith. Dissatisfied with his reply the King turns to a Christian scholastic and then to a Muslim Doctor. Both begin with an appeal to God as Creator of heaven and earth and both refer in the course of their exposition to the Jews. This leads the King to consult the Rabbi who, unlike the other two, appeals to human history, to 'The God of Abraham, Isaac and Israel, who led the children of Israel out of Egypt with signs and miracles'.[3] When the King expresses his surprise at this unconventional approach the Rabbi retorts that when God revealed Himself to Israel He did not announce Himself as Creator of the world and their Creator but as the God who had redeemed them from bondage. 'Now in the same style I spake to thee, a Prince of the Khazars, when thou didst ask me about my creed. I answered thee as was fitting and is fitting for the whole of Israel, who knows these things, first from personal experience, and afterwards through uninterrupted tradition, which is equal to the former.'[4]

There is a modern ring to Ha-Levi's realisation that the God of vital religion is not to be approached through reflections on how the world was created or similarly abstract questions remote from the living concerns of men. In Ha-Levi the way of tradition is wedded to the way of experience. Man's own experience of the divine is strengthened by his appreciation

[1] 'Guide', I, 33.
[2] Trans. by Hartwig Hirschfeld.
[3] *'Kuzari'*, I, 11.
[4] *'Kuzari'*, I, 25.

that this experience has been shared by many others before him and that the Jew is following in a great tradition which speaks to him of the way in which his ancestors came face to face with the living God.

Joseph Albo in the fifteenth century similarly bases his faith in tradition.[5] After defining belief as 'a firm conception of the thing in mind, so that the latter cannot in any way imagine its opposite, even though it may not be able to prove it', Albo goes on to apply this in relation to a matter the believer did not himself observe but which was seen by reliable witnesses who handed it down by tradition. Says Albo: 'This is worthy of belief almost as much as that to which the believer's own senses testify, though he cannot prove it by reason.' It is, according to Albo, for this reason that the *Torah* was not given in its completeness to the Patriarchs. For these were individuals and suspicion might have attended a faith handed down by individuals, however eminent and trustworthy. The *Torah* was revealed to all the people of Israel, who handed it down through the tradition. It is extremely unlikely that a whole people suffered from mass delusion.

The appeal to tradition has persisted down to the present among many Jews as the most powerful spur to faith far superior, in their opinion, to any other. The pietistic movement of Hasidism, which arose in the eighteenth century and still attracts many adherents and admirers, favoured the way of tradition above all others, though many of the Hasidic leaders were mystics and personally relied on the way of experience. The *Hasidim* had on the whole a powerful mistrust of philosophy (what did the Greeks know of God? was their constant complaint against the mediaeval Jewish thinkers) and they frowned particularly on attempts to prove God's existence. Rabbi Nahman of Bratzlav (1772-1811), great-grandson of the founder of the movement and one of its most perceptive thinkers, has the following maxims on faith in his brief dictionary of the spiritual life, the *Sepher Ha-Middoth*.[6] In these aphorisms Rabbi Nahman's intense mystical fervour is seen wedded to the appeal to tradition:

[5] '*Sepher Ha-Ikkarim*', ed. and trans. by Isaac Husik, Book I, Chapters 19-20, pp. 165-173.
[6] Warsaw, 1912, *s.v. emunah*, Part I, pp. 18-23; Part II, pp. 22-23.

'Belief in God should be attained by the method of faith not of demonstration.'

'Through humility man attains to faith.'

'Through faith man becomes as beloved to God as a wife to her husband.'

'If a man has lost his faith let him go to Jewish graves there to declare the kindnesses God has wrought for him.'

'Through Torah study every denial of God is shattered.'

'Indulgence in eating leads to decline in faith.'

'If you have problems regarding faith in God keep silent and your own thoughts will provide the answers.'

'Faith makes a man wise.'

'Man should at first believe in God and he will later enjoy the merit of understanding Him intellectually.'

'Denial enters the heart as the result of sin.'

'Man should weep when he falls from faith.'

'Faith is the fruit of silence.'

'Envy is one of the causes of loss of faith.'

'It is through faith that man comes to understand God.'

'Flattery leads to denial of God.'

'It is necessary for man always to strengthen himself in faith whenever he goes from one teacher to another since to sit at the feet of many teachers is harmful to the belief in God's unity.'

'Faith produces serenity of mind.'

In another of his works[7] Rabbi Nahman remarks: 'It is essential to avoid reading even those works on the philosophy of religion compiled by Jewish thinkers for these are extremely harmful to faith. The faith we have received from our holy ancestors is sufficient. It is a great principle and foundation in God's worship to be innocent and whole-hearted, to serve God without any philosophical investigation whatsoever.' It is remarkable how close Rabbi Nahman is to his near contemporary Kierkegaard, though there is no question of any contact between the two. In Rabbi Nahman's thought as in Kierkegaard's there is denial of the role of rational demonstration in the life of faith and there is constant awareness of faith's tensions. Rabbi Nahman does not write as a serene

[7] *'Likkute Moharan'*, 1808-1811, *Tinyana*, No. 44.

character, unharried by doubt. Where he differs from Kierkegaard is in his intense reliance on tradition, a concept which
has no appeal for the more individualistic Dane.

An interesting discussion on this whole question of faith-
through-tradition versus faith-through-reason is found in the
small volume by the Hasidic master and Kabbalist Rabbi
Zewi Hirsch of Zhydatchov (d. 1831). The little book is in the
form of a guide to the preparations necessary before one can
begin to study the Kabbalah. It includes extensive notes by
another Hasidic master Rabbi Zewi Elimelech Spira (d.
1841).[8] The author attacks[9] those Jewish thinkers who use
Greek philosophy as an aid to the understanding of the doctrine of God's unity. Since most Greeks were unbelievers, how,
asks the author, can they possibly serve as guides to the divine?
He takes particular issue with Bahya Ibn Pakudah who, in
his 'Duties of the Heart',[10] states that man can only ask *if* God
is, not *what* He is, i.e. that it is possible and desirable for man
to engage in philosophical investigation into whether God
exists but once reason has convinced him that there is a God
it is futile to use reason to discover God's true nature, for this
is incomprehensible.

Zewi Hirsch argues that the exact opposite is true. One may
ask what God is since Moses teaches us that He is compassionate and merciful. But to ask *if* God exists is to repeat the
sin of 'the generation of the wilderness' who asked: 'Is the
Lord among us, or not?' (Ex. 17:7). In an impassioned attack
on the whole philosophical approach, Zewi Hirsch writes:[11]
'Was it for nothing that the Lord our God brought us out of
Egypt and showed us His greatness and His strong hand with
signs and wonders? Was it for nothing that He parted the sea
for us, gave us His manna and the Sabbath? The Lord our God
opened for us the stores of His precious instrument (the
Torah), the delight of His treasure-house, at Sinai. He made
His Divine Presence rest upon us when the Temple was
erected. He sent His prophets to us and our feet stood at Sinai.

[8] '*Sur Me-Ra We-Aseh Tobh*', *Kether*, no date, but the approbation of
Zewi Hirsch Spira of Munkacs (great-nephew of Zewi Elimelech) is dated
Tebheth 5661 (1902).

[9] *Ibid.*, pp. 119f.

[10] '*Shaar Ha-Yihud*', Chapter 4.

[11] *Op. cit.*, p. 121.

And in each generation a man is obliged to see himself as if he himself went out of Egypt. Furthermore, there are all the events we have seen with our own eyes. To this day His loving kindness has not forsaken us. These, indeed, are His great and powerful acts, that a lonely sheep etc.[12] Shall we, then, ask *if* He is?'

Zewi Elimelech, on the other hand, agrees with Bahya.[13] Bahya is correct in saying that we cannot ask *what* God is because His true nature is known to Him alone. But man may ask *if* God is and this is irrelevant to the sin of 'the generation of the wilderness'. For their sin was in asking whether God was in their midst after they had already seen the truth for themselves. But if a man wishes to love God sincerely but wants to convince himself that God is (so that he may never subsequently doubt) he is permitted in these circumstances to ask *if* God is. Is not Abraham admired in the Jewish tradition for discovering God by unaided reason? Zewi Elimelech concludes, however, that this applied only to the mediaeval thinkers. In their day the esoteric wisdom of the *Kabbalah* (the word itself means 'tradition') was not yet fully revealed. Consequently, in the absence of a proper tradition the mediaeval thinkers had necessarily to rely on reason and, at least, the philosophical inquiry did help to refine man's ideas of God. But now that we have the *Kabbalah* it is forbidden (and here Zewi Elimelech agrees with Zewi Hirsch) to engage in philosophical discussion in order to prove God's existence.

The argument from tradition has come under heavy fire in modern times. It was all very well for the mediaeval thinkers to refer to the powerful evidence provided by two million eye-witnesses. In their day no one doubted the events in the book of Exodus as having actually happened as described. This was the firm belief of Christian, Muslim and Jew. Even the exceedingly rare unbeliever did not doubt that the events took place. The unbeliever was consequently obliged to conclude that the two million were all mistaken, suffering from mass delusion. This was hardly credible, as the mediaeval thinkers were quick to remark.

But, as we touched upon at the beginning of this chapter, in

[12] 'Should exist among the devouring wolves' as in *Yom.* 69b.
[13] *Op. cit.*, p. 121 note 113.

our day Biblical criticism and historical investigation into the sources of Judaism have had their say. Few today accept the Biblical account of the Revelation at Sinai as factual in all its details. Except by the fundamentalists, it is generally acknowledged that what we have in Exodus is not a tradition handed down by two million witnesses but a tradition that there was a tradition. In other respects, for example with regard to the age of the earth and man's span on it, the tradition is now known to have been in error. What guarantee therefore have we that the tradition is reliable even in its basic contention that there is a God who has revealed Himself to man? The answer must proceed on the lines we have already indicated, that it is not a matter of simply relying on an ancient tradition but of hearing for ourselves the great echoes of the original series of encounters between God and man as recorded in that tradition.

Whatever its origins, the Bible is with us still and in this marvellous collection of books, for all the errors and crudities (which cannot be overlooked), the Presence of God can yet be felt by the spiritually sensitive reader. It is exceedingly difficult, if not impossible, to account for the lofty teachings of the Hebrew prophets, the civilising influence of the great Law of Moses, the history of a small people who found God and brought Him to mankind, the Sinaitic revelation itself and the spiritual power these books continue to exercise over men's souls, unless Israel really met with God and recorded in immortal language the meaning of that encounter. We can be sceptical of individual details in the Bible. We can dwell on the numerous parallels with Egyptian, Babylonian and Assyrian *mores*. We can point out the striking resemblances between Hebrew poetry in the Bible and Canaanite hymns in praise of the pagan gods. We are forced to recognise, to a degree quite beyond the imagination of our ancestors, the human element in the Biblical record. What cannot be seriously doubted is the 'something else', which has ensured that this and no other collection of books has become the sacred Scripture of a large proportion of mankind; that there are living Jews who regard themselves as the heirs to the Bible and no living Babylonians, Canaanites and Assyrians; that there is a Voice which speaks here in promise of great vision, of dreams of world peace, of holiness, justice and mercy, of freedom and the unique worth of each individual as a child of God.

Bishop Gore's famous statement of this position cannot be faulted.[14] 'Here, then, we find a succession of wonderful men, mostly conscious of profound unpopularity in their contemporary world, who nevertheless, even in the face of the most determined hostility of courts and people, delivered a message which we feel to be self-consistent and to involve the same great principles throughout, about God—His nature, His will, His purposes—and about human nature—its dignity, its responsibility, and its sin; a message which they declare, with the fullest conviction, to be derived not from their own reasoning or speculation, nor from tradition (though they would have indignantly repudiated that they were its first recipients), nor from any external source at all, but from God, the God of Israel, speaking in their own souls, so intensely and clearly that there could be no mistake about it.'

The older view of revelation as divine information conveyed to man in the form of propositions has yielded in many circles to an interpretation in terms of process. But it is still revelation and the Bible is still its record. From the historical point of view the mediaeval thinkers were trying, no doubt inadequately, to state systematically their conception of God and His nature in a way which equated it with the tremendous Presence encountered by the Biblical authors. And the Biblical insights were fostered and developed by the subsequent Jewish teachers who vindicated their faith by the quality of their lives.

In this sense one can, indeed, speak, as did the mediaeval thinkers, of a *continuous tradition*. No one with any feel for history will, nowadays, conceive of that tradition in static terms. It can no longer honestly be held that in generation after generation, reaching back to Moses himself and even beyond him, a series of ideas, beliefs and practices were handed down unchanged with no internal development or external influence. But for all our recognition of the dynamic rather than static quality of the tradition, the basic belief that it is all the work of God in co-operation with the humans who

[14] 'Belief in God', Chapter IV, pp. 78-80.

sought Him can reasonably be said to be based on experience, the experience of the prophets and law-makers in the first instance and the later experience of sages, thinkers and undistinguished people who lived by the great truths. The existence of the Jews does explain the existence of God. The Jews are the most powerful proof for God's existence. There is still great power in the appeal to tradition. *'This is my God, and I will glorify Him: My father's God and I will exalt Him'* (Ex. 15:2).

We have examined here and in previous chapters the four main ways by which men are led to faith in God: the way of reason, the existentialist encounter, the way of experience and the way of revelation-tradition. In actual life, of course, there is no such neat division, one man calmly and deliberately choosing one way and another man a different way, as if the would-be believer goes shopping in the market for ways to God. Questions of individual temperament are undoubtedly involved. The rationalist favours the way of reason, the mystic the way of experience. But the ways do converge, the different approaches are complementary. It would probably be true to say that most Theists did not begin their quest in a vacuum. In the first instance belief stems from their particular religious tradition. When the speculative stage is reached and there is a tendency to question the truth of the tradition, the other ways serve to reinforce the initial premise. The existentialist emphasis on involvement checks the purely intellectual approach in which the bare assent to God's existence has little religious vitality and less personal concern. Religious experience serves to validate in an intensely personal way the belief in God held through the approach by reason or tradition or through the leap of faith. The way of reason shows how belief in God affords the most satisfactory explanation of existence. Thus the ways converge to produce complete conviction.

These four 'ways' are not 'proofs' for the existence of God nor, for that matter, can the traditional 'proofs' really be treated as such. They are better treated as 'indications' which converge to produce conviction. It has frequently been objected that this manner of approaching the question of faith is unsatisfactory, because if each particular 'proof' is invalid it is logically unsound to treat their sum total as more valid. A number of noughts added to one another still yield nought. No stronger proof is forthcoming simply by adding up a series of invalid proofs. But, as we have suggested earlier, the argument gains by treating the various ways as 'indications'. A further, not unhelpful, analogy is that of a man suspected of murder. If the crime had actually been witnessed this would constitute proof. But what if he had only been observed at the scene of the crime when it was committed? Further, that he had motive and opportunity and that there is also other circumstantial evidence. Depending on the strength of the converging pieces of evidence it might eventually be proved that he was, in fact, guilty. The analogy is not, of course, exact and is in part offensive. For one thing it omits the element of personal encounter stressed by the existentialists. For faith in God we are not as detectives seeking an arrest but rather lovers hoping for an acceptance to our proposal. For all that, the analogy does help us to see how in the dynamic of faith man attains complete conviction through the different approaches.

PART III

Objections to Faith

Chapter 7

The Existence of Evil

THE fact of evil in the universe is undoubtedly the most serious obstacle to faith in God. The problem involves far more than the suffering of the righteous and the prosperity of the wicked. It is rather the question of the necessity for any suffering or for any wickedness. God as the Creator of the universe has made everything that is in it—including evil—and it is difficult to avoid the conclusion of His responsibility.

There have been many formulations of the basic problem but they all come to this: Theistic faith generally involves belief in an all-good and all-powerful God. Even those Theists who permit only the use of negative attributes when speaking of God must at least mean that although God's real nature is unknown, we do know that He is neither evil nor lacking in power. If, therefore, God is good He must wish to prevent evil, for a Being who is good must by definition be one who wishes to prevent evil. If He is all-powerful He can prevent it. And yet God has evidently not chosen to prevent evil since there is obvious evil in the universe He has created. From life as we know it, either there is no God or, if there is, conventional Theism has been mistaken as to His nature. If He exists He is either not all-good and *can*, therefore, tolerate evil; or He is not all-powerful and, therefore, *must* tolerate evil.

Today when this question is discussed, the particular evils of the past few decades must form a large part of the burning **problem**; the murder of six million Jews by the Nazis, for example. Mankind has known tragedy and pain before the twentieth century. But while the problem is as acute if only one innocent child expires in agony the colossal scale of the more recent horror and the fiendish nature of its execution has forcibly taught our generation what is involved in affirming that God is good in spite of contrary evidence. To put it brutally, it was God who gave evil men the skills to perfect instruments of destruction. It was His gas which choked to death infants in arms, His cattle trucks in which starved men and women were packed so closely together that many of them died before even reaching their final destination, His bullets which penetrated the backs of the innocent victims lined up before the massed graves. And yet many of those victims went to their death singing a haunting song, which has come down to us, of faith in God, of belief in perfect faith that He is good. A groping theodicy today seeks to discover how it is at all possible for such faith not to be unfounded. In the words of the title of a book by Dr. I. Maybaum, how is it possible still to see 'the face of God after Auschwitz'?

Very few, if any, Theists have been prepared to solve the problem by accepting that revision of the normative Theistic position which would accept God as not wholly good and, therefore, prepared to tolerate evil or so unconcerned with it as to be indifferent to its effects. This would be a drastic revision, indeed, depriving Theism of most of its content and meaning. A Being so intelligent as to have created the universe cannot be indifferent to evil, for this is an attitude which stems from lack of sensitivity and imagination. On the human level even though it is possible to find highly intelligent people deficient in moral sensitivity we nevertheless rightly conclude that in spite of their intelligence in some areas of life they have, basically, a strong element of stupidity. More to the point is that human beings, created by God, do protest vehemently against evil and would destroy it if they had the power so to do. How, then, did a Being indifferent to evil bring the human protest into existence? It would moreover be impossible to worship a Being indifferent to suffering and thereby inferior to His worshippers. This is the reason that Theists have always spoken of God as their ally in the struggle against evil. However the existence of evil is explained or understood, it cannot be because God is Himself indifferent to evil.

Nor can a solution be found by trying to minimise the extent of evil or by denying that it exists. Maimonides, for instance,

believed that there is more good than evil in the universe.[1]
But, even if this is so, the problem remains of the reason for
any evil at all. Similarly, to argue that evil is only the absence
of the good is merely playing with words. The problem is just
as severe that the all-good and all-powerful God permits the
absence of the good. A victim tortured by the Gestapo suffered
no less if his pain was attributed not to positive evil but to the
absence of the good. As for the argument that evil is only an
illusion and does not really exist, the *coup de grace* was given
to this by MacTaggart[2] who rightly observes that the word
'really' has no meaning in this context. For even if evil is
delusion the delusion at least is real and this is in itself evil.
One can speak of some particular instance of pain as illu-
sionary, as when we refer to an imaginary headache. The
imaginary pain is a delusion in relation to a real pain, though
it may hurt equally. But what sense does it make to speak of
all pain as a delusion? If we do this we are simply substituting
the word 'delusion' for the word 'pain' or 'evil' and the reality
it represents remains the same. The Gestapo victim suffers
no less if his pain is called 'delusion' rather than 'evil'.

If, then, evil is real and God all-good, and the Theist is not
prepared to qualify either of these propositions, it would seem
that the only way out of the dilemma is to grapple with the
meaning of an 'all-powerful' God. Are there limits to God's
power? The most favoured attempt by traditional Theists at
dealing with the problem of evil tries to see a purpose in evil,
i.e. to see evil as necessary in serving the good. But it can then
be argued that even if it is true that evil serves good (that there
are certain supremely worthwhile goods which cannot be
attained in a universe where there is no evil) what is the reason
for an omnipotent God not creating the required good without
the prior evil?

Obviously a great deal depends on what we mean by 'omnipotent'. If the particular good required cannot *logically* be
said to be possible without the evil on which it depends then
even God cannot create it without that evil. The mediaeval
thinkers discussed whether God can do the impossible. Can
He, for example, will Himself out of existence? Many reply

[1] 'Guide', III, 12.
[2] 'Some Dogmas of Religion', section 171, pp. 209-210.

that while God can do that which seems impossible to us He cannot do the absolutely impossible precisely because it is absolutely impossible. It is no limit, they argue, on God's power to do the possible if we admit that He cannot do the impossible.[3] These thinkers were correct in this contention. What they sometimes failed to see is that the question involved here is not of God but of human language. God cannot do the absolutely impossible not because there are limits to His powers but because—the expression 'doing the absolutely impossible' is a nonsense expression. Nothing can make *possible* that which is by definition absolutely impossible. There is an evident contradiction in the language used. A God who did not exist would not be God. It is consequently not to impose limits on God's powers to say that He cannot will Himself out of existence or create a stone so heavy that even He cannot move it. These are nonsense sentences, no different in their logical structure from sentences like: Can God brillig or brollig? It can be argued, of course, that the promotion of certain goods without prior evils does not involve us in a logical absurdity and this must be discussed separately. This we shall presently do but first we must examine two different attempts at a solution to the basic problem which have sometimes been advanced.

The first of these is to qualify 'omnipotence' more radically than by mere linguistic analysis of its meaning. In short, some Theists have accepted that God is really limited in power in some respects, so that He is not *all*-powerful. Evil is real and God is all-good and would, indeed, have prevented evil if He could have done so, but this is not in His power. This is the doctrine of the finite God who is all-good, very wise and very powerful but who is limited by 'something' over which He has no control and it is from this that evil emerges. This 'something' can be thought of in different ways, as part of the stuff of the universe against which God struggles[4] (and He is then thought of not as a Creator but as a fashioner of a sub-

---

[3] See Saadiah: '*Emunoth We-De'oth*', II, 13. Aquinas similarly says: 'Nothing that implies a contradiction falls under the scope of God's omnipotence', '*Summa Theologica*', Part I, Question 25, 4. *Cf.* Appendix II; *infra*, p. 203.

[4] See John Stuart Mill: 'Three Essays on Religion', who argues vigorously for a finite God.

stance co-eternal with Him) or, as E. S. Brightman calls[5] it, 'the Given' belonging to the nature of God Himself. According to Brightman there is a random element in the universe, a 'dysteleological surd'. A 'surd' in mathematics is a non-rational number. The random element in the universe prevents us, on the view, from explaining everything teleologically, i.e. of seeing the end and purpose for which everything was created. There are some things for which no reason at all can be given. God, in this view, is seen as constantly perfecting the universe, calling upon His creatures to assist Him in conquering more and more of its evil. The dramatic quality of the religious life is thus greatly heightened since a real battle is being waged with God and man as allies for the good, against the evil which threatens both their aims.

But for all its grandeur the objection to this solution is that a Being who does not wish evil, but is powerless to prevent it, would not be God. Whence comes the evil over which He has no control? Whether the limitation is in the very stuff of the universe or in Himself, such a Theistic philosophy eventually reduces itself to dualism and lies open to the standard objection to dualism. This is, that the universe exhibits unity and co-operation between its parts but if there is more than one divine power how is such unity possible? When Judaism, for instance, speaks of God as Creator of the universe it implies that the whole universe is subordinate to Him and to Him alone.

The second and even more drastic solution, particularly popular in some theological circles today, is to deny that personal terms like 'all-good' and 'all-powerful' can be applied to God who is thought of rather as a Force or Power or as the impersonal Ground of Being. On this view the whole problem is unreal. It is only because we think of God as a Person that we are bothered by why *He* permits evil. But if God is the name we give to those forces in the universe which make for righteousness and for the enobling of human life there is no problem at all. When man speaks of God as his ally in the struggle against evil he means, on this view, that he believes

[5] E. S. Brightman: 'The Problem of God', 'A Philosophy of Religion', Chapter X, pp. 170-180; P. A. Bertocci: 'Introduction to the Philosophy of Religion', Chapter 17, pp. 420-441.

that good will eventually triumph, that it is a force stronger than the evil. But he must not think of a Person who controls the universe that this should be so, a Person of whom it is possible to ask why should he not have created things differently.

Certainly if such a view is held then there is no problem of evil but this is only because the Theistic sense of the name 'God' has been abandoned. There is no problem of evil any more than there is for an atheistic philosophy, but then we are faced with the problem of atheism itself. For, in truth, this view is essentially atheistic. It accepts the existence of evil as a final obstacle to Theistic faith but continues to use the term 'God' to represent something other than that which it represents for Theism.

We have noted earlier in this chapter that it is no way out of the dilemma to argue that evil is less extensive than it seems. Even a little evil needs to be explained. But it might be here remarked that, in fact, Judaism never tries to minimise the extent and power of evil.[6] The Bible knows of human misery and tragedy, seeing the human situation in which evil befalls men as a necessary pre-requisite for the good to be realised. In many Biblical passages the complaint is made to God that evil has achieved the victory, a complaint made in the very name of God's justice. 'Thou that art of eyes too pure to behold evil, And that canst not look on mischief, Wherefor lookest Thou, when they deal treacherously, And holdest Thy peace when the wicked swalloweth up The man that is more righteous than he' (Hab. 1: 13). 'Right wouldest Thou be, O Lord, Were I to contend with Thee, Yet will I reason with Thee: Wherefore doth the way of the wicked prosper? Wherefore are all they secure that deal very treacherously' (Jer. 12: 1). 'Why standest Thou afar off, O Lord? Why hidest Thou Thyself in times of trouble?' (Ps. 10: 1).

Pervading the Bible is the recognition that human life is short and frail, that man's existence is insecure, his lot misery. 'Lord, what is man, that Thou takest knowledge of him? Or the son of man, that Thou makest account of him? Man is like unto a breath; His days are as a shadow that passeth away' (Ps. 144: 3-4). 'As for man, his days are as grass; As a flower

---

[6] See Hillel Zeitlin: *'Ha-Tobh We-Ha-Ra'* ('Good and Evil'), pp. 15-23.

of the field, so he flourisheth. For the wind passeth over it, and it is gone; And the place thereof knoweth it no more' (Ps. 103: 15-16).

The pessimism of Ecclesiastes is well-known but this nevertheless did not result in its exclusion from the Canon. In ancient or modern literature nowhere are there to be found such mighty probings of the question of evil than in the book of Job. Hillel Zeitlin is justified in concluding: [7] 'We can see from the severe complaints of the prophets and the weighty arguments of the book of Job that they understood only too well that there is much to complain about in life, that much happens in the world which should not happen and much does not happen which should. If we give any thought to this matter we can only conclude that whoever argues that Judaism is a philosophy of absolute optimism is entirely in error. Certainly on the popular, national and legal level Judaism is optimistic, and here Schopenhauer was perfectly correct, but Judaism at its elevated moral level, in the prophetic understanding, is as remote from absolute optimism as from complete pessimism. It cannot be denied that the Hindus had a better understanding of the great power of evil, of destruction, of the transient and the changing, than the Jews but the Jews, too, understood and sensed this to a great extent. The difference between the two philosophies lies only in this: that the Hindus produced one set of conclusions from their views on good and evil, the Hebrew prophets a different set of conclusions. The faith of the prophets was exceedingly powerful. Even though they complained at the insufficiencies in the ordering of things—whether life is good or bad—for them life was God-given and man must live to improve matters, he must go and examine his ways. Their strong faith gave them the energy and courage to suffer much. Even as they complain they believe. The prophet says to God: "Right wouldest Thou be, O Lord, Were I to contend with Thee, Yet will I reason with Thee." "Right wouldest Thou be"—on this the prophet can cast no doubt even though he sees with his own eyes that the "way of the wicked prospers" for his sense of the moral imperative to set justice on the throne of glory has a greater control over him than that which his eyes see. "Yet will I

[7] *Ibid.*, pp. 20-21.

reason with Thee" cries, without fear and trembling, the justice here below to the justice on high. So, too, Habakkuk says:
"Thou that art of eyes too pure to behold evil, And that canst
not look at mischief, Wherefore lookest Thou, when they deal
treacherously, And holdest Thy peace, When the wicked
swalloweth up The man that is more righteous than he." At
the same time that he complains: "Wherefore lookest Thou,
When they deal treacherously" he believes that: "Thou art
of eyes too pure. . .".'

Those who follow the prophets and the Jewish tradition
generally do not minimise the extent and intensity of evil,
nor live in a fool's Paradise, but courageously face the terrible
problem of evil and still live by faith.

We must turn, therefore, to the solution that evil exists because it serves the good and that to expect God to produce
the good without the evil upon which it depends is to demand
a logical impossibility. It must first be realised, however, that
very few Theists would speak in this connection of a complete
solution. For there is an element of absurdity in imagining
that finite man can grasp fully God's ways. 'For my thoughts
are not your thoughts, neither are your ways my ways, saith the
Lord. For as the heavens are higher than the earth, so are my
ways higher than your ways, and my thoughts than your
thoughts' (Is. 55: 8-9). At the most the Theist claims that he
can obtain some faint glimpse of the reason for God permitting
evil and why it is asking for the logically impossible to demand
that the world in which we live should be other than it
actually is?

If we think of the good things we particularly value we see
that these could not be realised in a world without evil. Sym-
pathy, kindliness, heroism, courage, wisdom and skill, all require for their realisation situations in which there is an
element of evil. At the very heart of Theistic faith is the idea
of man making the good his own by freely choosing it, by
preferring the good to its opposite. This is man's glory. By
helping to destroy evil he becomes God-like and worthy of
sharing God's goodness for ever. But what meaning can there
be in the idea of a free choice of good in a world in which
there are no evils to be conquered? This kind of argument is
sometimes said to apply only to moral evils, to evils caused

by man. If a man could never cheat or steal there would be no possibility of his leading a life of honesty and integrity. But what of the evils in nature? What of earthquakes, disease, floods, and other catastrophes? Yet in reality these, too, are part of the background of struggle against which man finds the good to make it his own. Involved in the very idea of the creation of a finite world in which man strives for perfection is the existence of evil and imperfection. This is not to say, of course, that we can see clearly in all circumstances how particular evils serve particular goods. The ultimate point of this type of explanation is that man cannot have his freedom and yet live in an environment which is so constituted that he cannot exercise it. Unless there is evil there can be no good.

It is all too easy, however, in a discussion of this nature to fall into the trap of interpreting the whole purpose of the universe as for man's benefit. The more we stress, as we should, the need for human freedom the greater the temptation to see man as the sole aim of creation. There have been, in fact, many Theists who have been prepared to adopt the view that man is God's only ultimate purpose in creation. It would probably be true to say that this attitude is so widespread and always has been that it might be considered the conventional Theistic view. But it is important to realise that it is not an essential doctrine for Theism. Not a few great Theists have denied that God's sole purpose in creation is for the sake of man. Maimonides, for example, devotes much space to a refutation of the doctrine.[8] Today when the exploration of outer Space is imminent we must be prepared for the discovery that other worlds are inhabited by non-human intelligent beings and these cannot have been created for man's sake. It will not do, however, to invoke God's other unknown purposes as an explanation for evil in the world, for omnipotence is surely capable of achieving these purposes without human suffering. It is extremely difficult to see how an all-good Being could have purposes for some of His creatures which can only be achieved through human suffering. And here there seems to be no logical contradiction involved as there is in the idea of *man* having freedom and yet having no choice.

[8] 'Guide', III, 13.

One of the most profound discussions of the inevitability of evil for a world in which moral values can be realised is that of F. R. Tennant.[9] Tennant points out that for the world to be a theatre of the moral life there must be a regular operation of natural forces, there must be a lawabidingness in the universe. A topsy-turvey world in which anything can happen or a fairy-tale world in which the ugly brute always turns into a prince would not be the requisite background for the emergence of man's moral qualities. 'Without such regularity in physical phenomena,' writes Tennant, 'there could be no probability to guide us: no prediction, no prudence, no accumulation of ordered experience, no pursuit of premeditated ends, no formation of habit, no possibility of character or of culture. Our intellectual faculties could not have developed. And, had they been innate, they would have wasted themselves, as Comte remarked, in wild extravagances and sunk rapidly into incurable sloth; while our nobler feelings would have been unable to prevent the ascendancy of the lower instincts, and our active powers would have abandoned themselves to purposeless agitation. All this is obvious; but it has often been ignored in discussion of the problem of physical evil. Nevertheless, Nature's regularity is the key to this problem. Once let it be admitted that, in order to be a theatre for moral life, the world must be largely characterised by uniformity or constancy, and most significant consequences will be seen to follow. It becomes idle to complain, as some writers have done, that the orderliness of the world is too dear at the cost of suffering and hardship which it entails, and might more or less be dispensed with for the benefit of the sentient and rational beings which people the world. As Hume admitted, if the "conducting of the world by general laws" were superseded by particular volitions, no man could employ his reason in the conduct of his life. And without rationality morality is impossible: so, if the moral status of man be the goal of the evolutionary process, the reign of law is a *sine qûa non*. It is a condition of the forthcomingness of the highest good, in spite of the fact that it is not an unmixed good but a source of suffering. We cannot have the advantages of a determinate

[9] 'Philosophical Theology', Vol. II, pp. 197-205. *Cf.* Ninian Smart: 'Philosophers and Religious Truth', Chapters VI, pp. 167-196.

order of things without its logically or its causally necessary disadvantages.'

A recent criticism of this point of view[10] is to the effect that there is no logical impossibility in the notion of a world containing evil in which man, nevertheless, always chooses the good any more than on determinist theories there is a logical impossibility in the notion of man's freedom. The determinist may be faulted on other grounds but surely not on those of logic. Even determinists use the word 'freedom'. But in the world as it is at present constituted, a world which contains evil as well as good, it is not logically absurd for a determinist to speak of freedom and to believe in it. It is quite otherwise with regard to a world in which there is not even the determinist choice between good and evil (which is the kind of world required by the anti-Theistic argument on the question of freedom) for then it would be logically absurd to speak of human freedom.

A difficulty seldom considered by Theists who advance the free-will defence is that if evil is necessary for the development of the free moral personality what becomes of the human personality in Heaven where there is no evil? John Hick,[11] one of the very few defenders of Theism to discuss this problem, states: 'It is claimed—reducing the argument to its bare bones—that the evils of this life are necessary to prepare us as moral personalities for the life of the future heavenly Kingdom, and that they are justified by the fact that in that Kingdom all evil will have been left behind and unimaginable good will fill our lives. But if only challenges and obstacles and sufferings can evoke the highest moral qualities within us, will not these evils still be necessary in heaven? If, for example, courage presupposes danger on earth, why does it not also presuppose danger in heaven? If love is at its strongest and deepest amidst trials and difficulties, must there not be trials and difficulties in heaven also? And so with all the other virtues.'

We are admittedly on highly speculative ground here but if

[10] Antony Flew: 'Divine Omnipotence and Human Freedom' in 'New Essays in Philosophical Theology', pp. 144-169. For a fuller treatment of this problem see John Hick: 'Evil and the God of Love', pp. 302-311.
[11] 'Evil and the God of Love', pp. 387f.

eternity is conceived of not as mere endless duration in time but as beyond time, if the soul we make here is thought of as being ours in the eternal Now, then there has to be a period of soul-making in time (the duration of which in the case of each individual is, as it were, God's decision for him) to equip us for eternal life. Once eternal life has been attained through the free choice of the good in a world containing evil it is the possession of its owner for all eternity. This kind of argument does not rule out the possibility of progress in Heaven, though in speaking of progress we are bound by the limitations of our language to impose a time sequence on our experiences in the eternal Now.

The problem is not, of course, solved. Most of us feel that the good results could have been achieved without the *amount* of actual suffering wrought. And what of animal suffering and the sheer pointlessness of some human suffering? Nevertheless it is not an abandonment of the Theistic position to recognise this frankly as a mystery. We cannot hope as finite human beings to see all of God's ways. Here is where faith enters the picture. Very well, it might be retorted, if faith is to be invoked what is the purpose of the whole discussion? But the use of our reason to take us as far as it can is surely not without value. It enables us to see that our faith is not entirely blind and it helps us to distinguish between valid indications and invalid attempts at a solution.

For if on the Theistic view there is a problem of evil, on the atheistic view there is a problem of good. Man's protest against evil and his struggle to overcome it have themselves to be explained. Which is the ultimate reality, the good or the evil? When Theists declare their belief that God is good they are affirming by faith that good is inherent in the very structure of things in a way in which evil is not. Evil belongs to the temporal, good to the eternal. Evil is allowed to exist by God's fiat but ultimately vanquished.

To sum up: It is no solution to the problem of evil to deny that it is real. This is a meaningless assertion and contributes nothing to the problem. Indeed, conventional Theism is rightly at pains to stress the real severity of evil and to treat the fight against it as a battle. Nor is it at all satisfactory to attempt to solve the problem of postulating that God is other than all-good. A God indifferent to evil would not be God. A valid solution must concentrate on exploring the meaning of the term 'omnipotence' when applied to God. This has meant traditionally that God is Infinite. Doctrines of a finite deity or a description of God in terms of force, power or process alone are rejected. But omnipotence cannot mean that God can do the logically impossible because this is a logically meaningless assertion. Consequently, the best defence of the Theistic position is that which sees evil in the universe as the price we have to pay for the type of world in which moral values can be realised. To ask that God should provide for the realisation of these values through man's free choice in a universe in which there is no evil is to demand the logically impossible. The purpose of such realisation, according to traditional Theism, is for man to become God-like for all eternity by his free choice of the good in the world of time. This naturally leads to a consideration of what eternity can mean if we do not limit the concept to endless duration in time. There can be no full and complete solution in which all difficulties are neatly tied up. If we are able to catch some brief glimpse into the fringes of God's ways it is not unreasonable to conclude that the rest must be obscure since if the Infinite were capable of being grasped by the finite mind it would not be Infinite. Man can see enough of the way for him to walk along it in faith without his faith being blind and pointless. If he follows the Jewish tradition in this matter he will never cease from pursuit of the good and war against evil, confident that he does God's work. God has created man with a spirit of proud independence so that he spurns a gratuitous good bestowed upon him even if it comes as a gift from God Himself. He becomes the recipient of the highest good by the glory of his constant choice of it in perfect freedom.

Chapter 8

The Marxist Attack

MANY Theists in the past may have believed their faith to be true because, among other reasons, there seemed no other explanation for its persistence. So many men, wise and good, had believed in God. If Theism was false how did it come to exercise so powerful a fascination over the human mind and stir such profound longings in the human heart? Why did no one see through it? Can a false idea have such a capacity for endurance?

In modern times, however, various attempts have been made to explain the social and psychological appeal of Theism independently of its truth or falsity. According to these theories the persistence of Theism is no evidence of its truth. Men have believed in God because for one reason or another it was convenient and comfortable for them to do so. The older position was turned on its head. Precisely because the appeal was so strong in the past, it has been suggested, there was the strongest temptation to overlook the question of truth in holding on to a doctrine which was of help to mankind or, at least, to many individuals and social classes. Prominent among these attempts is the Marxist interpretation of human history and its critique of religious belief. To explain the appeal of Theism on grounds other than truth does nothing to demonstrate that it is, in fact, false. But if the alternative explanation is convincing, it does serve to defeat the generally subconscious argument that it must be true otherwise it would not have survived. Its survival can be understood on the grounds that influential groups found it useful, comfortable and an aid to their more mundane strivings.

Whether Marx was influenced in his thought by his Jewish ancestry is debatable. His enthusiasm for social reform has been said to owe a great deal to the heritage of the Hebrew prophets, while attempts have been made to trace his dialectic not only to Hegel but also to Talmudic methods of reasoning. (Marx was descended from Rabbinical families on both paternal and maternal side.) Neither of these influences can easily be dismissed but there is no doubt at all that his thought on religion is utterly opposed to Jewish Theism. His followers fought bitterly against every religious interpretation of life, Jewish, Christian, Muslim, Hindu and Buddhist. Orthodox Marxism is virulently atheistic and anti-religious.

Karl Marx was born at Trier in Germany on May 5th, 1818. Though he was born a Jew his father embraced Christianity when the boy was six years old. Marx declared himself to be an atheist as soon as he grew to manhood. He studied at the Universities of Bonn and Berlin. It is highly significant that he received his doctorate in philosophy in 1841 for a thesis on the philosophy of Epicurus, the ancient Greek thinker who denied the power of the Greek gods. In the Rabbinic literature the word formed from the Greek thinker's name—*epikoros*—became the term used to denote the unbeliever, the rebel against faith. Together with Engels Marx wrote the 'Communist Manifesto', published in 1848 and containing the influential exhortation: 'Workers of the World, Unite!' Marx later settled in England. His patient researches in the British Museum are well-known. These culminated in his *'Das Kapital'*, the first volume of which was published in 1873, the second in 1885 and the third in 1894. Marx died in London on March 14th, 1883. He was buried in the Highgate Cemetery where his grave, with its huge memorial stone, has become a place of pilgrimage (!) for Marxists the world over.

It has frequently been remarked that for all its negative attitude towards religion Marxism is itself a religion of a kind, with Marx as its prophet and *'Das Kapital'* as its sacred Scripture, the latter sharing the fate of all such writings in having its orthodox interpreters as well as its deviationists. Marxism resembles other religious systems, too, in its eschatological hope and its dogmas which it is forbidden to question. There is no doubt of the force of the Marxist viewpoint as an obstacle to Theistic belief and in fact many religious believers have been attracted by the 'religion' of Marxism.

In speaking of Marxism in this connection it is necessary to draw a distinction between the atheism of Marx himself (which derives almost entirely from Feuerbach) and the full attack on Theistic faith in the Communist philosophy as developed by Marx, Engels and Lenin.[1] It is as a result of this latter philosophy that Marxism has become an obstacle to Theistic faith and it is this that we must discuss.

For the God of traditional Theism Marxism substitutes Dialectical Materialism. Dialectic is the process of thought which moves from thesis to antithesis to synthesis. An idea is propounded as a thesis but another idea challenges it in antithesis. Eventually the new idea is seen as one which does not contradict entirely the old and a synthesis is attained. Basically the Dialectic is Hegel's but something akin to it is found in ancient literature particularly in the Talmud, a fact which, as we have noted, may be of significance in a discussion of Marx's thought.[2] But for Marxists the Dialectic is wedded to the concept of matter as all that there is, hence Dialectical Materialism. More than one critic of Marxism has noted the logical absurdity in the whole concept of Dialectical Materialism since Dialectic is a process of thought and it is extremely difficult to see how matter can be engaged in thesis, antithesis and synthesis.

Be that as it may, in Marxism man's economic needs are responsible for his philosophy. All movement in society, however buttressed by appeals to reason, is, in fact, the working out of the class struggle between those who have, the capitalists, and the have-nots, the proletariat, the workers and producers. According to the interpretation of Dialectical Materialism, history must move from the thesis of Capitalism to the antithesis of its overthrow by the proletariat. Class warfare is involved in the struggle between thesis and antithesis but the process cannot be arrested and eventually the dictatorship of

[1] See James Collins: 'God in Modern Philosophy', pp. 249-257.

[2] The dialectic of this kind is found in numerous Talmudic passages. A statement advocates a certain point of view without qualification. Another source is then quoted in contradiction. The solution is that the second statement shows that the first is limited in application and that for a full picture both statements have to be taken into account. The formula generally here is: 1. Statement A, which seems to be categorical. 2. But statement B contradicts it? 3. There is no contradiction; A applies only to cases x whereas B applies to cases y.

the proletariat will be fully established. When this happens class warfare will be at an end since in the absence of private property there will be no cause for economic strife. Thus the synthesis will eventually be attained and the state will wither away in a classless brotherhood.

Lenin, Marx's chief disciple, put Marx's ideas into operation after the Russian revolution of 1917. The Communist Party provides the antithesis to Capitalism. Today a large proportion of the world's inhabitants are in the Communist camp. As a result, since Marxism is doctrinaire and must be accepted in its entirety, millions of people are today not only fighters against Capitalism but also against Theism; though within limits religion may still be practised in Soviet Russia. No one can be a member of the Communist Party unless he affirms atheism.

In the Marxist scheme there is obviously no room for God. But Marxism goes further, treating belief in God as positively harmful. Marxism holds that men adhere to Theistic religion not because it is true but because it acts as a tool for the preservation of the economic and social *status quo*. This is particularly so since in the Theistic faiths man's final bliss is not in this world at all but is reserved for him in the Hereafter. The priests of Theism, it is argued, help those in power to exploit the poor by directing their hearts to an other-worldly existence in which they will find compensation for their misery here on earth. By turning men's eyes heavenwards Theism encourages indifference to the economic struggle in the here and now. Religion thus becomes 'opium for the people' (the expression, incidentally, seems to have been used by Charles Kingsley before Marx). The strong appeal of religion is the appeal of any drug, providing a contentment through vain dreams and producing a stupor from which man cannot awake to better himself. By dreaming of a God who helps him man is effectively prevented from helping himself.

The Marxist critique hits hard because Theists recognise that it is not entirely without foundation. It is within the experience of most of us that some people do use their religion to further their own grasping ends, to still their social conscience, to act as a palliative against guilt feelings if they are exploiters, or as a tranquilliser if they are exploited. But the mistake of the Marxist is to imagine that all Theists use their religion in this way and to overlook the fact that Theistic faiths themselves have been at least as condemnatory as Marxism of the abuses, as mentioned above, to which religion can be subjected. The sweeping denunciation that one's philosophy of life is inexorably determined by one's economic needs can be turned only too easily against Marxism itself. It is incredible that some Marxists speak as if the Communist philosophy is never used to further injustice, selfishness and greed.

It would be incorrect to suggest that social and economic exploitation in the name of religion is entirely unknown in the history of Judaism. But it is true to say that the demands of social justice feature prominently in Jewish teaching and that other-worldly tendencies, pronounced though these are in Rabbinic Judaism, have rarely been allowed so to dominate Jewish thought as to obscure the need to improve human society in the here and now. The virtual silence on the whole question of the Hereafter among the great Hebrew prophets, and the prophetic demand for justice, righteousness and loving kindness are too well-known to require much reiteration. And, for all its other-worldliness, Rabbinic Judaism does not normally think of this life only as a 'vale of soul-making', a mere preparation for the World to Come, but as good in its own right, a precious gift of God. The ancient Rabbis were pioneers in the field of social justice, stressing the equality of men and protecting the worker against exploitation.

There is little point in comparing Rabbinic thought in the Talmudic period on economic problems with modern theories concerned with the problems of capital and labour in the kind of society which has merged since the Industrial Revolution. All that is required to refute the Marxist claim that religion has always been a reactionary force in the social field is to show that the Rabbis, inspired by their religious faith and acting on its teachings, tried successfully to make their religion a power for social betterment. This can be done without any apology and without reading into the Rabbinic sources ideas which are not there. In an admirable short study of 'Social Legislation in the Talmud' Dr. I. Epstein[3] gives the following

[3] *Cf.* the interesting pamphlet in the same series by H. Heinemann: 'Torah and Social Order'.

examples of how the Talmudic Rabbis introduced social legislation to act as a check against exploitation. The profit motive,
for instance, was controlled. An over-charge or under-charge
of a sixth of the market price was sufficient to have the scale
cancelled (*B.M.* 50b). Attempts were made to legislate against
the middle-man's profit in commodities such as eggs (*B.B.*
91a). Attempts at cornering the market in important commodities were severely frowned upon (*B.B.* 90b and *Yom.*
83a). Quoting the verse: 'For unto Me the children of Israel
are servants' (Lev. 25:55) a Rabbi ruled (*B.M.* 77a-b) that a
workman who had hired himself for the day had the right of
retracting half way through his work. For, said the Rabbi, the
worker is not a slave—' "unto Me" they are servants and not
servants to servants'. The buyer of property sold by the court
to pay the debts of a bankrupt was obliged to sell it back to
the bankrupt if the latter subsequently had the purchase price
(*B.M.* 16b). Dr. Epstein concludes: 'Living amidst a mixed
and unfriendly population, subject to violent currents of hate
and persecution, the Jewish communities had a severe struggle
to maintain the ideals of justice and mercy, righteousness and
equity which they drew from the Bible. It was not always
possible for them to regulate the social relations of rich and
poor, employer and employed, debtor and creditor, rulers and
ruled, buyer and seller, sinner and saint on the lines they
desired. But the Jewish leaders, undaunted by all obstacles and
difficulties, struggled bravely on, and thus kept their people
from being submerged; and in what they accomplished they
not only anticipated much that is best in the social ethics of
modern civilisation, but what is more, have provided the
Jewish state of the future with valuable material for setting
upon earth a Kingdom of God.' Epstein wrote this before the
establishment of the State of Israel. The new State without
doubt has many faults but those familiar with social conditions in Israel know that a mighty attempt is being made to
apply Biblical and Rabbinic teachings on social justice to the
lives of its citizens.

In discussing Rabbinic social legislation the temptation
must be resisted to paint the picture of a unique system based
on principles of social justice operating in a vacuum. It is
abundantly clear that the Rabbis found in both Palestine and

Babylon (the second great centre of Jewish life in Talmudic times) a highly developed social system with its own institutions and that they had no hesitation in using and adapting it. A good illustration of this is the institution of market commissioners. Everywhere in the Near East these, known as *agoranomi*, were appointed to control weights and measures.[4] In ancient Athens ten *agoranomi* were chosen by lot every year. Here they were particularly responsible for the retail trade, giving strangers permission to engage in it, testing weights and measures as well as the quality of goods, and confiscating and destroying what was spoilt. They settled disputes between buyers and sellers on the spot or, if a lawsuit was necessary, provided it.[5] The very name *agoranomi* was retained by the Jewish teachers when they adopted the institution. In Palestine, in the Talmudic period, it was the function of the *agoranomi* to control weights and measures; prices, however, were left to find their own level (*B.B.* 89a). In Babylon too, prices had long been controlled. There is evidence of such control, quite independent of any Jewish associations, dating as far back as the early Seleucid Empire. This inheritance from the Seleucids was the norm in Parthan times after 141 B.C.E. as well as in Sassanian times, the period of the great Babylonian Jewish academies.[6] The responsibility for the appointment of the *agoranomi* in the Jewish Community belonged to the Exilarch, the lay head of the Community, who had the position in the Persian Empire of a minor king with his own police force. The famous Babylonian teacher Rab, on his return from Palestine to his native Babylon in 219, was appointed by the Exilarch to the position of market-commissioner. Rab refused to control the market prices, preferring the Palestinian system, for which he was imprisoned by the Exilarch (Jer. Talmud, *B.B.*, V, 2). From these and similar details the picture which emerges is of Jewish Communities availing themselves of the institutions of their day in the furtherance of social justice. In any event these facts go a long way in rendering ridiculous the Marxist claim that the Jewish

[4] See F. M. Heichelheim: 'Syria', pp. 205-206.

[5] See *'Pauly-Wissowa'*, Vol. I, p. 883.

[6] See R. H. MacDowell: 'Stamped and Inscribed Objects From Seleucia on the Tigris', pp. 127-155 and p. 263.

faith is a convenient tool for the exploitation of the poor.

As for the Marxist claim that the doctrine of the Hereafter is opposed to the need for social concern and responsibility in his life, it is difficult to see how Judaism is affected. As we have noted, the whole conception of a Hereafter occupies a very insignificant role in Biblical thought. It is certain that when the Hebrew prophets spoke in God's name their chief interest was with justice and righteousness in the here and now. Rabbinic Judaism, which does have a very strong other-worldly emphasis, is, nevertheless, an heir to the Biblical message; it could hardly have been anything else. For the Rabbis and their followers there is no contradiction between the claims of social justice and the longing of the individual to attain spiritual bliss in Heaven after the death of the body. On the contrary it is only through 'good deeds', which include social and benevolent acts, that man can, for the Rabbis, attain to the state described by them as 'basking in the radiance of the Divine Presence'. One of the Rabbis characteristically stated that the first question a man is asked on judgment day is: 'Did you conduct your business affairs honestly?' (*Sabb.* 31a). Another Rabbi gave expression to the paradox in this way: 'Better is one hour of repentance and good deeds in this world than the whole life of the World to Come; and better is one hour of bliss in the World to Come than the whole of this world' (*Abhoth*, IV, 17).

With very few exceptions even the most determined other-worldly exponents of Judaism never forsook the Biblical insight. The mystic Rabbi Moses Hayyim Luzzatto (1707-1747) in his famous moralistic work: *'Mesillath Yesharim'* ('The Path of the Upright')[7] bases his entire system of moral and spiritual advancement on firm belief in the Hereafter as the ultimate goal of man. In the very first chapter he writes: 'It is fundamentally necessary both for saintliness and for the perfect worship of God to realise clearly what constitutes man's duty in this world, and what goal is worthy of his endeavours throughout all the days of his life. Our Sages have taught us that man was created only to find delight in the Lord, and to bask in the radiance of His Presence. But the real place for

[7] Ed. M. M. Kaplan, Jewish Publication Society of America, Philadelphia, 1936.

such happiness is the World to Come, which has been created for that very purpose. The present world is only a path to that goal.' Though 'only a path', this world is, for Luzzatto, the place where man acquires his immortality by engaging in good deeds, prominent among which are acts of justice and equity. One does not find in Luzzatto a fully developed system of applied social justice. But it remains true that he devotes three chapters of his work (X-XII) to the acquisition of what he calls the trait of 'Cleanness' and, as he is at pains to point out, this embraces in large measure the need for sound social conduct based on the Biblical and Rabbinic ideal of justice.

Another extremely eloquent refutation of the Marxist view is the famous saying of the Hasidic master Rabbi Jacob Isaac of Pzhysha (d. 1814) known as the 'holy Jew'. According to Hasidic teaching there is nothing on earth without its good aspect, there are 'holy sparks' in everything. In that case, asks R. Jacob Isaac, what is the good in atheism? His answer is that in man's social duties and obligations he should behave as if he were an atheist, assuming that God did not exist to help the poor and the needy, so that if he did not help them they would remain destitute. Faith is a virtue when applied to one's own life. It is wrong to have it on behalf of others. There is yet something of value in atheism, for even the believer has to be a small doubter when called upon to alleviate human suffering.[8]

Judaism has staunchly defended the claims of justice and has advocated the freedom of the individual as a God-created personality in other spheres of life. Precisely because Judaism is a freedom-loving and just faith it continues to protest against every form of slavery, including the denial of basic human rights in totalitarian systems.

---

[8] See 'Rabbi Jacob Isaac of Pzhysha' (Hebrew) by Z. M. Rabbinowitz, Piotrkow, 1932, pp. 59-60.

Chapter 9

The Freudian Attack

T H E Freudian sees religious faith as wishful thinking. His basic critique of religion would run as follows:

At some stage, the knowledge acquired by a child during his earliest years, that he can rely on his father, is rudely shattered. His father may die, leaving him to cope with life unaided. Or even if his father lives the son comes to understand that his father, too, has fears, that he is not infallible or omnipotent, that his actual power to help is extremely limited. With a burning need for a father in whom he can trust he eventually creates out of his imagination a father-figure real enough to take the place of his genuine father. He projects his need onto the cosmos and comes to believe in an undying and unfailing Father in Heaven to offer him comfort and solace and to enable him to cope with life's problems. Rather than face the painful process of growing up he prefers to remain a child, crying in the dark for the reassuring voice and hand. He becomes a believer in God.

Since, however, the belief in God is a projection of the childish need, the ambivalence of the child to his human father is also projected. On the one hand man wishes to hear the voice of God and to obey it, on the other hand he wishes to be free of God and live his own life. Thus religion is associated with feelings of guilt and sin and the need for atonement.

We do not believe because it is true but because it is comforting, the Freudian argues. Religion is an illusion, albeit a necessary illusion for the immature. But eventually, it is to be hoped, man will learn to stand on his own feet, to live with his fears rather than seek an unreal solace, to face life heroically as an adult rather than timidly as a child.

The criticism hits Theists uncommonly hard because it is

undoubtedly true that for some of them all of the time and for most of them some of the time their belief does cater to the strong emotional need for security and relief from tension and anxiety. Freud's description of religious faith as universal neurosis (healthier, to be sure, than individual neurosis in that it does not isolate the individual from society but a neurosis nonetheless) does present the Theist with a severe challenge. One of the most unacceptable ego-punctures is calling an adult naïve. It is not surprising that Theists have reacted vehemently to Freud. They have been sorely tempted to dismiss it all with a refusal to argue, which plays into the hands of the opposition in demonstrating the basic irrationality of their faith. The better course is to examine critically the Freudian attack and to note that reason is not at all on one side.

Sigmund Freud (1856-1939)[1] was born a Jew and remained conscious, even proud, of his Jewish background all his life but it would seem that from an early age his attitude to the Jewish religion was entirely negative. Leslie D. Weatherhead[2] is wrong in suggesting that the origin of Freud's opposition to religion may have been as a rebellion against the tyranny of an orthodox background, for we have reliable evidence[3] that Freud's father, while possessing some knowledge of Hebrew literature and Jewish religion, was very far from orthodox and had no deep religious faith. Whatever the reason, Freud was

[1] Freud's three main books on religion are: 'Totem and Taboo', 'The Future of an Illusion', 'Moses and Monotheism', Ernest Jones: 'Sigmund Freud' in three volumes, is an indispensable work by a disciple for the understanding of Freud and the background to his theories.

[2] 'Psychology, Religion and Healing', p. 408.

[3] Freud's niece in an autobiographical sketch ('Commentary' May, 1956, pp. 418f.) denies that Freud's parents were Orthodox or that their household was pious. H. L. Philp: 'Freud and Religious Belief', adopts the opposite attitude that Freud's bias in favour of atheism was the product of his 'freethinking' home background, pp. 2-4. Cf. Ernest Jones, op. cit., Vol. 111, p. 376: 'Nevertheless he (Freud) went through his life from beginning to end as a natural atheist . . . that is to say, one who saw no reason for believing in the existence of any supernatural Being and who felt no emotional need for such a belief. The world of Nature seemed all-embracing and he could find no evidence of anything outside it'. Cf. Chapter IV: 'Freudian Religion' in G. Stephen Spinks: 'Psychology and Religion', pp. 75-89. D. Bakan's: 'Sigmund Freud and the Jewish Mystical Tradition', is an unsuccessful attempt to demonstrate that Freud's work has its unconscious origin in the Jewish mystical tradition.

one of those men who feel no attraction for religion and never have anything that can be remotely described as a religious experience. This is an important key to the understanding of the whole Freudian attack on religion. For it cannot be too strongly emphasised that Freud, in his writings on religion, was not advancing reasons to show that religion is false. The question Freud tried to answer was why, *since* religion is false (a position he had arrived at on other grounds), do people believe in it? It will not do therefore to speak of psychoanalysis *versus* religion. Freud's eminence in the sphere of psychology and as one of the great pioneers of thought cannot be invoked as 'scientific' opposition to religion. Freud's atheism was philosophical and in the sphere of philosophy he was an amateur and not a particularly capable one at that. If Freud were right that religion is false on purely philosophical grounds his explanation of why religion nonetheless survives would perhaps be convincing. It is also possible that man does become aware of God in the manner in which Freud suggests. But the believer rejects Freud's basic premise. For the believer religion persists because it is true. The mechanism by which man recognises God may possibly be that described by Freud, but what is arrived at is a true belief. Men have a hunger for God because there really is a God who is the source of that hunger and who alone can satisfy it.

Freud is not content with describing why people today hold fast to religious belief even though it is, from his point of view, false. He seeks to describe how the belief arose originally in the prehistoric dawn of human society. Briefly stated, Freud's view is that primitive man hunted for food and sought shelter in small groups presided over by the old man of the tribe, the father. The price the younger men had to pay for the protection of the old man was subjection to him. The women of the tribe, for example, belonged exclusively to him. When the domination of the old man became too unbearable he was slain by the younger men and eaten. But they continued to see him in their dreams and, being afraid of retribution, sought to propitiate him. In this way the basic ideas associated with religion were born: the undying God, the father-figure, feelings of guilt and sin and the taboo on incest (the women of the family continue to belong to the old man of the tribe). There is, in fact, no evidence at all that any of this actually happened. Most anthropologists reject the whole theory as entirely without foundation. No one can claim that Freud was scientific in his anthropology.

It must, however, be repeated that the Theist can keep an open mind on theories such as these to account for the growth of religious consciousness in the human race in general and among individuals in particular. Whatever the cause of the belief, whatever its history and psychological explanation, the philosophical question concerns the truth or falsity of the proposition and on this neither psychology nor anthropology has anything to say. The Theist believes on other grounds that his belief is true. In the long history of mankind men have arrived at true beliefs by irrational means and false beliefs by rational ones. But to acknowledge this is to recognise that the Theist must be prepared to test the rationality and truth of his belief and the refined Theist will not fail to do this. It is only when the Theist refuses to reason at all <u>about his belief</u> that he is vulnerable to the Freudian attack.[4]

The refined Theist ought to be grateful to Freud for pointing out that man's religious beliefs are perhaps due to wish-fulfilment alone. For one thing this means that the Theist must constantly be on guard against religion as a childish escapism from life. He must grow in religious maturity so that his faith enables him to face life courageously with his God challenging him at every turn. Again it is salutory for man to recognise the irrational side of his nature, that he is not as reasonable as he likes to pretend he is. (Theism has always taught the value of humility.) The harm is done only when it is argued that *all* man's convictions are arrived at by irrational means. If this were so it would be true of the Freudian attack itself. An argument which relies on reason to attack *reason* is obviously self-defeating. Similarly it is unfair for the Theist to claim, as some Theists do, that the atheist always denies God because of wish-fulfilment because, for example, it is a good excuse to avoid the moral responsibility which religion enjoins. This may be true, and probably is, of some atheists just as the wish-fulfilment motive applies to the belief

---

[4] See the chapter on 'Religious Belief and Psychological Explanation' in 'Difficulties in Christian Belief' by Alasdair C. MacIntyre, pp. 88-101.

of many Theists. But ultimately the question is one of truth. The Theist holds fast to the truth that there is a God.

In more recent years there has been evident an attempt by a number of psychologists to combat the Freudian critique of religion as an illusion without necessarily rejecting the many Freudian insights of permanent value. Even in an earlier period a clergyman who was a disciple of Freud tried to show how Freudian views can be reconciled with a Theistic belief.[5] Gordon W. Allport[6] has a very positive attitude towards religion as the most satisfactory way of unifying man's separate activities. He contrasts what he calls 'growth religion' with 'safety religion'. Allport points out that higher education rightly teaches people not to be duped. However, many of them fail to go beyond this first lesson and, he continues, because in their youth they had accepted religion uncritically they tend to imagine that religion itself is obscurantist. Atheism also has its dupes. The vehemence with which some atheists attack religion makes one suspect that they are governed by an emotionally over-determined negativism. If, as Freud has said, the religious sentiment is basically an extension of one's attitude towards one's physical father, then we must expect repressed animosity towards this father occasionally to be reflected in a hatred of religion. It seems curious that while Freud insists that belief in God is a projection of dependence and love associated with the earthly father, he overlooks the fact that by the same token atheism may be construed as the prejection of ambivalence or hatred associated with the father. Probably the truest statement would be that on occasion, probably not often, both belief and doubt may reflect unconsciously one's attitude towards one's parents.

And, of course, C. G. Jung, Freud's rival, far from accepting Freud's analysis of religion as an obsessional neurosis believes that it is in fact religion which saves man from mental disorders. Jung was an empiricist; his interest was chiefly in the psychological value of religion, not in its truth or falsity. In an oft-quoted passage—probably over-quoted and out of context but still not without significance—Jung remarks:[7] 'I should

[5] Oskar Pfister: 'Christianity and Fear'.
[6] 'The Individual and His Religion', pp. 115f.
[7] 'Modern Man in Search of a Soul', p. 264.

like to call attention to the following facts. During the past thirty years people from all civilised countries of the earth have consulted me. I have treated many hundreds of patients, the larger number being Protestants, the smaller number Jews, and not more than five or six believing Catholics. Among all my patients in the second half of life—that is to say, over thirty-five—there has not been one whose problem in the last resort was not that of finding a religious outlook on life. It is safe to say that every one of them fell ill because he had lost that which the living religions of every age have given to their followers, and none of them has been really healed who did not regain his religious outlook.'

The acknowledgment of the truth of Jung's contention that religion can bring 'peace of mind' may however encourage its pursuit for that very reason and to do this is to miss the point of the meaning of religion. If it is true that there is a God then man's greatest privilege is to serve Him and have a relationship with Him. The result of this may well be peace of mind but to make it the aim of religion is to substitute self-worship for the worship of God. This is of vital concern to the now much-debated 'death of God' question.[8] Modern secular man, it is claimed, conducts his life as if he had no need for God; thus it frequently appears that when religious people do invoke God's help it is for the purpose of placing the responsibility on to Him instead of facing it for themselves.

The truth is that there are two views of what religion means. Some see it as a means of escape, an ever present refuge in times of trouble, a relief from pain, hopelessness and anxiety. Others, while acknowledging these aspects, prefer to lay greater stress on the idea of religion as a challenge.

The escapist view of religion tends to dwell on the transient nature of man's earthly span, its brevity and brutishness. At every turn man is confronted with obstacles to his desires and ambitions, his hopes for a better life are constantly frustrated,

[8] On this there is fast developing a huge literature; see e.g. the now famous books by the Bishop of Woolwich: 'Honest to God' and 'The New Reformation', and 'The Honest to God Debate' by John A. T. Robinson and David L. Edwards; 'Faith, Fact and Fantasy' by C. F. D. Moule and others; Dietrich Bonhoeffer: 'Letters and Papers from Prison'; Paul Van Buren: 'The Secular Meaning of the Gospel'; Harvey Cox: 'The Secular City'.

his dreams are often so far beyond realisation. If this way of looking at life is stressed it is understandable that relief is sought in the life of another, altogether richer, completely unassailable world, the world of the spirit. In prayer, for example, when man reflects on God's perfection, all the petty irritations, imperfections, inadequacies and injustices of the mundane world are transcended. In the pursuit of the beauty of holiness man finds refuge from the prevailing ugliness.

There is sufficient power in this view of religion to make it exceedingly attractive for many people. Moreover, it is right that we be reminded periodically of the existence of a higher world. But this view fails on two counts as a satisfactory philosophy of life. First, it is psychologically unhealthy in that it encourages immaturity and hinders moral and spiritual growth. It arrests the development of its followers, allowing them to remain at the childish level. When life becomes too difficult the child seeks comfort in the parents' embrace. The Freudian critique of religion is here not without its justification. Secondly, the escapist approach is theologically unsound because it tends to see God basically as at war with His creation. Once admit that religion is chiefly a matter to be engaged in away and apart from man's daily and worldly concerns and you banish God from the totality of His world into the mere corner of it that we call the house of worship.

This is why so many great Jewish teachers have favoured a different approach to religion, seeing it as mainly a profound challenge to men and women who willingly accept this world with all its imperfections as the arena where they can grow in maturity, spiritual depth and constant battle. Certainly such was the religion of the great Hebrew prophets. Their experience of God, mysterious and intensely personal, nevertheless expressed itself in terms of human values and in actual human situations. They spoke in the name of the 'holy One' of justice, righteousness and holiness in human society with all its imperfections. Rabbinic teaching generally follows the same tendency.

Bonhoeffer speaks of man 'coming of age'. The secular society is the greatest challenge to religion today and religious people can react to this challenge by rejecting the secular world, seeking the more refined world of the spirit. But if they do this they fight a losing battle for they surrender the sublime conception of God as King of the Universe. Far better that they live as citizens of this imperfect world and strive to bring the light of God's truth to shine on the whole of human existence. The Rabbinic ideal is well known; man is co-partner with God in the work of creation.[9]

Apart from the critique of religious faith itself, other Freudian views on man's nature are of significance to religion. Freud divides the mind into three, the *ego*, the *super-ego*, the *id*. The *ego* is the mind of man as it is aware of himself, the conscious mind. The *id* is the unconscious mass of repressed impulses. From infancy we repress our impulses pushing them out of conscious into the subconscious where they continue to enjoy existence and influence our conduct. The process starts in infancy because it is then that parents and teachers begin to teach the child to control feelings and desires. The *id*, then, represents man's basic impulses and desires, many of them infantile but with later additions. These have been controlled by a censorship partly of the conscious mind, partly of the sub-conscious, based largely on parental discipline by which the infant is taught how to behave. Since the infant cannot understand the meaning of parental rules this censorship is exercised in an irrational way. This controlling force is the *super-ego*. Thus man is seen as engaged in constant struggle within himself. His *ego* is in the middle pulled downwards by his *id* and upwards by his *super-ego*. Neither will be thwarted and most mental disturbance is generally due to a failure to attain the correct balance. It is fatal to allow the *ego* to become completely dominated by either the *id* or the *super-ego*. Stability and harmony in life are achieved by the frank recognition of man's aggressive and animal instincts as represented

[9] See e.g. *Sabb.* 119b: R. Hamnuna said: 'He who prays on the eve of the Sabbath and recites *"and the heaven and the earth were finished"* Scripture treats of him as though he had become a partner with the Holy One, blessed be He, in the work of creation', and *Sabb* 10a: 'Every judge who judges with complete fairness even for a single hour Scripture gives him credit as though he had become a partner with the Holy One, blessed be He, in the work of creation.' Without evident awareness of the Rabbinic view, Harvey Cox, *op. cit.*, p. 264 remarks: 'Recent discussions of the concept of the covenant in the Old Testament suggest it means that Yahweh was willing to stoop so low as to work in tandem with man, to work on a team, no matter how poorly the human partner was working out.'

by the *id*. These man can and should control but not eradicate for they are essential if life is not to be deprived of its driving force.

In the book mentioned above, Leslie Weatherhead compares man to one who inhabits a room, on the ceiling of which the *super-ego* in the attic knocks, demanding him to come up, and on the floor of which the *id* in the cellar knocks, demanding him to come down and respond to needs, so that he is distracted and torn asunder. The way to mental health is to recognise both elements, and then come to terms with them. A man must not yield to either completely, for neither would let the other have it all his own way. That which man *ought* to do and that which he *wants* to do must be co-ordinated in an 'ego-ideal', and then harmony can be restored. The implications of all this for religion are clear. Some religions seek to encourage the *super-ego* at the expense of the *id*, urging man to do that which the *id* will not allow him to do, obviously with neurotic results. A healthy-minded religious outlook panders neither to the *id* nor *super-ego* but encourages man to attain to his ego-ideal. This is so even if Freud's precise analysis is incorrect. Even on the superficial level it is clear that a religion which fails to challenge man at all has no vitality and little meaning, while one whose challenges are too high submits its adherents to unbearable strain.

No one who has read Freud and Rabbinic teachings on the good and evil inclination can have failed to notice their remarkable resemblances. It would, of course, be grossly anachronistic to speak of Rabbinic anticipation of Freud. Although the notion of the subconscious was known long before Freud, and is found in various literatures of the world, Freud's contribution gave it a scientific basis, through his empirical method. To compare Freud and the Rabbis on this subject is not to try to equate their opinions but to note that the faith of the Rabbis was not based on too high a view of human nature, nor did they normally encourage man ruthlessly to suppress his basic instincts. The religion of the Rabbis, however it fared among some of its later interpreters, is a challenging faith but one fully in accord with the idea of balance and harmony in human life.

In the Rabbinic scheme man is influenced by his two 'in-

clinations', the *yetzer tobh* ('the good inclination') and the
yetzer ha-ra ('the evil inclination'). His task is to follow the
dictates of the good inclination and to control the evil inclination, though the latter, too, has its place in human life. Avoid-
ing the implication of anticipation in a direct sense, as we
have said, the Rabbinic scheme does roughly correspond to
the Freudian in this way. The *ego* is man faced with the
struggle within him, the evil inclination is the *id* that pulls
him in one direction, the good inclination is the *super-ego*
that pulls him in the opposite direction.[10]

The evil inclination, *yetzer ha-ra* (sometimes simply called
'the *yetzer*'), frequently denotes in Rabbinic literature the
sex impulse, but it is used also of the bodily instincts in general
as well as man's aggressive drives and ambitions. Although it
is called evil this is not so much because it is evil in itself but
because it can easily lead to evil. Indeed it is evident from a
number of Rabbinic passages that the Rabbis saw positive
value in the *yetzer ha-ra*. It is stated, for example, in a rather
curious passage (*Yom.* 69b) that the *yetzer ha-ra* was delivered
into the hands of the 'Men of the Great Synagogue' (Ezra and
his associates) who wanted to kill him (the *yetzer ha-ra*—he is
personified in the story). The *yetzer* said that if he were killed
'the world would go down'. They therefore imprisoned him
for three days, and then searched the entire land of Israel for
a new-laid egg and could not find it. Instead of killing him
they put out his eyes so that at least he could no longer entice
men to incest. Demythologising his passage, the very interesting thought remains that the 'Men of the Great Synagogue',
despite their mighty efforts to further and establish Judaism,

[10] For a useful selection of some of the relevant material on the Rabbinic
views of the *yetzer ha-ra* see Solomon Schechter: 'Aspects of Rabbinic Theology', Chapters XV and XVI and Montefiore and Loewe: 'A Rabbinic Anthology', Chapter XI. There is an interesting essay on Freud and the Rabbinic
views by Arnold J. Wolfe in the book edited by him: 'Rediscovering Judaism',
Quadrangle Books, Chicago, 1965 ('Psychoanalysis and the Temperaments of
Man', pp. 133-162), but this is vitiated by Wolf's equation of the *yetzer ha-ra*
with the *ego* rather than the *id*. On the question of specific Jewish rituals
and psychoanalysis see: Abraham Cronbach: 'Psychoanalytic Study of
Judaism' in the 'Hebrew Union College Annual', Vols. VIII-IX, pp. 1931-2;
Alter Druyanov in the magazine: '*Reshumoth*', Vol. I, Odessa, 1918, pp.
199-204, Vol. II, Tel-Aviv, pp. 303-357; Theodor Reik's two volumes of
studies; 'Ritual', London, 1931 and 'Dogma and Compulsion', New York,
1951, and my criticism of these in: 'We Have Reason to Believe', pp. 33-43.

were not permitted to be so 'successful' in their fight against the evil inclination as to destroy it completely; for then the world would die. They, however, succeeded in combating the grosser kinds of sin and depravity. Israel is no longer tempted to commit incest or, as the same passage declares, to worship idols. Similarly, in another passage (*Midrash*, Gen. R., 9:7) there is a comment on the verse: 'And God saw everything that He had made and behold, it was very good' (Gen. 1:31). Had the verse have said simply: 'it was good' it would have referred to the good inclination. Since it says *very* good' it refers to the evil inclination. For were it not that man has a *yetzer ha-ra* he would neither build a house, nor marry a wife, nor beget children, nor engage in commerce. In other words 'good' though the world would undoubtedly be without the *yetzer ha-ra*, it would be an unexciting, colourless, uncreative good. God sees that the world is *very good* by creating the *yetzer ha-ra*. It is in this spirit that Rabbinic references to the *yetzer ha-ra* as the 'leaven in the dough' (*Ber.* 17a) are possibly to be understood. Although the leaven can be responsible for over-fermentation without it the bread would be unpalatable.[11]

One of the most remarkable Rabbinic passages in this connection states that the *Torah* is the antidote to the poison of the *yetzer ha-ra* (*Kidd.* 30b). The meaning appears to be that when man submits to *Torah* discipline he becomes free of morbid guilt feelings, his life unclouded by the oppressive fear that the evil within him will drag him down and bring about his ruin. There is no need to flee from life or, with reference to the modern problem, reject the 'secular city'. The famous parable tells of a king who struck his son, later urging his son to keep a plaster on the wound. While the wound is covered the prince may eat and drink whatever he desires without coming to harm. Only if the plaster is removed will the wound fester. God has 'wounded' man by creating him with the evil inclination. But the *Torah* is the plaster which, by preventing the wound from festering, enables him to welcome life without fear.

Judaism is very conscious of man's sinfulness. The great Day of Atonement, *Yom Kippur*, is sufficient evidence of this.

[11] See the discussion of this point in Schechter, *op. cit.*, pp. 264f.

It is noteworthy, however, that the liturgy of *Yom Kippur* subtly suggests the mere commonplace nature of most of our sins. They are, in the main, the sins of ordinary men and women. We are offered no encouragement to indulge in an orgy of masochistic self-recrimination. Of the three main Hebrew words for sin *het*, which means literally a missing of the mark, *avon*, sin resulting from a perverse twist of character, and *pesha*, wilful rebellion against God's laws, it is the most innocuous that is used in the lengthy *Al Het* formula of confession. As Rabbi Dr. Hertz remarks in his Commentary to the Prayer Book the more vicious crimes such as brutal assault, bestial cruelty and murder, are omitted from the list of sins to be confessed. We humbly abase ourselves before the divine Throne not as dissolute sinners, but as unworthy, ignorant bunglers. Indeed, almost at the beginning of the Yom Kippur service there occurs the threefold repetition of: 'for in respect of all the people it was done *unwittingly*'.

It is not suggested that attitudes of introspection or of encouragement to morbid guilt feelings are completely unknown among Jewish teachers. But the Rabbinic view of the *yetzer ha-ra* which, after all, was probably the most influential in determining subsequent Jewish attitudes, is one which is helpful in preserving the correct balance. On this view Judaism controls but does not deny life. Every part of human nature can find fulfilment within its range. The recognition of the tension which exists in the human soul, far from being detrimental to the religious life, is an essential ingredient.

PART IV

The Life of Faith

Chapter 10

Faith and Trust

T H E Hebrew word for 'faith', *emunah*, was, in the Biblical period, a synonym for 'trust' in God. When, during the Middle Ages, *'emunah'* became reserved for the cognitive aspect of faith, for belief that there is a God, the Biblical term *bittahon* continued to serve, as it did in the earlier period, for the idea of trust in and reliance on God. *Emunah* has now come to mean that man affirms God's existence, *bittahon* that man places his trust in God. The famous mediaeval work on this theme, *'Sepher Ha-Emunah We-Ha-Bittahon'* ('The Book on Faith and Trust', written by Jacob Ibn Shesheth though incorrectly attributed to Nahmanides) states: Faith (*emunah*) is the tree, trust (*bittahon*) the fruit.[1] There can be no fruit without a tree, there can be no trust without faith. Man cannot trust in God unless he believes that there is a God to be trusted. But there can be a tree without fruit. It is possible for man to believe that there is a God and yet fail to trust in Him.

This may be for a variety of reasons. It may be that his belief in God is too weak and vague to produce the more passionate, committed affirmative relationship suggested by trust. Or, as Ibn Shesheth writes,[2] it may be because, while believing without reservation in God's power to help, man cannot bring himself to believe that he, in his sinfulness, is worthy of being helped. This latter reason is the heart of the problem of trust in God. How far should the believer rely on God and how much reliance should he place on his own efforts? If it is irreligious to fail to place one's trust in God is

---

[1] *'Sepher Ha-Emunah We-Ha-Bittahon'*, ed. B. Chavel, in *'Kithbhe Ha-Ramban'*, Vol. II, pp. 341-448. The illustration of the tree and its fruit is given in Chapter 1, ed. Chavel, p. 353. The author illustrates this by Hillel's saying (*Abhoth*, I, 5) that the unlearned man cannot be a saint. The saint must be learned but it does not follow that the learned man is a saint.

[2] *Op. cit.*, Chapter 1, ed. Chavel, p. 353.

it not either arrogance or naïvety to believe that God will
help in all circumstances? This is the central religious problem regarding the life of trust. When is trust a virtue and
when does it cease to be a virtue? When is trust to be embraced and when rejected? No sane believer would face an
oncoming express train trusting God to save him from injury. He would regard this as an act of impiety, of testing
God, of failing in the God-ordained duty that he take care
of himself. Where, then, is the line to be drawn between
courageous reliance and foolhardiness? Religious teachers
have given to this question various answers ranging from the
most extreme attitude of complete quietism, in which man
does nothing for himself, to so great a confidence in the power
of human effort as to nullify trust in God.[3]

'Trust in God and keep your powder dry.' This implies
that it is both proper and desirable to strike the correct balance between the view that only human effort avails and that
which sees all human effort as futile. But, as in all matters
regarding the attainment of a delicate balance, the problem is
extremely complicated. Where is the emphasis to be placed?
On the whole it is correct to say that during the Middle Ages
the stress was on the 'trust in God' while in modern times
even the most religious of men have been rather more concerned with keeping the powder dry.[4]

[3] For a splendid summary of the whole question see R. J. Zvi Werblowski:
'Faith, Hope and Trust: A Study in the Concept of Bittahon' in 'Papers of
the Institute of Jewish Studies London' ed. J. G. Weiss, Magnes Press,
Hebrew University, Jer., 1964, pp. 95-139.

[4] See the very interesting Responsum of Rabbi Moshe Feinstein (Vol.
'Hoshen Mishpat etc.,' New York, 1963, section O.H., No. 111, pp. 299-300)
dated Heshvan 27th, 5724 (1963) on whether it is indicative of lack of trust
in God to take out a life insurance policy. The question is posed as follows:
'Is there any advantage in, or is there a prohibition against, taking out an
insurance policy because, God forfend, it may appear to be a lack of trust in
God in whose power it lies to make a man rich enough to leave a substantial
sum to his heirs?' The reply is that it is obviously permitted and is no
different from any other business enterprise. Rabbi Feinstein quotes Ber.
60 that it is a 'vain prayer' to pray for a miracle. Bittahon, he argues, means
that all is from God but on condition that human effort is first expended. The
whole idea of insurance is God's 'advice' to this generation on how to prosper.
Bittahon comes into it, too, that one will be able to pay the premiums. The
same applies to other forms of insurance e.g. car insurance and against fire
and theft. All God-fearing people, concludes Rabbi Feinstein, who take out
insurance policies understand this.

The historical background to the marked shift in emphasis is not at all difficult to trace. From the Renaissance, man's newly discovered powers of self-expression led him increasingly from a God-centred to a man-centred universe, with man acquiring progressively greater self-confidence. The view that this life was a school where man had to train himself to enjoy God for ever yielded increasingly to the view that this life was good in itself. There was a new flowering of the human spirit, expressing itself in the beginnings of accurate scientific investigation and in new forms in art, literature and music. With the advent of modern science and technology and their world-transforming achievements, from the building of great roads, railways, bridges and ships to the splitting of the atom, it is not surprising that the mediaeval view of human effort as a mere concession to human frailty, as a necessary evil,[5] receded more and more into the background. There is obviously a vast difference in outlook between the mediaeval Islamic view that a man should regard himself as a corpse in the hand of God, with no will of his own at all, to the *religious* motivation behind the rise of modern capitalism.[6] For the modern believer the whole idea of trust in God has been called into question in a way inconceivable in the Middle Ages. And yet, unless they are spiritually insensitive, modern men must surely see that such a tremendous idea cannot be abandoned by the believer without the greatest impoverishment. They must sense the incongruity between their protestations in the house of worship that all depends on God and their daily conduct of life as if they had no need of that hypothesis.

In making this distinction between the modern and the mediaeval attitude we are not suggesting that the distinction is always neatly chronological. An attitude of quietism is not entirely unknown among modern Jews and famous mediaeval

[5] See the sources quoted by Werblowski, *op. cit.*, pp. 124-125.

[6] See R. H. Tawney: 'Religion and the Rise of Capitalism'. For the Islamic doctrine of *tawakkul* ('trust', 'contentment', 'resignation') see Werblowski *op. cit.*, p. 121 who quotes the famous saying of Sahl of Tustari: 'The first stage of *tawakkul* is that one should be in God's hand like a corpse in the hand of the washer, which he turns to and fro as he wills without any movement or volition on his part.' Werblowski rightly points out that this attitude is incompatible with that of the Bible and the Rabbis.

thinkers like Saadiah Gaon rejected it. In Sadiah's chapter on 'Worship'[7] there is a very modern-sounding analysis of the whole question. Many assert, observes Saadiah, that the highest endeavour of the servant of God ought to be to devote himself exclusively to God's service, singing His praises and worshipping Him in prayer and study, while abandoning all mundane concerns in his confidence that God will provide. Saadiah does not deny that the ideal is a lofty one but he takes strong exception to its exclusiveness. If, for instance, man takes no concern for his food he will die. If all the members of a particular generation failed to concern themselves with the begetting of offspring divine worship would eventually cease altogether for there would be no one left to engage in it. Furthermore, the hermit saint is unable to fulfil what Saadiah calls the 'rational' commands of the *Torah* such as the laws governing business relations and the conduct of man in society, the laws of just measures and the duties of charity. Nor will Saadiah allow an exception to be made for the individual saint on the grounds that his special kind of devotion will equip him the better to serve as a teacher of others and thus repay his debt to society. For this would mean that it is not he but those others who serve God in the particular way the *Torah* enjoins, that is the way in which God wishes to be served. Nor is attention to one's material needs in any way irreligious since this is the way God has laid it down for man to follow. If one is to be consistent in an attitude of quietism it would have to be applied to man's spiritual as well as his material concerns. Unless one accepts that there is a God-ordained way for man why pray or study? Why not remain entirely inactive, trusting God to reward man with eternal bliss without his being obliged to engage in any effort whatsoever? But if one accepts the idea of a God-ordained way then it can only be the way of the *Torah* and this is clearly not that of quietism.

Saadiah, then, is a mediaeval opponent of quietism. One of the most influential of modern religious thinkers, Kierkegaard, holds the opposite view to that of Saadiah. In comparing these two thinkers we are not suggesting that there is a

[7] '*Emunoth We-Deoth*' ('The Book of Beliefs and Opinions'), X, 15, trans. S. Rosenblatt, pp. 395-397.

clear-cut distinction in this matter between Judaism and Christianity. The problem is far too complicated for any such neat distinction and it is obvious that individual temperament enters into the picture. The point of the comparison is to demonstrate that while, generally speaking, our distinction between the mediaeval and the modern world on this question of trust in God is sound, it must not be pressed too far. Saadiah, the mediaevalist, is very modern while Kierkegaard, the modern, is completely mediaeval. Moreover, it is significant that, rightly or wrongly, Kierkegaard states that his own position is the only authentic Christian doctrine and that the opposite view is pure Judaism.

'Judaism,' writes Kierkegaard,[8] 'is really of all religions outspoken optimism. Certainly Greek paganism was also an enjoyment of life, but it was uncertain and filled with melancholy, and above all it had not divine authority. But Judaism is divinely sanctioned optimism, sheer promise for this life.' On the question of marriage he observes: 'That Christ was born of a Virgin would not have scandalised the pagans, but for Judaism it was bound to be a scandal. For Judaism culminates in regarding marriage as so divine that it is God himself who has instituted it. Judaism has ideas of the propagation of the species as a kind of religion. And then to be born of a Virgin! Basically this is a denial of the whole of the Old Testament, a removal of its essential powers.' Kierkegaard's determined opposition to marriage is expressed with the vehemence so typical of this existentialist thinker: 'The error in Catholicism is not that the priest is celibate; no, the error is that a qualitative difference between the layman and the priest has been introduced, which goes clean against the New Testament, and is a concession of weakness in relation to numbers. Certainly the error is not that the priest is celibate —a Christian should be celibate. "But if you hold to this you will have no Christians at all!" If that is so, it is all one to me. "And on the other hand, if you make Christianity consist of marriage, then you will get millions of Christians!" It is all one to me.'

[8] This and the following quotations are from 'The Last Years—Journals 1853-55' by Søren Kierkegaard, edited and trans., by Ronald Gregor Smith, (p. 67; p. 79; p. 264; pp. 119-120).

Protestant Orthodoxy, with its demand that man marry and propagate the species, Kierkegaard considers to be 'heart twaddle, mediocrity with a dash of sugar'. In another passage he remarks: 'But in Christianity married people are consecrated, and the ceremony sanctifies this relation. How charming! So bandits in the south sanctify murder by kneeling down beforehand at the altar.' Saadiah, as any representative Jewish teacher, would have been horrified that marriage could be compared, even by illustration, with murder. In the Talmud (*Yeb.* 63b) it is said that R. Eliezer stated that he who does *not* engage in the propagation of the race is as though he sheds blood.

It is worth noting, however, that the ideal of the hermit saint is not entirely unknown in Rabbinic Judaism, as evidenced by the example of Ben Azzai (second cent.) who preached eloquently on the virtues of marriage while himself remaining unmarried. Excusing his lack of consistency this teacher is said to have protested that his soul was in love with the *Torah* and the world would have to be established by others.[9] It is strange that Saadiah makes no mention of this at all and he may have been influenced by the need to combat contemporary ideas of quietism. But his silence is further evidence that on a complex issue such as this it is precarious to talk of *the* Jewish point of view.

Prior to the time of Saadiah there is a debate, recorded in the Talmudic literature,[10] in which the second-century teacher, Rabbi Simeon ben Yohai, taught that the man who 'does God's will' can afford to neglect his material responsibilities, relying on God to provide. Rabbi Ishmael, his contemporary, retorted by quoting: '*That thou gather in thy corn*' (Deut. 11:14) to demonstrate that human effort is indispensable. A later teacher remarked[11] that many have tried to follow Rabbi Simeon without success but many have followed Rabbi Ishmael with success. The background to the debate should not be overlooked. Both teachers lived at a time when the

[9] *Yeb.* 63b. See Maimonides, *Yad, Hil. 'Ishuth'*, XV, 3 and '*Shulhan Arukh*', Ebhen Ha-Ezer, I, 5, that this attitude did not entirely die out even at a much later date.

[10] *Siphre, Ekebh*, sec. 42, *Ber.* 35b. See my 'Jewish Values' pp. 86-98, for a fuller discussion.

[11] *Ber., ibid.*

wars with Rome and the sporadic attempts at Jewish revolt had brought great devastation to the land. At this period there was so considerable an economic decline in Palestine that there are sparse references in the sources of the period to commercial undertakings there. In such periods it is usual to find teachers like Rabbi Simeon advocating a completely negative attitude towards human effort, rejecting it as fruitless in favour of a life of prayer and contemplation. What does emerge clearly from the earlier sources is that both quietism and its opposite had their advocates among Jewish teachers and that the differing attitudes were not uninfluenced by cultural and economic considerations.

Even into the twentieth century the more extreme attitude on trust found its exponent in the saintly Rabbi Yoizel Hurwitz of Novogrudok (called Navaradok) in the Government of Minsk. Rabbi Yoizel (c. 1848-1919) was a distinguished representative of the *Musar* movement, the Lithuanian moralistic movement founded in the last century by Rabbi Israel Lipkin of Salant.

Rabbi Yoizel, a successful business man in his youth, came under the influence of the *Musar* movement and eventually relinquished his commercial interests to devote himself entirely to moral improvement and divine worship. For a time he lived as a hermit in a little hut with two holes in the wall, through which sympathisers would place meat or dairy dishes (the two apertures were for the purpose of keeping the two separate in compliance with the dietary laws which forbid the mixing of meat and milk). He became the particular target of *Maskillim*, the advocates of Westernisation among the Russian Jews. Eventually Rabbi Yoizel emerged from seclusion to found a Talmudical Academy in Navaradok in which his particular approach to Judaism was extensively cultivated. Chaim Grade's short Yiddish story: 'My Quarrel with Hirsh Rasseyner' is a vivid account of the views of the Navaradok students.[12] Rabbi Yoizel's ideas on trust in God are to be

[12] Published in an English translation in: 'A Treasury of Yiddish Stories' edited by Irving Howe and Eliezer Greenberg, pp. 579-606. On Rabbi Yoizel see: 'Rabbi Israel Salanter: Religious-Ethical Thinker' by Menahem G. Glenn, pp. 82-90 and Dobh Katz: *'Tenuath Ha-Musar'*, Vol. IV, Tel-Aviv, 1957, Chapters 10-24, pp. 179-351.

found chiefly in his *'Madregath Ha-Adam'* ('Man's Spiritual Stage') published for the first time just before his death and reprinted some years ago.[13]

Rabbi Yoizel was particularly concerned that men with the necessary qualifications should devote themselves unreservedly to *Torah* study, taking no thought of the morrow, ready to sacrifice every worldly ambition and thought of career. It is said that in Rabbi Yoizel's extremism he prayed for the economic downfall of those of his pupils who engaged in trade so that they would be obliged to devote themselves to *Torah* study. A pupil of Rabbi Yoizel named Joel Barantschick once opened a small shop in Riga. When the master heard of it he prayed that Rabbi Barantschick would become bankrupt.[14] Two typical sayings of Rabbi Yoizel are: 'Man must be capable of giving up all his tomorrows for today; so that he should not have to spend all his todays for one tomorrow.' 'He who worries about this world may be likened to one who sits in a train and pushes his finger against the carriage wall to make the train go faster.'[15]

It is notorious that the Navaradok students engaged in bizarre practices inviting ridicule so as to cultivate an attitude of complete indifference to worldly opinion. Some would dress as tramps, neglecting cleanliness. Some would go to a chemist's shop and ask for nails. Others again would make ridiculous proclamations in public. It was believed that by thus inviting scorn a man learned to view with equanimity the disdain and praise of others and so equip himself for a life of sincere devotion to the truth regardless of public opinion.[16] Navaradok, however, did not preach quietism in spiritual matters. Here, it was taught, all depends on human effort. The Navaradok students came to a Jewish hamlet and lodged in one of the Study Houses; when the resident Jews came to Synagogue they found chalked on its doors: 'Jews, Repent!' A Navaradok student would stand in the market place publicly confessing his sins, particularly that in his endeavours on behalf of others the ego had reared its

[13] *'Madregath Ha-Adam'*, Kedem Press Co., New York, 1947.
[14] Katz, *op. cit.*, p. 238 note 10.
[15] Glenn, *op. cit.*, p. 87.
[16] For further details see Katz, *op. cit.*, pp. 257f.

head and he therefore was the lowest of the low.[17] In this way trust in God served the interests of a strong revivalist movement.

To the question, widely discussed by the mediaeval thinkers, of why human effort is required if God provides, Rabbi Yoizel replies that it all depends on man's own attitude. Rabbi Yoizel advocated the most extreme attitude of trust. He believed that if a man really has this strong sense of God's power to help and relies upon it without qualification then God provides without any human effort being required. Human effort only becomes obligatory when trust in God is weak.[18] Rabbi Yoizel knows, of course, that the Talmudic authorities quoted earlier state that many have followed Rabbi Simeon ben Yohai without success but he replies that, indeed, his way is not for the *many*. The few chosen individuals, however, prepared to follow this way can proceed in complete safety. When a man wishes to swim, observes Rabbi Yoizel,[19] he must plunge into the water and surrender to the experience. If his hand or foot is always groping for the security of a hold he will never learn to swim. The pious man who trusts in God with reservations, always leaving scope for human effort, will never know what it really means to trust in God. Rabbi Yoizel, a great master of the parable, had a favourite illustration in reply to the objection that human experience teaches that success is only possible through human effort.[20] A blacksmith said that it was a good thing he had never taken up the trade of goldsmith for he would have starved, since during his whole career no one had ever brought him gold to fashion. The man who lives without complete trust in God does, indeed, require human effort but a higher life is possible for those courageous enough to cast their burdens on the Lord.

To come to the contemporary attitude, it is clear that trust in God cannot be equated with a facile optimism that because God is in His heaven all will be well in the physical or material sense. Such an attitude, psychologically and theo-

---

[17] Glenn, *op. cit.*, pp. 89-90.
[18] See Katz, *op. cit.*, Chapter 15, pp. 241-251.
[19] '*Madregath Ha-Adam*', p. 196.
[20] Katz, *op. cit.*, p. 243.

logically unsound, despite Rabbi Yoizel, is totally unsupported by experience. Trust in God cannot mean this. It is obvious that however we understand the difficult question of divine providence, there is no guarantee that justice and righteousness will immediately win out. Moreover, even if a man believed his cause to be just he would have no right to expect God to come to his immediate vindication. There may be a large number of complex factors, which the believer is bound to take into account (the needs of others, the divine economy in which nature is not suspended by the prayers of the just, etc.) preventing an immediate remedy in an unjust situation. Further, the man so sure that his cause is right as to demand immediate vindication is lacking in the humility that should be the hallmark of the religious man, if the accounts of Theistic faith are to be trusted. Confidence that one's needs will be satisfied partakes more of trust in oneself than trust in God. To trust in God without the slightest attempt at keeping the powder dry is to trust in Him without using powder at all. It is to step in the path of the oncoming train. It is to rely on a miracle, which, as the Rabbis remind us, is an act of impiety.[21]

Trust in God is best seen not as a course of action to be pursued but as an attitude of mind to be cultivated. The man who trusts in his friend is aware that sometimes there may be reasons for the friend being of little help, but this does not affect the trustful relationship between them. Each is fortified by the knowledge that there he has an ally. Indeed, the very notion of trust implies a degree of uncertainty. It is an affirmation in spite of circumstances. By analogy it is possible to see one's attitude towards trust in God in this way. It is an attitude based on the Theistic premise that God loves man and is not at war with His creation. It does not ignore the Rabbinic idea that man is co-partner with God,[22] that human effort is itself God-ordained. The man of faith believes that in any ultimate sense his pursuit of the good and rejection of evil will conquer, will bring him nearer to God, will make its contribution to the fulfilment of God's purposes. The chief concern of the man of faith is to have that relationship with

[21] See *Pes.* 64b.
[22] *Sabb.* 119b. See *supra*, p. 142.

God which makes him live as God's ally, as it were, in the struggle against evil.

Tillich[23] has defined 'faith' as ultimate concern' and rightly sees this as the Biblical meaning of trust in God. He remarks[24] that idolatrous faiths (the worship of the nation or of success) fail precisely because they try to make ultimate that which is finite and they therefore *ultimately* disillusion the believer. Of Biblical faith Tillich says: [25] 'An example—and more than an example—is the faith manifest in the religion of the Old Testament. It also has the character of ultimate concern in demand, threat and promise. The content of the concern is not the nation—although Jewish nationalism has sometimes tried to distort it into that—but the content is the God of justice, who, because he represents justice for everybody, and every nation, is called the universal God, the God of the universe. He is the ultimate concern of every pious Jew, and therefore in his name the great commandment is given: "You shall love the Lord your God with all your heart, and with all your soul, and with all your might" (Deut. 6:5). This is what ultimate concern means and from these words the term "ultimate concern" is derived. They state unambiguously the character of genuine faith, the demand of total surrender to the object of ultimate concern.'

The tension between reliance on God and the need for human effort is never entirely abolished. If it were the dynamics of faith would be at an end. And the true man of faith would not wish it to be otherwise. For trust in God, as any other vital relationship, is a matter of constant challenge and response, approach and withdrawal, relinquishing and possessing. Something of this is without doubt implied in the most famous statement in the Bible on trust in God:

'Blessed is the man that trusteth in the Lord,
And whose trust the Lord is.
For he shall be as a tree planted by the waters,
And that spreadeth out its roots by the river,
And shall not be anxious in the year of drought,
Neither shall cease from yielding fruit'

(Jer. 17:7-8).

[23] Paul Tillich: 'Dynamics of Faith'.
[24] *Op. cit.*, pp. 11-12.　　　　[25] *Op. cit.*, pp. 2-3.

Or, in the words of another prophet:

> *'For though the fig-tree shall not blossom,*
> *Neither shall fruit be in the vines;*
> *The labour of the olive shall fail,*
> *And the fields shall yield no food;*
> *The flock shall be cut off from the fold,*
> *And there shall be no herd in the stalls;*
> *Yet I will rejoice in the Lord,*
> *I will exult in the God of my salvation'*

(Hab. 3: 17-18).

Chapter 11

Faith in Action

THIS chapter has been deliberately titled ambiguously in order to call attention to the two typically Jewish attitudes in matters of faith. The first of these wishes to see faith *realised*, given concrete expression, brought down from heaven to earth. It wishes faith to be acted upon, it is faith in *action*. The second attitude, stemming from the first, has confidence in the effects for faith of the practical life enjoined by Judaism. Belief is nourished through the deed regularly sustained and constantly practised. Judaism believes in the power of the deed in promoting a religious attitude towards life. Judaism places its trust in the deed, it has *faith* in action.

It is true that over-much emphasis on the deed can lead only too easily to mere mechanical observance, to soulless routine, to indifference to the deeper meaning and significance of religious belief. Taken to extremes, it comes to see belief as irrelevant. The good Jew then becomes one who has succeeded in achieving the highest score of good deeds. But here two things require to be said. First, the most representative Jewish teachers have always been on guard against the degeneration of true religious feeling into mere behaviourism. Not for nothing are there so many injunctions in the literature of Jewish piety on the need for inwardness when carrying out the precepts. Proper intention, the pure motive, the correct understanding of why things are to be done, the direction of the heart to God—these are, for the Jewish teachers, of the essence of true religion even when it is taught that in any event the deed should not be rejected if the motive is not yet as pure as it might be. Secondly, when Judaism stresses the value of action this is not to be taken in any narrow physical

sense. The Jewish emphasis on action is in reality an emphasis on the expression of ideals but the nature of this expression is to be intellectual and emotional as well as physical.
It is not merely the hand that is to become engaged. There is
the demand that the mind be engaged in study and the heart
in prayer. An important part of the 'action' Judaism requires
is the intensive study of the *Torah*, of the classical sources of
Judaism, in which God's will is revealed. Certainly the
emphasis on action is not for a feverish busy-ness which leaves
no room for contemplation but is rather a recognition
that faith is not of much use unless it is put to work, operating in the whole of man's life. The righteous *lives* by his
faith.

The literature on inwardness is immense; but for our purpose Maimonides' statement, one of the best, will suffice for
illustration. Towards the end of the 'Guide for the Perplexed'
he writes: [1] 'Know that all the practices of the worship, such
as reading the *Torah*, prayer, and the performance of the
other *commandments*, have only the end of training you to
occupy yourself with His commandments, may He be exalted,
rather than with matters pertaining to this world; you should
act as if you were occupied with Him, may He be exalted, and
not with that which is other than He. If, however, you pray
merely by moving your lips while facing a wall, and at the
same time think about your buying and selling; or if you
read the Torah with your tongue while your heart is set upon
the building of your habitation and does not consider what
you read; and similarly in all cases in which you perform a
commandment merely with your limbs—as if you were dig-
ging a hole in the ground or hewing wood in the forest—
without reflecting either upon the meaning of that action or
upon Him from whom the commandment proceeds or upon
the end of the action, you should not think that you have
achieved the end. Rather you will then be similar to those of
whom it is said: *Thou art near in their mouth, and far from
their reins* (Jer: 12:2).'

There is no stronger refutation of the criticism that Jewish
legalism suffocates faith than the fact that the three great

[1] III, 51, translation of Shlomo Pines, p. 622, The University of Chicago Press, 1963.

Codes of Jewish law, those of Maimonides, Jacob b. Asher (d. *c.* 1340) and Joseph Karo (1488-1575)—begin with an appeal to faith:

1. Maimonides: *'It is the Foundation of foundations and the Pillar of sciences to know that there is a Primal Being who is the Cause of all that exists and all beings in heaven and earth and that which is between them owe their existence solely to His true being.'*

2. Jacob b. Asher in the Tur: *'Judah, the son of Tema, said Be strong as a leopard, light as an eagle, fleet as a hart, and strong as a lion, to do the will of thy Father who is in heaven. He specifies four things regarding the service of God, blessed be He, beginning with 'strong as a leopard' since this is a great principle in the service of God, blessed be He. For it happens at times that a man wishes to perform a good deed but refrains because people may ridicule him. He, therefore, warns you to be stubborn in the face of scoffers and not to refrain from doing the good deed.'*

3. Joseph Karo in the *Shulhan Arukh*: *'One should be as strong as a lion to rise up in the morning to worship his Creator, that he should be up before dawn.'*

A remarkable passage in the Talmud (*Makk.* 23b-24a) deals with the formulation of principles of Judaism but serves incidentally to shed a good deal of light on typical Rabbinic thinking in this matter of the relationship between belief and action. Here it is stated that the third-century Palestinian teacher, R. Simlai, preached that six hundred and thirteen precepts were given to Moses, three hundred and sixty-five negative precepts, corresponding to the number of days in the solar year, and two hundred and forty-eight positive precepts, corresponding to the number of members of man's body. (The meaning is evidently that the *Torah* embraces the whole of a man's life and covers all his days.) David came and reduced them to eleven principles in Psalm 15. (The meaning here appears to be that the detailed rules and regulations are the concrete expression of certain basic principles of virtue.) *'He that walketh uprightly, and worketh righteousness, and speaketh truth in his heart; that hath no slander upon his tongue, nor doeth evil to his fellow nor taketh up a reproach against his neighbour, in whose eyes a vile person is despised, but he honoureth them that fear the Lord, He sweareth to his own hurt and changeth not, He putteth not out his money on interest, nor taketh a bribe against the innocent. He that doeth these things shall never be moved.'* Then Isaiah came and reduced them to six principles (Is. 33: 15-16): *'He that walketh righteously, and speaketh uprightly, He that despiseth the gain of oppressions, that shaketh his hand from holding of bribes, that stoppeth his ear from hearing of blood, and shutteth his eyes from looking upon evil; he shall dwell on high.'* Then Micah came and reduced them to three (Micah 6: 8): *'It hath been told thee, O man, what is good, and what the Lord doth require of thee: only to do justly, and to love mercy and to walk humbly with thy God.'* Isaiah (Is. 56: 1) later reduced them to two: *'Keep ye justice and do righteousness.'* Finally, Habakkuk (2: 4) based them on one: *'But the righteous shall live by his faith.'*

The editors of this passage were thinking primarily of the principle of reduction according to which the detailed rules are 'reduced' to basic ideas. But it is possible to read this backwards, the great principle of faith can be extended to two, to six, to eleven ideas and eventually to find expression in the detailed observances of the Jewish faith. But the foundation of the whole is faith.

To try to consider in detail how the faith of Judaism applies in practice demands a comprehensive study of Jewish life and observances, beyond the scope of a book concerned chiefly with the question of faith. What can be done is to examine a typically Jewish institution such as the Sabbath as representing the life of faith in the human world. The same approach can then be seen to be relevant to other Jewish institutions but, for the details of these, works of a more immediate practical nature should be consulted.

Although it is hoped that this book has been written to express the Jewish ideal of faith as represented among the majority of believers, the particular position of the author cannot, and should not be omitted. Nowhere is this more to be noted than in a discussion of Jewish practice and observance as reflecting the will of God. It must be said, then, quite clearly and unambiguously that in the following I do not share the fundamentalistic view according to which the will of God is conceived of as communicated in direct fashion leaving no room for the human element.

Among Jews who keep the Sabbath three different attitudes are to be observed. These may be called: (1) the fundamentalistic, (2) the naturalistic, (3) the theological. The first approach is completely God-orientated but, owing to its conception of revelation, feels compelled to take the Biblical passages dealing with the Sabbath and creation as factually accurate, making Sabbath observance dependent on a view of the evolution of the physical universe which most moderns find incredible. The second approach, rejecting the first in the name of intellectual integrity, throws out the baby with the bath water. Rejecting all supernaturalism it prefers to see the values of Sabbath observance purely in human terms. Our purpose here is to examine and offer criticisms of both these approaches and to advocate the third approach in which the Sabbath is seen as a day of divine worship with an interpretation of its history that does not conflict with the present state of human knowledge. This third approach sees the Sabbath as a particularly significant illustration of faith in action.

For the fundamentalist the Sabbath is to be observed because God has so ordained it in the Bible, communicating the command directly to Moses. The fundamentalist refuses even to consider the opinion that any of the Pentateuchal passages dealing with the Sabbath are post-Mosaic or that there are contradictions between the passages or even that they contain different versions of the same command. Moreover, he refuses to admit error of any kind in the Biblical record and therefore feels obliged to accept as factually correct those passages which speak of God creating the world in six days and resting on the Sabbath.[2] He may be prepared to interpret the six days of creation as six very lengthy periods of time but he insists that the Bible contains a factual account of the age of

[2] Gen. 1:1-2:3; Ex. 20:8-11; Ex. 31:12-17. It has often been noted that in the version of the Decalogue in Deuteronomy the reason for Sabbath observance is connected with the Exodus, not with creation (Deut. 5:12-15). But in the Qumran fragment (4 Q Deut. n) of the Deuteronomic Decalogue the creation reason is added, though it is impossible to know whether this is an authentic, different version or a mere combination of the two ideas for liturgical purposes.

the earth and the emergence of creatures upon it and it is upon this that his whole concept of Sabbath observance is based. The seventh day of the week is distinguished from other days as the day on which God rested and this distinction corresponds to the reality of God's actual creative process when He brought the world into being. This is not to say that the fundamentalist necessarily adopts an anthropomorphic picture. He will probably affirm that God does not 'work' and requires no 'rest', so that 'rest' in this context implies no more than the cessation of the divine creative activity.

The objections to fundamentalism are weighty. Biblical scholarship presents an astonishing wide range of views on the question of the authorship, transmission and compilation of the Pentateuch. While some of the problems connected with these may never be solved, nevertheless there is a consensus of opinion among scholars based on the soundest evidence and extremely unlikely to be upset, that the Pentateuch is a composite work with its parts deriving from diverse geographical and cultural centres and that some of these parts, at least, are post-Mosaic. This is to state a very conservative position. In the opinion of many scholars the first chapter of Genesis is not only post-Mosaic but post-Exilic. Nor can the first chapter of Genesis accord with our present-day knowledge even if the six days of creation are taken to represent vast periods of time. No adequate reply has yet been made to the overwhelming objections to fundamentalism presented fairly and with reverence for the Biblical record in, for instance, S. R. Driver's Commentary to Genesis[3] first published over sixty years ago. Most informed students of the Bible, including believers who see it as in some sense the word of God, today accept as axiomatic that the Biblical writers shared the views of their contemporaries in the Near East on cosmogony. They could only have anticipated the science of our day by a miracle, which all the evidence goes to show was not performed on their behalf. On this view the sublime account in Genesis, for all its errors regarding the precise nature of the evolution of the world and the creatures which inhabit it, still conveys the eternal truth that God is the Creator of

[3] 'The Book of Genesis' in the Westminster Commentaries, Methuen, 12th ed., 1926, pp. xxxi-xlii and pp. 19-33.

the universe. To observe the Sabbath is to acknowledge this by affirming it week by week. It is faith in action.

It would be anachronistic to pretend that the Talmudic Rabbis had our views on this question. Their views are what we would today call fundamentalistic but it cannot be too strongly stressed that the state of knowledge regarding the material universe in Rabbinic times was such that they had no reason whatsoever for rejecting what is today known as fundamentalism. Nevertheless, there are some indications that, even in Rabbinic times, the purpose of Sabbath observance was held to be that of hailing God as Creator, not as a human re-enactment of the divine cessation from work on the seventh day.[4] In Rabbinic literature generally Sabbath observance does not belong in the category of acts enjoined in *Imitatio Dei*. 'Just as He is called merciful be thou merciful. Just as He is called compassionate be thou compassionate.' This we find in the Rabbinic literature. But it is nowhere stated in that literature: 'Just as He rested on the seventh day rest thou on the seventh day.' The believer who rejects fundamentalism only departs from tradition—with good reason—in this particular rejection. In his determination to keep the Sabbath, whatever its origins, as a day on which God is acknowledged as Creator he is completely within the tradition.

The naturalistic approach to Judaism argues, without justification, that the acceptance of the scientific method and the increase of knowledge resulting from its application compels us to abandon not alone fundamentalism but every kind of supernaturalism. On this view, religious institutions such as the Sabbath may still have great value but this value is to be seen in purely human terms, the enrichment and ennoblement of human life, without reference to any supernatural

---

[4] See '*Mekhilta De-Rabbi Simeon ben Yohai*' to Ex. 20:11, ed. Hoffmann, Frankfurt, 1905, p. 109 that God before whom there is neither labour nor weariness 'wrote about Himself' that He rested and Maimonides' observations in 'Guide', II, 31. In an interesting Responsum, Rabbi J. J. Weinberg concludes on the basis on these and similar passages ('*Seride Esh*', Vol. II, Mosad Ha Rav Kook, Jer., 1962, No. 20, pp. 43-4): 'The result of our investigation is that it does not mean that we are obliged to rest (on the Sabbath) because God rested on that day but that God blessed and sanctified this day so as to provide us with the opportunity of testifying to His creation of the world during the six days of creation'.

order or entity. This is the Jewish version of what is today
called in certain Protestant circles 'religionless Christianity'.
Some Christian critics of this position have described it (perhaps unfairly) as the view that there is no God but Jesus is
His Son! The similar critique for Jews would be: There is
no God but the *Torah* is the way He has ordained! Those
Jewish religious naturalists who observe the Sabbath have no
difficulty in pointing to the human values enhanced by Sabbath observance. Man needs a day of rest from his labours to
enable him to recuperate and to find time for the pursuit of
higher aims. He needs, too, a link with his past and a sense of
belonging provided by an institution so rich in historical association as the Jewish Sabbath. Above all the Sabbath ensures
Jewish survival. As Ahad Ha-Am's famous aphorism has it:
'More than the Jews kept the Sabbath the Sabbath kept the
Jews.'[5]

The Jew who accepts traditional Theism is not necessarily
obliged to try to expose the inadequacy of naturalism for the
Jewish naturalist. He may well argue that if he did not
believe in God he would still keep the Sabbath on the grounds
the naturalist indicates. He may well feel, as the naturalist
does, that if this was so the term 'God' should continue to
be used to convey the idea of those forces in the universe which
make for righteousness and for human betterment. The super-
naturalist would not wish to deny that the purely human
values of which the naturalist speaks can be realised as by-
products of Sabbath observance. But for the believer they are
by-products and not the aim of the Sabbath. For the believer
God *is*. The Sabbath is the particular day on which He is
affirmed as Creator. Because this is so it can be said without
distortion or subterfuge (even if fundamentalism is rejected)
that God commands the Jew to keep the Sabbath, the command being conveyed through the historical experiences of
the people of Israel.

There is a fallacy, however, in the naturalistic assumption
that religious values, hitherto associated with religious institutions, can still be furthered by those institutions even when
the supernaturalistic basis for them is rejected. It is, of
course, possible for the naturalist to try to keep people in

[5] *'Al Parashath Derakhim'*, Vol. 3, p. 79.

ignorance of the falsity, from his point of view, of the super-naturalistic basis and he may justify this in order to preserve the resulting values (but would he really wish to keep people in ignorance?) but once let them into the secret and the institution loses its sanction. In any event no Theist should wish to defend religious institutions because they cater to secular values, for in so doing he tacitly admits that there is nothing left to defend. There is no point in trying to make faith attractive by surrendering that which makes it faith.

I have called the third approach to the Sabbath the theological because, while rejecting an untenable fundamentalism, it considers the Sabbath to be man's path to God. *'It is a sign between Me and the children of Israel forever'* (Ex. 31:17). The Hebrew word for 'sign' *(oth)* is the one used in the Bible for 'miracle', as in the expression 'signs and wonders'. The word denotes an indication or pointer. The Sabbath is a pointer to the reality that there is a God. We proceed to explore further the significance of this theological approach to the Sabbath.

Many among the wise and good have taught that man has a greater chance of knowing the spiritual side of existence in tranquillity rather than in effort, in repose rather than in activity, in peace and quietude rather than in restlessness and noise. Judaism has a strong bias in favour of the active and social life. It teaches that God is to be encountered in the world, not in escape from it. But Judaism, of course, knows of the great virtues of serenity. The name for the Sabbath in the traditional Jewish literature is *yom menuhah*, 'a day of rest'. The Hebrew word is that used by the Psalmist when he speaks of God leading him by 'the still waters' *(mey menuhoth,* Ps. 23:2). One's reflection can be seen in disturbed waters but there it is confused and indistinct. It is in the still waters that a clear undimmed reflection is seen. The tempo of modern life is such that man can find neither his God nor himself, except with the utmost effort, amid its distractions. Only through the day of rest, involving a complete cessation from the manipulation of the material world, can man come to know life in its spiritual depths. Judaism does not encourage us to see man's week-day pursuits as a mad and futile scramble but there is spiritual wholesomeness in a periodic acknowledgment of the ridiculous element in man's ceaseless pre-occupation with means rather than ends. If the hound of heaven pursues the Jew unsuccessfully during the other six days of the week, on the Sabbath it has a greater chance of overtaking him.

The Sabbath ideal of rest is not purely passive, a mere stoppage of labour. A special atmosphere of difference from other days is cultivated by refraining from week-day pursuits as well as by the wearing of special Sabbath clothes, the lighted candles on the best white tablecloth, the cup of wine, over which God is hailed as Creator, and the two freshly-baked loaves. Traditionally even speech is controlled so that there are no references to mundane matters.[6] There were Jews so conscious of the day's sanctity that they conversed only in Hebrew, the 'sacred tongue'.

The Rabbis compare the Sabbath to Paradise in miniature.[7] On the Sabbath we obtain a foretaste of the bliss reserved for the righteous in heaven. There is a certain ambivalence in the Jewish sources towards the state expressed by this Hebrew word for 'repose', *menuhah*, to which we have called attention. On the one hand it represents, as we have seen, the ideal of Sabbath rest and is used in the prayers for the dead to suggest bliss in the Hereafter 'under the wings of the Divine Presence'.[8] On the other hand a Talmudic passage states that scholars have rest (*menuhah*) neither in this world nor in the next because they 'go from strength to strength'.[9] For there is repose and repose. No human soul can find serenity in the rest of stagnation. A human being is not a vegetable. His peace of mind is gained through struggle and effort. The

---

[6] See Isaiah 58:13: 'If thou turn away thy foot because of the Sabbath, From pursuing thy business on My holy day; And call the Sabbath a delight, And the holy of the Lord honourable; And shalt honour it, not doing thy wonted ways, Nor pursuing thy business, nor speaking thereof.' The Rabbinic comment on this verse is: '*And shalt honour it*, that thy Sabbath garments should not be like thy week-day garments. *Not doing thy wonted ways*, that thy walking on the Sabbath shall not be like thy walking on week-days. *Nor speaking thereof*, that thy conversation on the Sabbath shall not be like thy conversation on week-days' (*Sabb.* 113a-b).

[7] 'The Sabbath is a sixtieth of the World to Come' (*Ber.* 57b). Cf. *A.Z.* 3a.

[8] See Prayer Book '*Otzar Ha-Tephilloth*', Vilna, 1914, p. 714 and commentaries.

[9] *Ber.* 64a.

genius of the traditional Jewish Sabbath solves the problem
by calling a halt for the duration of the day to man's physical
efforts, particularly those of a creative kind, while encourag-
ing him to engage in mental and spiritual effort. The Sabbath
thus becomes a day of prayer and reflection and a day of *Torah*
study. The Jewish mystics are eloquent on the duty of discovering new ideas in the *Torah* (*hiddushe Torah*) on the
Sabbath.[10]

A fine modern *Midrash* on the first chapter of Genesis
is the account by Edwyn Bevan in his notable book: 'Symbolism and Belief'.[11] Bevan remarks that the ancient Hebrew
writer makes God create the world in six days and rest on
the seventh because he wishes to express the idea that God
is in the Time process but also beyond it. Man is obliged to
rest on the Sabbath and treat the Sabbath as a holy day because
he, too, is made for more than the six days. The implication
is that the potential being of man extends beyond the world,
and that he must therefore seek to meet God in God's own
quiet beyond the world. The old Rabbinic notion of the
'extra soul' with which the Jew is endowed on the Sabbath[12]
has been interpreted in more prosaic fashion but it suits to
express what it is that the Sabbath is supposed to do for man
in terms of heightened spiritual experience. Man needs the
'extra soul' provided by the Sabbath to prevent him losing his
ordinary soul during the remainder of the week.

One of the insights of Rabbinic Judaism is that man need
not be a 'holy man' or 'saint' in order to enjoy religious experience. Max Kadushin[13] has coined the helpful term 'normal mysticism' to denote this awareness of the divine by
average men with no claims to any extraordinary sanctity.
A latter-day Jewish mystic has said: [14] 'There is a form of faith
which belongs to experience in which man tastes the sweet-
ness of God's remembrance, as Scripture says: "Taste ye and
see that the Lord is good." God sometimes gives this into the
hearts of those that seek Him but even ordinary folk experi-

---

[10] *Zohar*, III, 173a.
[11] Fontana Library, Collins, London, 1962, pp. 108-110.
[12] *Betz*. 16a.
[13] 'The Rabbinic Mind', Chapter VI, pp. 194-272.
[14] Rabbi Aaron Roth: *'Shomer Emunim'*, Vol. I, p. 169a.

ence on the Sabbath and the Festivals some special joy and divine vitality.'

This then is the traditional Jewish Sabbath as seen by those who favour our third approach. It is a day of rest, of heightened spirituality, of religious experience. We cannot better this description in the hymn for Sabbath afternoon:

'*A rest granted in generous love,*
A rest true and faithful,
A rest of peace and tranquility, of quietude and safety,
A perfect rest wherein Thou delightest.
Let Thy children perceive and know that this their rest is
*   from Thee,*
And by their rest may they hallow Thy name.'

And this approach to the Sabbath can be extended throughout the whole of practical Judaism as faith in action. The Jewish man of faith remembers his God in prayers, when he conforms to the dietary laws, in the marriage relationship with its lofty standards, in business and profession by the strict code of honesty and integrity, by the inculcation through teachings of compassion and benevolence, by the exercise of his mind in the study of the *Torah*. A fundamentalistic approach sees all these as static; naturalism is too man-orientated, prayer is a superior form of auto-suggestion. The non-fundamentalist can lead a complete life of faith in the God who guides him as He has guided the people of Israel in the past. In this approach the observances of Judaism are seen neither as mere colourful ceremonies nor as direct commands in the fundamentalist sense but as tried ways to God.

Chapter 12

Faith and its Tensions

I N the previous chapters of this book we have been concerned chiefly with the basic issue of faith in God. This is not a specifically Jewish question but universal. Although our discussion has proceeded from the Jewish point of view its object is the God in whom all Theists believe. Faith does not, however, remain very significant if pursued in the abstract. It generally receives its concrete expression within particular human situations and in the context of a definite religious tradition, in our case the Jewish. For most Theists, therefore, in addition to the basic belief in God there are a number of secondary beliefs more or less peculiar to the religious tradition to which they belong.

It has been suggested earlier that there are frequent tensions around faith's basic issue. It is certainly true that there are severe tensions around the secondary issues. Judaism is a religion with God at its centre. But it is, too, the religious expression of the Jewish people, an expression that is varied and approached in diverse ways. It is consequently proper in a book on Jewish faith to examine the various facets of Jewish belief. This chapter seeks to answer the question: what kind of religion is Judaism? It is an attempt at demonstrating Judaism's rich variety. Such variety produces tensions which can be, and have been in the past, creative. Hence the title of this chapter: 'Faith and its Tensions'. An alternative title could be: 'The Comprehensiveness of Judaism'.

Is Judaism optimistic or pessimistic, rational or non-rational, particularistic or universalistic, for the group or for the individual, this-worldly or other-worldly? It is sometimes assumed that with regard to such questions we must choose between two contraries, coming down firmly on the side of one. But another, far more effective, way of looking at the question, and one far more in accord with Jewish historical experience, is to see Judaism as a rich and comprehensive faith embracing various moods and differing attitudes. There is no necessity for us to choose between an either/or when we can have a both/and.

On the basic issue we cannot, of course, have it both ways. Here we are compelled to make a choice, though faith's tensions are such that this choice is not necessarily for all time but must be made again and again. The idea of a choice in this sense is very prevalent in Jewish teaching. *'I call heaven and earth to witness against you this day, that I have set before thee life and death, the blessing and the curse; therefore choose life, that thou mayest live, thou and thy seed'* (Deut. 30: 19). Elijah's admonition brooks no escape: *'And Elijah came near unto all the people, and said: "How long halt ye between two opinions? If the Lord be God, follow Him; but if Baal, follow him"'* (I Kings 18: 21). The whole question of whether one can choose within Judaism only arises if one has first chosen Judaism.

Elijah's challenge implies that an outright acceptance of Baal and rejection of God is better than a vague intention of having both. In honest and complete rejection of God a decision has at least been made. The contrast between the two is highlighted. Black and white are seen for what they are and no longer reduced to a colourless grey. Elijah's prime concern is with a choosing people because such a people, he is convinced, will not permanently prefer Baal. As it is, the addiction to Baal while professing God has the result that faith in God becomes Baal-infected. Baal-worship in itself is stupid, false and demoralising and becomes even more so when joined in unholy wedlock with worship of the God for whom Baal-worship and all it stands for is an abomination.

Within Judaism, however, there are many ways and we are not obliged to choose only one. In the Bible itself, for instance, side by side with the fiery zeal of an Elijah there is the more serene approach of an Isaiah. Over two thousand teachers are named in the vast Talmudic literature, each differing, each with his own particular approach to life and faith within the broad framework of Judaism. Modern Jews are the heirs to it all and can draw on all these teachings. Such an attitude is uncongenial to some minds, particularly the severely logical and uncompromising. Truth loses much of its power, they argue, when it comes fragmented. Maimonides in his most famous work, the gigantic compendium of Jewish law and faith, strove mightily to present a digest of all the Jewish teachings up to his day, extracting the essence of the great spiritual leaders of the past, rejecting, on the basis of well-founded rules, opinions which should not be followed and presenting it all in systematic fashion. In Maimonides' great Code the names of the Rabbis, the authors of the doctrines he records, are omitted. During his lifetime Maimonides was criticised for this valiant though, fortunately for the Jewish dynamic, unsuccessful attempt. After his death the work was given the title: 'The Strong Hand'. Indeed, there is power in the notion of Judaism as one great uncomplicated whole. But it is simply untrue to the history of the Jewish faith. Those individual Rabbis refuse to be effaced. Their voice still speaks to remind us that there is room in Judaism for differing opinions and that unless this is acknowledged the strong hand is in the greatest danger of becoming a mailed fist. The *Midrash* tells us that just as many sparks fly from the anvil when it is struck by a mighty hammer so Scripture is capable of many different interpretations (*Sanh.* 34a).

The reasons for Judaism being rich in its variety are not far to seek. For one thing the traditional name for the *'Torah'* is *'The Torah of Life'* and life is complex. There are times when one's mood is optimistic, others when it is pessimistic. One man is an extrovert, another an introvert and some men are both at different times. There are occasions in life which call for strength and unyielding principle, there are others which demand a pliant, accommodating attitude. Furthermore, Judaism is inconceivable without the Jewish people and Jews, as other men, are influenced by their surroundings. Judaism teaches that man should always try to arise above both heredity and environment as did Abraham, the progenitor of the Jewish people, since man is free and a child of God. But no man can escape heredity and environment entirely. We are what we are partly because of our birth and cultural background. Those who teach Judaism and those who

live by it are bound to find the teaching and the living determined to some extent by what they are. One of the most significant and influential works of Jewish devotion is Bahya Ibn
Pakudah's 'Duties of the Heart', to which reference has earlier
been made. Bahya, from the little we know, appears to have
been a lonely, sombre man. And he was greatly influenced in
this thinking by the Islamic Sufis who taught the virtues of
ascetism and self-denial. As a result, Bahya's work is in some
respects far more life-denying than life-affirming, so much so
that it has been described as 'un-Jewish'. But Bahya and his
book testify to Judaism's capacity for varied expression.

A Hasidic tale illustrates this dynamic quality of the Jewish
faith. The hero is the Hasidic saint and humourist Rabbi
Naphtali of Ropchitz (d. 1827) who said that before his birth
an angel showed him two lists containing rules of behaviour,
all culled from classical Jewish sources. In one list he read:
'If man wishes to make the *Torah* his own he must be as cruel
to his family as the raven is to its young'. In the other list he
read that a man must care for his family beyond his strength
and love and respect his wife more than himself. One list said
that a scholar should burn with the fire of righteous indigna-
tion; in the other, a man merits the Hereafter by being meek
and humble. 'Be cunning in God's service' said one list; 'Be
simple-hearted before God' (Deut. 18:13) said the other. In
one list he read that a man should be satisfied with a bare
minimum as the Talmudic Rabbi Hanina ben Dosa whose
staple diet was a portion of beans. In the other list he read
that a man will be obliged to render an account to heaven
for every legitimate pleasure he denied himself. The Rabbi
said that his soul was profoundly disturbed at the thought
that when he came down to earth he would be obliged to live
according to the rules in both lists. How would he be able
to reconcile them? But as he was pondering on the question
he suddenly heard the words: 'A male child is born' and there
he was in the world. Ever since, he concluded, he has been
preoccupied with this very question.

There is no simple, uncomplicated rule of conduct to fit
every human situation. For all the detailed guidance in the
Jewish sources there is still much room for individual
initiative. There are always new situations in which the true

way is to be sought and to be discovered only after a prolonged quest. Only the narrow-minded and the timid, lacking confidence in themselves and in the capacity of Judaism to inspire as well as to direct, would wish it to be otherwise.

Judaism, optimistic or pessimistic?

We have touched on this question in the chapter on the problem of evil. Here we try to examine it in more detail.

A Buddhist story tells of a mother who had lost her only son and came to the Buddha to find comfort. He advised her to obtain some mustard seed from a house which had never known death. After a while the woman came to the Buddha to tell him that she was unable to find such a house and the great teacher indicated that this was the key to her anguish. Pain and suffering are the lot of mankind. None can escape them and resignation is the only satisfactory philosophy of life. Man can never find rest until he has succeeded in rising above all desires to enter the bliss of Nirvana.

The Buddhist approach is typical of Far-Eastern religious philosophy. A pessimistic attitude towards life has been very wide-spread in the Far East and not a few Western thinkers (Schopenhauer particularly) have been fascinated by the view that man must accept his lot from which he cannot escape and to which in wisdom he should submit. In our day, too, a number of thinkers continue to be attracted by what they consider to be the only realistic assessment of the human situation.

The opposite extreme of Far Eastern pessimism is Western optimism as found particularly in the Victorian age. At the end of the last century the belief in human progress was so strong that many were convinced of the impending millennium. And, it must be said, there were good reasons for this conviction. Science and technology were beginning to take rapid strides towards the improvement of the human lot. Disease was slowly but surely retreating before the advance of modern medicine and hygiene. Social conditions were being improved and there was a great increase in education which augured well for the future. It appeared quite reasonable to hold the view that man had at last found himself and was capable of creating a brave new world for himself and for posterity. It is tragic that this noble dream should have been shattered. Some contemporary religious thinkers are too prone to gloat over its discomfiture without appreciating its solid worth. Moreover, for all the new emphasis our age requires, it would be a pity if the liberal vision were to be banished completely in the name of realism or what passes for it.

It was natural for Jews to welcome this new optimistic spirit as offering them new hope for the future. All this accorded well with the Jewish religion which, it was held, is clearly optimistic as evidenced by the first chapter of Genesis in which God saw all that He had made and pronounced it very good. The Jewish doctrine of the Messiah, which looks forward to the Golden Age instead of projecting it into the past, was adduced as further evidence of the unyielding optimism of the Jewish faith.

A less superficial examination of the sources reveals that we are much nearer the truth if we refuse to make a neat distinction between a pessimistic and an optimistic faith. In the sources there is no facile hope that somehow good will automatically result from man's efforts. Indeed, in the Bible generally one finds a sombre assessment of man's capacity for self-improvement. On the other hand, a faith like Judaism, which believes that the universe is God-created, cannot surrender entirely to pessimism. In this, as in other matters, Judaism seems to encourage its followers to accept the tensions inevitable in the human situation although in matters of balance Judaism does tend to optimism. One or two examples should be given.

After the idyllic picture in the first chapter of Genesis a much more alarming view of man emerges. In Genesis Chapter 6, verses 5-8, we read: *'And the Lord saw that the wickedness of man was great in the earth, and that every imagination of the thoughts of his heart was only evil continually. And it repented the Lord that he had made man on the earth, and it grieved him at his heart. And the Lord said: "I will blot out man whom I have created from the face of the earth; both man and beast, and creeping thing, and fowl of the air; for it repenteth me that I have made them". But Noah found grace in the eyes of the Lord.'* With the exception of the last verse the passage is pure Buddhism in its philosophy. It is not by accident that it is quoted with full approval by the greatest exponent of Zen Buddhism, Professor Suzuki. But the last verse is there and is most typical of the Jewish spirit. No matter how much evil there is in the world, how depraved the human condition, there is always a Noah capable of seeing a vision of a better life and becoming the founder of a new race. Similarly, the Psalmist, for all his pessimism, feels compelled to conclude on a note of hope:

'The days of our years are three-score years and ten,
Or even by reason of strength four-score years;
Yet is their pride but travail and vanity;
For it is speedily gone, and we fly away.
Who knoweth the power of thine anger,
And thy wrath according to the fear that is due unto thee?
So teach us to number our days,
That we get us a heart of wisdom'

(Ps. 90: 10-12).

Relevant to our discussion is the frequently overlooked Talmudic passage (*Erub.* 13b) which tells of the two and a half year long debate between the rival schools of Hillel and Shammai at the beginning of the present era. One school held that it were better for man not to have been created than to have been created and the other that it is better that man has been created. Eventually, the passage concludes, the decision was reached that it were better for man not to have been created but now that he has been created he should scrutinise his deeds. It is this typical qualification which redeems the view from a surrender to utter pessimism. Life is grim enough most of the time. The most outstanding teachers of Judaism so long ago were prepared to admit that so far as human thought can take us the creation of man on earth is not really worthwhile from man's point of view. But as religious believers they were bound to conclude that since God had, in fact, placed man here on earth it must follow that man can, if he so desires and has the courage, come to grips with his circumstances with God's help. 'Now that he has been created he should scrutinise his deeds.'

The legends of a faith can at times be more revealing than

179

its more formal teachings. The Talmudic tale of Nahum of Gimzo (*Taan.* 21a) has become part of Jewish folklore. The folk etymology of the name Gimzo reads it as: '*gam zo*', meaning 'this also'. Nahum is the man who always said: *gam zo le-tobha*, 'this also is for good'. Whatever happened to him he would treat as ultimately for the good. The legend has it that the Jews had to send a tribute to the Roman Emperor and Nahum was chosen to deliver it safely. Nahum placed the gifts of gold and precious stones in a sack and journeyed to the Emperor's court. Thieves staying at his inn stole the gifts and replaced them with dust. On his arrival at the palace Nahum presented his sack to the Emperor only to find that it contained nothing but dust. Even when the ruler cried out that the Jews were mocking him Nahum continued to proclaim 'This also is for good'. Finally Elijah appeared in the nick of time disguised as a courtier and persuaded the Emperor that the dust belonged originally to Abraham who used it in his battles. At that time the Emperor was troubled by a province which refused to submit to him and he instructed his soldiers to use this secret weapon in their campaign, which they did with miraculous success. Nahum was suitably rewarded and on his return to the inn informed the innkeeper of his success. The innkeeper thereupon filled many sacks with the dust, which came from his own back yard, and presented them to the Emperor to discover, of course, that the dust no longer possessed its magical properties.

It might be thought absurd to quote this naïve little tale in a serious theological discussion but the spirit of a faith frequently resides in its fables. The legend appears to be affirming that in his long and chequered history the Jew has come to see that as a descendant of Abraham, the undaunted man of faith, he must not despair utterly even when all his hopes have been turned to dust. The dust remains dust and is not turned back to gold. The attitude of 'this also is for good' is far removed from a shallow looking on the bright side or a simple faith that because God's in His heaven all's right with the world. The Jew's bitter experience has taught him that all too often the world is very far from right. But on the deeper level of faith he turns to God confident that God's will for him is being fulfilled. The very dust becomes the means of his deliverance. But this magic only works for men like Nahum who really mean what they profess.

Judaism, particularistic or universalistic?

To ask whether Judaism is particularistic or universalistic is a very abstract way of putting a question of the utmost relevance to the future of Judaism. Does Judaism encourage its adherents to concentrate on the special needs and problems of the Jews or does it prefer them to look beyond the confines of their own group? The answer which emerges from an examination of the classical sources is that it does both. On the one hand there can be no Judaism without the Jewish people. But on the other hand the God the Jews worship is 'King of the Universe', the Father of all mankind.

Nowhere is the polarity of Jewish thought more clearly expressed than in the famous verse: *'Ye are My witnesses, saith the Lord, and My servant whom I have chosen'* (Is. 43: 10). A witness does not testify on his own behalf but on behalf of others. As the verse implies, the Jew, as the servant of God, is expected to be of service to all His children.

The real problem is where to place the emphasis. And here we find that at times the particularistic elements have been stressed, at others the universalistic. It cannot be denied that in the long history of Judaism there has been not infrequently an inbalance caused by over-emphasis on one of these.

Extreme emphasis on particularism results in the kind of absurdity in which every important event or movement, whether social, political or religious, is approached with 'Is it good for the Jews?' It is also unfortunately true that some of the finest Jewish minds in the past have lent themselves to an interpretation of the 'chosenness' of Israel in terms which suggest that there is a qualitative difference between the Jewish and Gentile soul. On this view Jews are seen as a race of spiritual supermen, not in Nietzschean terms that the weak should serve them but that they should serve the weak. Nonetheless there is something very offensive to the modern mind in the notion that God has somehow singled out a particular group to endow it with an unearned spiritual superiority over the rest of mankind. Judah Ha-Levi follows the conventional mediaeval division of all things into four groups. These are:

mineral, vegetable, animal and human. But, Ha-Levi goes on to say, Jews do not belong in the fourth group but form a special fifth group; they are different in kind from other humans in the same way in which humans are different from animals, animals from vegetables and vegetables from minerals. Ha-Levi's poems breathe a rich humanity and the deepest yearning for the restoration of his people to the land of its fathers. Yet his pseudo-biological interpretation of what it means to be a Jew strikes us as sheer nonsense. Quite apart from the theological difficulty in the belief in God arbitrarily favouring in this way the members of a particular group irrespective of their individual merits, there is no evidence at all that the Jew is automatically the spiritual superior of the Gentile. (This is not to say that the Jewish *way* is the same as the Gentile way. The question of how Judaism sees other faiths is a difficult one but in some senses at least an affirmation of Judaism must imply that the Jewish way is superior to that taught in other faiths). Judah Ha-Levi himself tries to avoid the difficulty by pointing out that the higher the species the greater its fall. A dead animal is more unpleasant to look at than a dead tree and, by the same token, he argues, a bad Jew is much worse than a bad Gentile.[1]

Curiously enough Judah Ha-Levi, in flat contradiction to the Rabbinic sources, puts forward the view that only a Jew can be a prophet. Modern scholars have noted that this idea is first found in the writings of the Church fathers who wished to restrict prophecy to Israel so as to be able to claim that when the Church became the new Israel prophecy in Israel came to an end. Thus the irony of the situation, that the great Jewish thinker in his effort to stress Jewish particularism is compelled to borrow ideas from sources hostile to Judaism.

A similar qualitative distinction is found in even more offensive terms in some of the Kabbalistic sources. These go to the extreme of limiting the 'divine spark' in man to Jews. Not content with this even the 'animal soul' (i.e. the vital principle, the animating force in human life) of Gentiles derives from 'evil' spiritual powers with the conclusion that

[1] *'Kuzari'*, I, 102-117; II, 43-66.

a Gentile is incapable of performing a disinterested action.[2] It is easy to apologise for this kind of sentiment on the grounds of reaction to fierce persecution and the need for Jews as a minority group in a hostile environment to retain confidence in itself by over-compensation. But the extremist doctrine remains offensive and must be rejected.

The late Professor Leon Roth was a valiant opponent of the narrow view and used his skill and erudition to emphasise the universalistic aspects of Judaism. Just before his death he wrote a penetrating essay pointing out how at times the narrow view effaced an original elevated one. There is, for example, a saying in the *Mishnah* (*Sanh.*, IV, 5) to the effect that whoever saves a single life it is accounted to him as if he had saved a whole world. It is clear from the context that the reference is to any human life, Jew or Gentile, but somewhere along the line a narrow-minded commentator qualified the saying to make it read: 'whoever saves a *Jewish* life'. Unfortunately this reading is retained in many texts so that a sublime universalistic teaching has been reduced to banality and worse.[3]

At the opposite extreme of particularism is the view of classical Reform Judaism. The early reformers in their justifiable zeal for universalism seem at times to have believed that the only way to achieve this was to reduce as far as possible all the particularistic elements in Judaism. References to the return to Zion were omitted from the Prayer Book, for instance, and the ninth day of Ab, the traditional day of mourning for the destruction of the Temple and Israel's exile, was abolished as a fast day. But time accomplishes what commonsense cannot. The terrible events in Jewish life in this century and the emergence of the State of Israel have brought the majority of Jews to a realisation that a vague universalism is no substitute for the concrete expression of Jewish faith and

---

[2] See '*Tanya*', *Liqqute Amarim*, Chapters 1-2, pp. 9-13 and my translation of Dobh Baer of Lübavitch's 'Tract on Ecstasy', pp. 16-17 and p. 51 note 51.

[3] See Leon Roth's essay: 'Moralization and Demoralization in Jewish Ethics' in '*Judaism*', Vol. XI, 4 (1962), pp. 291-302. Some of the essays in the memorial volume to Roth: 'Studies in Rationalism, Judaism and Universalism', ed. Raphael Loewe, Routledge and Kegan Paul, London, 1966, explore the significance of Jewish universalism.

values within the particularistic framework of the Jewish people with all the associations of the Jewish past.

An examination of Jewish history reveals that, on the whole, the narrower view tends to prevail in times of persecution and oppression while the wider view becomes influential in times of greater freedom. When Jews were compelled to wear the 'Jew badge' they wore it with pride and the victims retaliated in the only way possible for them by affirming in their souls their superiority to the oppressors. When Israel was allowed to emerge from a physical and spiritual ghetto the universalism of Judaism reasserted itself. One of the loftiest verses in the Bible is that in which the prophet, living in an age of comparative security and ease, saw the two great nations of Egypt and Assyria as co-partners with Israel in the fulfilment of God's purpose: *'In that day shall Israel be the third with Egypt and with Assyria, a blessing in the midst of the earth; for that the Lord of hosts hath blessed him, saying: "Blessed be Egypt My people, and Assyria the work of My hands, and Israel Mine inheritance"'* (Is. 19:24-25).

As in other spheres of Jewish life there are strong tensions here but it is the task of the Jew, one which demands far more thinking than is evident to date, to preserve the delicate balance between universalism and particularism. Israel is spoken of in the Bible as a 'kingdom of priests' (Ex. 19:6). The priest serving in the Temple was not an end in himself, his function was to serve God and the people. His particular role was not for himself. And yet he must have experienced a special sense of privilege that he had been chosen for the sacred duties although there were dangers in this as the history of the priestly caste in Israel demonstrates only too well. In the same way Israel must always be alert to the danger while rejoicing as a people which has brought God to mankind and is a permanent witness to God's truth. Yet Judaism believes that the day will come when all men will acknowledge the truth and all serve in God's Temple: *'And the Lord shall be King over all the earth; in that day shall the Lord be One and His name one'* (Zech. 14:9).

Judaism, for the group or for the individual?

The collected sermons and addresses have recently been

published of the famous nineteenth-century moralist and religious thinker Rabbi Simhah Züssel Zif of Kelm in Lithuania. Quoting: *'And one called unto another, and said: Holy, holy, holy is the Lord of hosts; The whole earth is full of His glory'* (Is. 6: 3) he remarks that before the seraphim sing God's praises they call one unto another because the purpose of worship is to see God's unity amid the diversity of His creation. The Jewish ideal is that individuals in their distinctiveness should meet together in affirming the oneness of God.[4]

Rabbi Zif is correct that Judaism places a good deal of emphasis on group worship and group life generally. Man is a social animal, says Aristotle. He can only find his proper fulfilment in society. Judaism, recognising this truth, builds many of its institutions on this foundation. Whatever spiritual values are furthered by the ideal of the hermit in isolation from his fellows, it is not normally the Jewish ideal. Whitehead's famous definition of religion as 'what a man does with his solitariness' is only half the picture. Many people today know of the sect in ancient Judea from whose library come the Dead Sea scrolls. These men, in a time of national crisis, fled into the desert to seek God. But even there, since they were Jews, they functioned as a group. And it is not impossible that when the great Hillel preached: 'Separate not thyself from the community' (*Abhoth*, II, 5) his preaching was directed against even the comparative isolation of such groups.

Few institutions are more typical of this stress on the role of the community of believers in Judaism than that of the *minyan* (the quorum for prayer). According to the tradition the most sacred prayers can only be recited when ten men are present. In all the stages of man's life it is through the *minyan* that he becomes associated with his fellows. A *minyan* is normally to be present at a circumcision, a marriage and a burial. On these and similar occasions the life of the individual Jew is linked in the prayers recited with the life of his people. The majority of the traditional Jewish prayers are in the plural: 'Grant *us*' not 'Grant *me*.' In view of all this it is not strange that Maimonides, quoting Aristotle, states as an important principle in *Judaism*: 'It is well known that friends are something that is necessary for man throughout

4 *'Hokhmah U-Musar'*, Vol. II, Jer. 1964, No. 63, pp. 50-51.

his whole life. . . . For in a state of health and happiness, a man takes pleasure in their familiar relationship with him: in adversity he has recourse to them; and in his old age, when his body is grown weak, he seeks their help.'[5]

In the Jewish mystical literature even more is made of the group. It is said to mirror the processes in the Godhead by means of which diverse potencies become reconciled in complete unity. In the *Zohar*, for example, the name for the *Shekhinah*, the Divine Presence, is 'the Community of Israel'. Without exploring the full meaning of this Zoharic concept it is clear that we have here the idea that where there is a *community*, composed of individuals who pool their spiritual resources for the common good, there the *Shekhinah*, symbolic of the unification of all the separate forces in God, finds rest.

Judaism reminds us, then, that we belong to one another but one can legitimately doubt whether this needs to be emphasised in the Jewish world today. The more subtle danger today is not that the individual Jew seeks to live in isolation from the community but that his individual needs tend to be overlooked. In an age when vast impersonal forces sway the lives of men, when totalitarian systems tend to see the individual as a cypher, we need more than ever to be reminded that it is the group which exists for the individual, not the other way round. Of course it is true that I am less than human if I refuse to become intimately involved in my group, that an important part of my being is then frustrated. But the group exists for me, not me for the group, and this applies to all the individuals of which the group is composed. Precisely because of the group emphasis in Judaism the faith must always be on guard against the abolition or effacement of the individual. In the State of Israel, for instance, it is not unknown for Rabbis to try to 'sell' Judaism by pointing out to the Israelis that the Jewish faith has been the most potent force for ensuring the survival of the Jewish people. But sensitive Israelis then retort that, granted this was so in the past, there is no need for it now when the survival of Jewish peoplehood is in any event assured by the existence of the State of Israel. Far better, surely, to recognise that what religious Israelis, and for that matter religious Jews everywhere,

[5] 'Guide', III, 49.

require is the assurance that Judaism is capable of catering to their spiritual needs as individuals seeking God.

It is not at all difficult to demonstrate that in Jewish teaching the individual is of supreme significance. Too much can be made of group emphasis in the Hebrew Bible. No careful reader of the Bible can fail to notice that the Biblical heroes and heroines are individuals, no two exactly alike. Abraham is different from Isaac, David from Solomon, Amos from Isaiah. The Biblical characters are not depicted as cyphers but as men and women of flesh and blood, each with his own distinctiveness. Moreover, many of the more important commands in the Bible are addressed to the individual—'*Thou* shalt love the Lord thy God', '*Thou* shalt love *thy* neighbour as thyself'.

In a striking Talmudic passage (*Ber.* 58a) it is said that when one meets a huge company of six hundred thousand (the number obviously reflects the six hundred thousand males of the Exodus) a special benediction is to be recited: 'Blessed art Thou, O Lord our God, who is wise in knowing the secrets.' It is explained that just as no two faces in that vast company are identical so, too, differ their minds. God alone knows their secret thoughts by which they differ as individuals. It has been established nowadays that no two persons in the world have the same set of fingerprints. Each man and woman is unique, each possesses a special fraction of the divine light. The Jews of Eastern Europe used to tell of Rabbi Israel Meir Kagan, known as the *Haphetz Hayyim*, that he would occasionally ask a small boy to tell him of Judaism. When Rabbi Kagan was asked what could he possibly hope to learn from a child the saint replied that every Jew has his own particular portion in God's *Torah* and that it may well be that the little boy has been entrusted with a tiny portion of truth denied to the greatest of scholars.

In answer, then, to the question whether Judaism is for the group or for the individual it can only be said that it is for both. Without his group the individual is nothing but the group is a collection of individuals. Buber has the last word: 'Individualism understands only a part of man; collectivism understands man only as a part, Neither advances to the wholeness of man, to man as a whole.'

Judaism, rational or non-rational?

The question whether Judaism is rational or non-rational is of intimate concern to thinking Jews. People who think about their faith soon come to see that emotion is basic to the religious life and yet they have no wish to leave their minds outside whenever they enter a place of worship. It is possible, of course, to have a purely emotional response to religion and even to argue that reason is not relevant. But those who argue in this way are, by using argument, accepting that reason has something to say. Moreover, such an attitude comes perilously near to saying that there is no reason at all why men should believe in God, that belief is ridiculous but should be embraced nonetheless. It is doubtful if anyone ever holds such a view and those who appear to do so probably mean that while religious belief may *seem* ridiculous it is not *really* so.

The problem of the relationship between faith and reason is discussed in some detail in other parts of this book, particularly in the chapter on the way of reason and in the appendix on the Tertullian paradox. Here we are concerned with the question of tension in this matter.

Judaism cannot afford to negate reason since the original Biblical command to love God with 'all thy heart' really means something like 'with all thy mind'. The duty of *Torah* study is a supreme religious duty according to the Rabbis. In the Middle Ages the great Jewish thinkers like Maimonides believed very strongly that man had a duty to investigate his faith rationally. Perhaps the most telling example is Maimonides' attitude to astrology. Astrology in the Middle Ages was held to be true and looked upon as a science. It had the support of the Talmudic Rabbis. Yet Maimonides was bold enough to reject it as false in obedience to reason. Maimonides, convinced that astrology is both unreasonable and belief in it unworthy of those who see God in complete control of His universe, rejects astrological beliefs as he rejects magical beliefs including these found in the Talmud. 'Man was created with eyes in the front of his head not the back.'[6]

We have earlier referred to Bahya Ibn Pakudah, that the

[6] See '*Jewish Encyclopedia*', Vol. II, p. 245, *Yad, Hil.* Akkum, XI, 8 and I. H. Weiss: '*Dor Dor Wedorshow*', Vol III, pp. 223-224, Vol. IV, pp. 297-298.

only two people who truly serve God are the prophet intuitively and the philosopher through reason. Gersonides in 'Wars of the Lord' states that his concern is not with those content to believe but those who wish to *know*. Our *Torah*, Gersonides proclaims, is not a law which compels us to believe that which we know to be false. There was another side to the picture, even in the Middle Ages. There were anti-Maimonists. Maimonides' opponents were convinced that his approach in the 'Guide for the Perplexed' was extremely harmful to faith. The opponents of philosophy dubbed Gersonides' book 'Wars *against* the Lord'. It remains true that in the so-called Dark Ages those who embraced the cause of reason were among the greatest names in the history of Jewish thought.

It is customary to refer in this context to Greek influence and this is certainly to be observed. But the Rabbis of the Talmud, too, though not systematic philosophers, had great respect for the human mind. They ruled that the first petitionary prayer the devout Jew recites should be a prayer for knowledge. When one meets a sage learned in the *Torah*, say the Rabbis, it is necessary to thank God for 'imparting of His wisdom to them that fear Him' and even when meeting a Gentile sage, learned in secular knowledge, God is to be thanked for 'giving of his wisdom to flesh and blood'.[7]

It would be far off the mark, however, to interpret this to mean that religion should cater only to man's intellect. Reason can take us a good part of the way to God if we are prepared to acknowledge reason as one of the ways to faith (we have seen earlier that many today would disagree even with this). But since religion involves a confrontation of the Infinite and man's mind is finite, reason cannot take us all the way. We have seen that Bahya, for all his rationalism, declares that while we can ask *if* God is we cannot ask *what* He is because this is beyond all human comprehension. Chesterton rightly remarks that the difference between the philosopher and the poet is that the philosopher tries to get the heavens into his head whereas the poet tries to get his head into the heavens. We do not begin to understand the meaning of

---

[7] See *Ber.* 33a: 'R. Ammi said: "Great is knowledge, since it was placed at the beginning of the weekday blessing"' and *Ber.* 58a on the benedictions for Jewish and Gentile sages.

religion, as Schleiermacher said long ago, unless we see that it has its poetry as well as its prose. Religion is concerned with the whole man in his response to God, emotions as well as mind, deeds as well as thoughts. Even a Maimonides, the upholder of the 'supremacy of reason', admits that we cannot know the answer to man's freewill and God's foreknowledge for, he says, to understand this one would have to know as God knows and this is impossible for man.[8] We have referred repeatedly to the fact that the Biblical writers do not argue for God's existence but experience God.

Judaism is a religion not a philosophy and is therefore concerned that men use more than their minds in God's service, but it does encourage men to use their minds. It is true that Judaism is realistic enough to appreciate that some men are incapable of this. Very frequent in our sources are references to the great value of simple, naïve faith if this is all that can be attained. There is, for example, the story which has come down to us from the famous sixteenth-century Kabbalist, Rabbi Isaac Luria.[9] In the days of Luria there lived an unlearned man who read in his Bible how the people in the Temple times brought the show-bread to God's table. In his crude belief the man thought that this meant that somehow God ate the bread and in his desire to serve his Maker he instructed his wife to bake each week twelve loaves of bread, which he would place in front of the Ark in the Synagogue. Unbeknown to the man, the Synagogue beadle, finding the loaves, would take them home thus confirming the man in his superstition that God had accepted his gift. When this eventually came to the notice of the town Rabbi he upbraided the man for his gross credulity and offensive conception of the divine. The man's world collapsed about him. His means of serving God had been rudely taken from him. The tale concludes that when Luria heard of it he cursed the Rabbi for depriving the man of his simple faith.

It is insufferable that a man blessed with a keen intellect should look with derision on those not so gifted. Simple faith is extremely valuable for the simpleton but only for the

---

[8] *Yad, Hil. 'Teshubhah'*, V, 5.
[9] The basis of the story is in Moses Hagiz: *'Mishnath Hakhamim'* No. 200, see A. Roth: *'Shomer Emunim'*, pp. 95b-97a.

simpleton. Many Jews today, while prepared to reason acutely and successfully in every other sphere of life, have come to believe that piety demands a suspension of their critical faculties in the sphere of religion. A faith challenging to mind as well as heart is then in danger of degenerating into soggy sentimentalism. Some advocates of the negation of reason in religion are men of high ability in the sciences, but it is equally true that such an attitude repels many intelligent people who could be won for Jewish thinking if they were aware that the Greek thinkers spoke of the Jews as 'a nation of philosophers'.

It can be summarised in this way: The mediaeval sources sometimes speak of three areas: (1) That of *sekhel*—'reason'. (2) *Le-maalah min ha-sekhel*—'higher than reason'. (3) *Le-matah min ha-sekhel*—'lower than reason'. In our terminology this is: the rational, the non-rational and the irrational. There is certainly room in any sound religious approach for the non-rational because of the element of wonder and mystery inseparable from the fact that it is faith in the Infinite, in the Ground of being. But to confuse the non-rational with the irrational and to embrace the latter means that we give ourselves license to believe in any nonsense provided we tag the name of religion onto it. The Deuteronomist clearly did not allow this: *'Observe, therefore and do them: for this is your wisdom and understanding in the sight of the nations, which shall hear all these statutes and say, Surely this great nation is a wise and understanding people'* (Deut. 4:6).

Judaism, this-worldly or after-worldly?

Many Jews today believe that the doctrine of the After-life is one on which Judaism and Catholicism are divided. Judaism, it is suggested, does not really teach that there is a Hereafter. If its adherents do nonetheless speak of immortality they mean by it that one's thoughts live on in others and that one's life is continued by one's children and grandchildren. Such a view is a complete travesty of any recognisable version of traditional Judaism. Belief in immortality, in the sense of individual survival after the death of the body, is as much part of Judaism as it is of Catholicism. There is little meaning to be extracted from the idea that immortality means that we live on in others. At the most this can only mean that our thoughts and influence are immortal, not we ourselves. It is the thoughts and influences which live on in our children. By no stretch of the imagination can the persistence of our ideas in the lives of those we leave behind on earth be considered as 'us'. When people speak in this way, and moderns often do, they should be clear in their own minds that they have, in fact, rejected the traditional belief in immortality and are trying, surely unsuccessfully, to retain the traditional imagery for something quite different. Shakespeare is only immortal if the individual who lived on earth as the great Elizabethan playwright still enjoys existence in the realms of the spirit. We can only describe *him* as immortal, because people still read his *plays*, in a very loose and imprecise sense. It is, in addition, psychologically uncertain that men who give any thought to the question derive comfort from contemplating that some of their ideas will influence human life when they themselves are no longer here to gain any satisfaction from it.

It is no doubt old-fashioned, some would say reactionary, to affirm nowadays the traditional belief. But the belief is so deeply rooted in Judaism and, to this author's mind, so bound up with the meaning of human life as seen in Theism that he has no hesitation in declaring that he shares the belief in its conventional form. The difficulties in the way of belief here should not be glossed over but they are not insurmountable.[10] Many of them are due to a failure to appreciate what traditional Theism is aiming at when it speaks of eternity. Eternity is outside time completely and although this concept is extremely hard to grasp we can obtain some intimations of what it can mean. The good we do on earth becomes part of ourselves and remains such when we leave the world of time to inhabit eternity. This is to be thought of as a state not a place. We do not go to Heaven but become Heaven.

It is often implied that our present-day knowledge of the dependence of mind on the body prevents us from affirming that the one can live on after death of the other. When a man sustains a brain injury his mind, his 'soul', is affected. Brain surgery can change a man's character. How, then, can mind

[10] For a fuller discussion including the question of resurrection see my: 'Principles of the Jewish faith', Chapter 14, pp. 398-454.

or soul inhabit eternity where there is no body? But it must be realised that there is nothing in our contemporary knowledge of the interaction of brain and mind to make untenable the theory that the mind *uses* the physical brain as the only means for its expression in the material world. In the world of the spirit there is no reason why the mind should not function without this particular instrument.

With the idea of eternity as a state not a location in space, we can, perhaps, give this illustration. When men eventually get to the moon they will be unable to move about or even to exist without their space suits. They are utterly dependent on their space suits while on the moon to the extent that people whose whole existence was on the moon might be moved to argue that it is impossible to live without a space suit. And this would, indeed, be true of life on the moon where even a slight perforation of the suit might bring death to the man inside it. But it would not be true of man in the totally different atmosphere of earth. Here the suit is a prison and he can only live fully when he divests himself of it.

We have noted in the chapter on the Marxist challenge to Theism that, historically considered, Jews are heirs to two distinct traditions, the one, the Biblical, 'this-worldly', the other, the Rabbinic, 'other-worldly'. The virtual silence of the Biblical writers on the whole question of the Hereafter cannot be because of their ignorance of this belief. They knew of the role of the After-life in Egyptian religion and of Egyptian preoccupation with this theme. Alone among the literatures of the ancient Near East, the Bible resolutely turns its back on the realm of the dead to concentrate entirely on the abode of man that is earth. This can only be understood as a conscious reaction against other-worldly aims in religion. It has been remarked by many scholars that whereas one of the chief functions of the Egyptian priest was to cater for the needs of the dead and a sacred book of the Egyptian religion was 'The Book of the Dead', the Jewish priest was forbidden to come into contact with a corpse and the sacred book of the Jews became known as the book of life. The passion of the Hebrew prophets was for justice, righteousness and holiness to be realised here on earth.

It is generally acknowledged that the full belief in a Hereafter came into Judaism at the time of the Maccabees. Here were good and worthy people, some of them very young, many of whom were giving their lives in defence of their religion. It became increasingly difficult to explain God's justice solely in terms of life in this world. Unless the souls of those who had died lived on in eternity, it was argued consciously or unconsciously, then God created only to waste. It is all too easy to declare that we have, then, a supreme example of wishful thinking. Since the Jew in the days of the Maccabees could not endure the thought of his death he forced himself into the belief that his soul was immortal. But religious faith does try to make sense of human existence and, granted the belief in God, the postulate of an After-life seemed most reasonable even if in former times conditions were such as not to demand so forcibly that man face up to the question of life's final goal.

By the time the great classics of Rabbinic Judaism were compiled, belief in the After-life had become the norm in Judaism. We find numerous sayings in the Rabbinic literature suggesting that this world is a kind of school in which man prepares for eternity. This world, say the Rabbis, is like the eve of the Sabbath and the world to come is like the Sabbath. One who prepares on the eve of the Sabbath can enjoy the Sabbath but one who does not prepare on the eve of the Sabbath—what is there for him to enjoy on the Sabbath? (*A.Z.* 3a). This world is like an ante-chamber to the world to come; prepare thyself in the ante-chamber, that thou mayest enter into the hall (*Abhoth*, IV, 16).

It follows from what has been said that the reply to the question whether Judaism is this-worldly or other-worldly is that it is both. Here, too, there are tensions and we must not allow ourselves to be stampeded into an either/or. Modern Jews are the heirs to the Biblical emphasis on justice, righteousness and holiness here on earth and they are, at the same time, heirs to the Rabbinic emphasis on this life as a preparation for eternity. Furthermore, Max Kadushin has correctly said that Rabbinic Judaism, for all its stress on the Hereafter, is not a 'religion of salvation'. Life on earth was not only of value for the Rabbis because it affords man the opportunities of acquiring immortality. It is good in itself. Even if we believed that this life were all, the Rabbis would still have urged us to live worthily, honestly and with dignity and to reject the philosophy of 'Let us eat and drink for to-morrow we must die'. And yet, without the belief in immortality, all the values we cherish are doomed to ultimate extinction. If this were truly the case we would still have to live resolutely and with courage. But Theism in its traditional form assures us that God does not create to waste, and that no good deed is permanently lost, and that the individual soul which pursued goodness in this life will have it for his own and be God-like for all eternity.

It would seem, therefore, that Judaism would have its followers live as if this life were all and yet paradoxically to affirm that man has an immortal soul and that 'underneath are the everlasting arms'. The paradox has never been put more forcibly than in the saying quoted earlier of the second century Rabbi (*Abhoth*, IV, 17): 'One hour of repentance and good deeds in this world is better than the whole life of the world to come; yet one hour of spiritual bliss in the world to come is better than the whole of this life.'

To conclude, Judaism is rich enough to embrace the contraries of human existence. Just as the tensions around the basic issue of faith can enrich the life of faith so, too, the tensions around the secondary beliefs need not be feared but should be welcomed as opportunities for creative faith in action.

Appendices

Amen

Amen, used as a liturgical response in Judaism, Christianity and Islam, has the same Hebrew root as *emunah* ('faith') and expresses the same idea of trust, firm acceptance, specificity, reliance and affirmation. It is found in the Hebrew Bible in Num. 5:22; Deut. 27:15, 16, 17, 18, 19, 20, 21, 22, 23, 24, 25, 26; I Kings 1:36; Is. 65:16; Jer. 11:5; 28:6; I Chron. 16:36; Neh. 5:13; 8:6; Ps. 41:14; 72:19; 89:52; 106:48. See: Louis Ginzberg: 'Amen' in 'Jewish Encyclopedia', Vol. I, pp. 491-2; H. Revel: 'Amen' in 'Universal Jewish Encyclopedia', Vol. I, pp. 223-4; *'Encyclopedia Talmudith'*, Vol. 2, *s.v. amen*, pp. 46-50; M. Guttman: *'Maphteah Ha-Talmud'*, Bresslau, 1924, Vol. III, *s.v.* amen, pp. 193-195; J. Hempel: 'Amen' in 'The Interpreter's Dictionary of the Bible', Abingdon Press, New York and Nashville, 1962, Vol. I, p. 105.

Among Jews the world is never used at the beginning of a sentence as it is in Matt. 5:18; 26; 6:2; Luke 4:24; John 1:51.

Ginzberg, *op. cit.*, translates 'Amen' in the response as 'So be it' or 'So shall it be' and describes it as 'perhaps the most widely known word in human speech'.

Hempel, *op. cit.*, translates it as 'Truly' or 'Surely'. The late second-century teacher Rabbi Hanina (*Sanh.* 110b; 111a; *Sheb.* 36a) takes the initial letters of *'Amen'* to represent *el melekh neeman*, 'God, Faithful King'. Hanoch Zundel ben Joseph in his short essay on prayer: *'Besamim Rosh'* (printed in *'Siddur Otzar Ha-Tephillath'* Vilna, 1914, Chapter 34, pp. 37-38) understands homiletically the initial letters of Amen to represent *ani moser naphshi,* 'I am hereby ready to sacrifice myself'.

The idea that it is more difficult and consequently more

praiseworthy to give assent to a truth first seen by others than to be a pioneer in discovering the truth for oneself is possibly behind the Rabbinic teaching that one who responds with 'Amen' to a benediction is greater than the one who recites the benediction (*Ber.* 53b, *Naz.* 66b). The importance the Rabbis attached to the response can be seen from the saying of Rabbi Meir (2nd cent.) that a child merits the world to come from the day he answers Amen (*Sanh.* 110b). Similarly Rabbi Simeon b. Lakish (3rd cent.) said that all the gates of Paradise open to one who answers Amen with his whole being (*Sabb.* 119b). There are references in the Rabbinic literature to inadequate responses of Amen (*Ber.* 47a). Thus, the *Amen* should not be 'snatched' (*hatuphah*) or 'curtailed' (*ketuphah*) or 'orphaned' (*yethomah*). Rashi understands the first fault to be that the first letter of the word is slurred, the second that the final letter is indistinct and the third that one responds without having heard the benediction (the Amen is 'orphaned' from the benediction to which it should serve as a response). Others understand the first fault to be that the Amen is answered prematurely, i.e., before the benediction has been completed (see *Shulhan Arukh, Orah Hayyim*, 124:8). Amen is to be recited only after another's benediction, not after one's own (*Jer. Ber.*, V, 4; *Ber.* 45b: *Shulhan Arukh, Orah Hayyim*, 124; 1). After a prayer of petition the intention should be: 'May it be Thy will that this purpose be realised' (*Shulhan Arukh, loc. cit.*).

The fourteenth century Spanish commentator, David Abudraham, in his Commentary to the Prayer Book (ed. Jer., 1959, p. 114) compares the response of Amen to the validation of a bond by a Court of Law. Without such validation the bond may be a forgery or otherwise incapable of performing its proper function. Behind the whole institution of Amen is the idea that faith may be vaccilating, that it requires confirmation and constant reinforcement.

Appendix II

Jewish Parallels to the Tertullian Paradox

DR. ISIDORE EPSTEIN ('The Faith of Judaism', Soncino Press, London, 1954, p. 117) has this to say on Tertullian: 'Applied to the doctrines of Judaism, we can say that though they may not all be in accord with understanding they are all in accord alike with reason and the established truths of scientific teaching. Contrast this with the Tertullian dicta: *"Credo quia absurdum"*, *"Credibile quia ineptum"*, *"Certum est quia impossibile est"* ("I believe because it is absurd", "To be believed because it is foolish", "It is certain because it is impossible"), making incredibility the test of credibility; see Tertullian, *On the Flesh of Christ, V.* Judaism, on the other hand, whilst having too much respect for human intelligence to subscribe to any proposition involving the total surrender of human reason, nevertheless rightly recognises the limitations of the human faculties and senses and may well proclaim as an act of revealed faith, *"Credibile quia non intellectum est"* ("To be believed because it is beyond the understanding")—quite a tenable and rational proposition which would be unscientific to assail or deny *a priori*.'

Milton Steinberg ('Anatomy of Faith', ed. Arthur A. Cohen, Harcourt, Brace, New York, 1960, pp. 145-6), discussing Kierkegaard, similarly writes: 'Like other men professing a revealed religion, Jews have debated whether speculative inquiry is necessary or permissible and, if so, what may be the status of its conclusions vis-à-vis religious verities. But the possibility that faith and reason should be ideally exclusive of each other has little troubled traditionally-minded Jewish thinkers. They neglected to consider that possibility for one

o

simple reason: they had no reason to. Paradox may inhere in all religious affirmation; but where Christianity must glory in it, Judaism need not. Its central position is neither "absurd" nor an "affront" to reason. It is involved in no mysteries like that of the Trinity-Unity, of which one has no choice but to say *credo quia absurdum est* ("I believe because it is absurd"). It sets forth no Gods who are yet mortals. . . . The anti-Maimunists sought to ban all philosophical inquiry. But these rabbis, whether ancient of the mediaeval, were motivated by a kind of anti-rationalism worlds apart from Kierkegaard's. Their objection to speculation was pragmatic: that with revelation available it is superfluous; or, by its stubborn questioning, disturbing to faith; or, given human limitations, foredoomed to failure. *No Jewish thinker is on record as advancing Kierkegaard's contention of the radical incompatibility of religious truth and reason.* To the contrary, the common Jewish assumption has always been that the two for God are one, as they would be one for man were his powers of comprehension equal to the theme' (*italics* mine).

Both Epstein and Steinberg, and many another Jewish apologist, while admitting that Judaism knows of things 'higher than reason', deny that *any* Jewish thinker has ever taught the incompatibility of faith and reason. Historically considered this is simply untrue. One is quite justified in rejecting an interpretation of Judaism which glories in the 'absurd'. I would agree with Epstein and Steinberg in rejecting such an approach as it seems to me to be logically meaningless; and in this rejecting there is ample support from the great Jewish thinkers of the past. What we must not do is to claim that Judaism has never had anti-rationalists to reject human reasoning completely, declaring it to be incompatible with faith. Certainly the particular motive of belief in the Incarnation is peculiar to Christianity, and since Judaism rejects this belief there is no cause *on this ground* to reject reason as contrary to faith. But on other grounds there have been just a few Jewish theologians who have adopted a position not far removed from that of Tertullian and Kiergegaard. In the interests of historical accuracy we examine here some of these thinkers although few of us can agree with their approach.

In the Bible and the Rabbinic literature, as we have seen, the conflict between faith and reason is ignored chiefly because Biblical and Rabbinic thinking is not systematic but organic, more in the nature of a response than an argument. During the Middle Ages when the problem was acute there were thinkers who had little confidence in unaided reason as an approach to God. But even they did not normally go so far as to suggest that faith was irrational. Here Steinberg is undoubtedly correct. But there were exceptions, particularly in the ranks of the mystics and particularly also in the later period of Jewish thought from the Renaissance onwards.

During the Middle Ages some thinkers discussed whether God could do the impossible. The two Biblical references (Gen. 18:14 and Jer. 32:27) are not strictly germane to the discussion because they have to do with the miraculous rather than the impossible. Aquinas as we noted earlier states: 'Nothing that implies a contradiction falls under the scope of God's omnipotence' (*Summa*, Part I, Quest, 25, 4). Long before Aquinas, Saadiah Gaon, in a very modern-sounding passage ('Beliefs and Opinions', II, 13, English trans. by Samuel Rosenblatt, Yale Judaica Series, Yale University Press, 1948, p. 134), wrote: 'It will furthermore laud and praise Him justly and uprightly not by attributing to Him exaggerations and absurdities. Thus Scripture says, in regard to those that uttered God's praises: *And Hezekiah spoke encouragingly to all the Levites that showed good understanding for the Lord* (II Chron. 30:22). It will not, therefore, praise Him for being able to cause five to be more than ten without adding anything to the former, nor for being able to put the world through the hollow of a signet ring without making the one narrower and the other wider, nor for being able to bring back the day gone in its original condition. For all these things are absurd. Of course, certain heretics often ask us about such matters, and we do indeed answer them that God is able to do everything. This thing, however, that they ask of Him is not anything because it is absurd, and the absurd is nothing. It is, therefore, as though they were to ask: "Is God capable of doing what is nothing?" which is, of course, a real question.' Saadiah appears to be aware that, as we would say, the question is a linguistic one. We must not imagine that there is an entity called the 'absurd' regarding which we may discuss whether or not God can do it. Saadiah does not deny that God can cause the world to pass through the hollow of a signet ring by making the one smaller or the other larger. But to demand that He should do this without making the one smaller or the other larger is not to say anything about God's power but to utter a meaningless sentence. For by definition when we talk of one thing *passing through* another we imply that one is smaller than the other. It is as if we were to ask whether God can make one thing smaller than the other without making it smaller than the other which is, of course, nonsense.

The founder of the *Habad* movement in Hasidism, Rabbi Schneor Zalman of Liady (1747-1813), writes: 'Faith is higher than knowledge and comprehension for: "The simpleton believeth every word" (Ps. 14: 15). In relation to God, who is higher than reason and knowledge and Whom no thought can grasp at all, everyone is a simpleton. As it is said: "But I was brutish, and ignorant; I was as a beast before Thee: Thou holdest my right hand" (Ps. 73: 22-23). This means: Because I am brutish and as a beast I am continually with Thee' (*'Tanya'*, ed. Vilna, 1930, Chapter 18, p. 47). The last sentence comes very close to the Tertullian paradox. Only the fool of God is always with God. Schneor Zalman seems to be saying that if reason could bring a man to God and if man were to rely on this there might be times when reason fails and then man will be without God. But since God is utterly beyond all human reason and since faith is God's gift to man and in no way dependent on human reasoning (indeed, faith is contrary to reason, hence man is a 'simpleton' in this respect) then man can always be with God. The English versions of the Psalm render the second verse: 'Nevertheless, I am continually with Thee.' Schneor Zalman clearly understands the verse to mean: *'Therefore*, I am continually with Thee.' It is not in spite of his brutishness that man can be with God always but because of it.

Rabbi Menahem Mendel of Lübavitch (1789-1866), Rabbi Schneor Zalman's grandson and ultimate successor as leader of the *Habad* group, comments at length on this passage in his notes to the *Tanya* (Kitzurim, New York, 1948, pp. 101-103).

The grandson, a subtle, speculative religious thinker like Schneor Zalman himself, and like him the leader of the intellectual branch of Hasidism, is obviously embarrassed by the grandfather's apparent surrender to unreason. R. Menahem Mendel first points out that the verse: 'The simpleton believeth every word' is applied in the Midrash (Ex. R. III, beg.) to Moses at the start of his mission. Moses, remarks the *Midrash*, was at that time a 'simpleton', a mere tyro in the realm of prophecy, so that God, in order not to startle him, was at first obliged to speak to him in the voice of his father. R. Menahem Mendel continues: 'This means that faith in God is to be compared to the case of the simpleton who believeth every word, that a man should not use his reason to question the true faith.' In his relationship with God man 'should consider himself to be a simpleton and a fool so as to have faith'.

But R. Menahem Mendel considers this to be a hard saying. Surely, he argues, faith and truth have the same root in Hebrew and it cannot be meritorious to believe something one knows to be false. Consequently, there is bound to be a world of difference between the believer's faith in God and the credulity of the fool. The faith of the fool stems from his folly. He is not clever enough to see that what he accepts as true is really false. He finds it easy to believe *anything* because his critical faculties are dormant. Faith in God, on the other hand, is right because it is true. The belief of the man of faith is not in defiance of truth or in a spirit of indifference to it as is the faith of the fool. How, then, can Schneor Zalman compare the two and even begin to imagine that the case of the simpleton can be a helpful analogy for the life of faith?

In reply Menahem Mendel at first suggests that Schneor Zalman does not refer to the basic belief in God but to such secondary beliefs as the resurrection of the dead and that God is wholly good in spite of the evil we witness in creation. With regard to these, man's intellect must be severely controlled because of his awareness that his finite mind is incapable of grasping the Infinite so that here, and here alone, he should be as the fool. But on further reflection Menahem Mendel decides that this is not sufficient to remove the difficulty. Even secondary beliefs are, after all, true beliefs and should be held because they are true rather than as the fool believes, irrespective of whether they are true or false.

Menahem Mendel tries, therefore, to soften the difficulty by suggesting that Schneor Zalman only refers to the analogy of the fool in a limited sense. He does not intend to praise credulity in matters of faith but only to call man to a realisation of his limitations. The comparison of the man of faith to the fool is not with regard to the *content* of faith but to its *quality*. The content is certainly quite different. The man of faith believes that which is true, the fool that which is false. But the man of faith should believe in the truth as intensely as the fool believes in the false. Since the fool never tests his beliefs by reason he holds fast to them without question. Therefore the man of faith should learn from the fool to acquire this powerful sense of a truth beyond refutation. Such an interpretation of Schneor Zalman's thought, of course, removes the whole matter from the realms of the paradoxical; it is far from certain, however, that the interpretation is correct.

It is in the writings of Schneor Zalman's favourite disciple, Rabbi Aaron b. Moses of Starosselje (1766-1828) that we come nearest to the idea that faith is bound to contradict reason because there is an 'absurdity' at the heart of faith. Rabbi Aaron is the most radical acosmist in Jewish thought. For him there is no world and there are no creatures from God's point of view (or rather they are, as Aaron puts it, 'included in His blessed unity'). It is only from our point of view that things are seen in their multiplicity and separateness. But, Aaron goes on to ask, how is this possible? How can there be at one and the same time a finite universe of multiplicity from our point of view? Aaron replies that this is a 'marvel' (*pelé*) utterly beyond all human comprehension. (See my study of Aaron's thought: 'Seeker of Unity', Vallentine, Mitchell, London, 1966, Index *s.v.* 'marvel').

Because of this Aaron is obliged to hold that God can not only do that which is impossible for us but the logically impossible. For it is logically impossible for there to be a finite universe and yet for there to be no universe at all. Faith is thus belief in the impossible. Aaron (*'Shaar Ha-Yihud We-*

Ha-Emunah', Shklov, 1820, *Shaar*, III, Chapter 14, pp. 15a-16a, 'Seeker of Unity', pp. 101-103) in fact, takes issue with the famous mediaeval Jewish thinkers (he does not, however, refer to Saadiah) on precisely this score. For to these thinkers, observes Aaron, when it is said that God is 'higher' than reason the meaning is that His wisdom is infinitely superior to human reason. But the difference is in degree not in kind. For Aaron, however, there is a qualitative difference. God is utterly beyond all human reason.

Because of their conception in this matter the mediaeval thinkers declared that God is bound by the rules of logic. Abraham Ibn Ezra, for instance, treats the Talmudic saying that the ark in the Temple was there and yet occupied no space as legendary on the grounds that this is a logical impossibility and hence impossible even for God. A cannot be both A and not-A. This Aaron rejects. God is not bound by the rules of conceptual thinking. He is utterly beyond reason and can do the logically impossible. (The critique of Aaron's view is, of course, that it is no limitation of God's powers to say that He cannot do the logically impossible since nonsense is not turned into sense simply by tagging onto it the word 'God'. This critique is sound but does not alter the fact that, as we are here trying to demonstrate, a Jewish thinker embraces paradox as basic to faith.)

Another Hasidic thinker who embraces paradox as essential to faith is Rabbi Nahman of Bratzlav (1772-1811). In Rabbi Nahman's dialectic of faith doubts and difficulties are essential ingredients in the life of faith because the finite human reason is bound to come into conflict with the Infinite. This is endemic to man's condition as a finite creature. (See the very important essay on this aspect of R. Nahman's thought by J. G. Weiss: *'Ha-Kushya Be-Torath R. Nahman Mi-Bratzlav'* in the Salman Schocken Jubilee Volume, *Alei Ayin*, Jer., 1952, pp. 245-291.) A particularly striking formulation by R. Nahman in this connection is: 'It is entirely proper that objections be found to God. It is right and suitable that this should be so because of God's greatness and exaltedness. Since in His exaltedness He is so elevated above our minds there are bound to be objections to Him' (Weiss, *op. cit.*, p. 248 from *Likkute Moharan, Tinyana*, 52). A God who raises no problems for human thought would not be God for the very reason that the Infinite is bound to offend the finite mind. Since God cannot be grasped by the human mind the human reason in itself must not only fail to bring man to God but must be in contradiction to God. Like Aaron of Starosselje, Nahman of Bratzlev denies that God is bound by the laws of logic and takes issue with the mediaeval thinkers who declare that He is so bound. 'They write in their books: "Is it possible for God to make a triangle into a square?" (*i.e.* to make a square triangle). But our master (= R. Nahman) said: "I believe that God can make a square triangle. For God's ways are concealed from us. He is omnipotent and nothing is impossible for Him".' (See Weiss, *op. cit.*, p. 248, from *'Kunteros Yeme Ha-Telaoth'*, Jer., 1933 p. 190.)

R. Nahman's thought is nourished by the Lurianic *Kabbalah*. According to this doctrine the finite world can only have come into existence because God 'withdrew from Himself into Himself' and yet the world requires God's power for its very existence. The great paradox here is that with God there cannot be a finite world, for the finite world is other than God, and yet without God there can be no finite world, for nothing can exist away from His presence. Thus we are obliged to postulate that God has withdrawn Himself and yet has not withdrawn Himself and this is the great contradiction at the heart of faith (see Weiss's analysis, *op. cit.*, pp. 258f.).

Thus, for Tertullian the paradox at the heart of faith is due to the doctrine of the Incarnation. It is impossible for God to become man and yet the Christian must believe this 'impossible' thing. No Jewish thinker is moved by this because Judaism rejects the doctrine of the Incarnation. But both R. Nahman and R. Aaron see a similar 'absurdity' which is bound to remove faith entirely from the realm of conceptual thought. For these thinkers the 'absurdity' is that faith is bound to postulate that there is and yet is not a finite world (Aaron) or that God is and yet is not present in the world (Nahman). For reason this is nonsense, but for faith all things are possible.

It remains only to be said that R. Schneor Zalman's idea of the 'simpleton' as superior to the sophisticate in matters of faith is anticipated in the work of a more conventional Jewish anti-rationalist. The famous opponent of philosophy in the area of faith, R. Joseph b. Hayyim Jabetz (fifteenth to six-teenth century) similarly refers to the 'simpleton' as exempli-fying faith at its highest. In his '*Or Ha-Hayyim*' (Amsterdam, 1781, Chapter 5 end, p. 12a) this author writes that during the persecutions in Spain, to which he was an eye-witness, the thinkers and philosophers were far less ready to offer their lives for their faith than were the ignorant. 'Those men who prided themselves on their knowledge of these sciences forsook their faith on the bitter day and this is a strong and powerful proof that if instead of mastering those studies they had belonged in the group of the simpletons their simplemindedness would have saved them and "The Lord preserveth the simpletons" (Ps. 147:6).'

Bibliography

Bibliography

Talmud and Midrash.

Mishnah, ed. Warsaw, 1882.
Talmud Babli, ed Vilna Rom.
Talmud Yerushalmi, ed. Krotoschin, 1886.
Siphre, ed. Friedmann, Vienna, 1864.
Mekhilta, ed. Lauterbach, Philadelphia, 1933.
Mekhilta De-Rabbi Simeon ben Yohai, ed. Hoffmann, Frankfurt, 1931.
Yalkut Shimeoni, ed Warsaw, 1877.
Midrash, Psalms, ed. Buber, Vilna, 1891, Eng. trans. by William. G. Braude, Yale University Press, 1955.
Tanna De-Bhe Elijahu, ed. Friedmann, Vienna, 1900.
Zohar, Vilna, 1882.
Philo: Loeb Classical Library, Vol. IV, 1949, Vol. VIII, 1950.

Abbreviation of Talmudic tractates:

Ber.: Berakhoth	*M.K.: Moed Katan*
Betz.: Betzah	*Ned.: Nedarim*
B.B.: Baba Bathra	*Nidd.: Niddah*
B.K.: Baba Kama	*Sanh.: Sanhedrin*
B.M.: Baba Metzia	*Sukk.: Sukkah*
Gitt.: Gittin	*A.Z.: Abhodah Zarah*
Hag.: Hagigah	*Erub.: Erubhin*
Hull.: Hullin	*Pes.: Pesahim*
Yeb.: Yebhamoth	*Kidd.: Kiddushin*
Yom.: Yoma	*R.H.: Rosh Ha-Shanah*
Keth.: Kethubhoth	*Sabb.: Shabbath*
Meg.: Megillah	*Taan.: Taanith*
Makk.: Makkoth	

English translation of the Talmud ed. I. Epstein, Soncino Press, Bournemouth, 1935-1949.

Mediaeval Jewish Classics

Aaron Ha-Levi of Barcelona: *'Sepher Ha-Hinnukh'*, 3rd. ed., ed. B. Chavel. Jer., 1956.

Abba Mari of Lunel: *'Minhath Kenaoth'*, Pressburg, 1839.

Abraham Ibn David: *'Emunah Ramah'*, with German trans. ed. S. Weil, Frankfurt, 1852.

Albo, Joseph: *'Sepher Ha-Ikkarim'*, ed. with Eng. trans. I. Husik, Philadelphia, 1946.

Bahya Ibn Asher: *'Kad Ha-Kemah'*, Lemberg, 1880.

Bahya Ibn Pakudah: *'Hobhoth Ha-Lebhabhoth'* ('Duties of the Heart'), ed. Warsaw, 1875.

Cordovero, Mosheh: *'Elimah Rabbathi'*, Lemberg, 1881.

Crescas, Hasdai: *'Or Adonai'*, Vienna, 1860.

de Vidas, Elijah: *'Reshith Hohkmah'*, Venice, 1578.

Gersonides: *'Milhamoth Ha-Shem'*, Riva di Trento, 1560.

Hagiz, Moses: *'Mishnath Hakhamim'*, Wandsbeck, 1733.

Ha-Levi, Judah: *'Kuzari'*, ed. H. Hirschfeld, Leipsic, 1887, Eng. trans. H. Hirschfeld, Cailingold, London, 1931.

Luzzatto, M. H.: *'Mesillath Yesharim'*, ed. with Eng. trans. M. M. Kaplan, Philadelphia, 1936.

Maimonides: *'Sepher Ha-Mitzwoth'*, ed. Warsaw, 1883.

  'Mishneh Torah' ('Yad Ha-Hazakah'), ed. Warsaw, 1882.

  'Moreh Nebhukhim' ('Guide for the Perplexed'), Arabic text, S. Munk: 'Le Guide des Egarés', Paris, 1856-1866, Heb. ed., Lemberg, 1866 and ed. J. Kaufmann, Tel-Aviv, 1935-1959, Eng. trans. M. Friedländer, London, 1936 and S. Pines; 'The Guide of the Perplexed', Chicago University Press, 1963.

Nahmanides: Commentary to the Pentateuch, ed. B. Chavel, Mosad Ha-Rav Kook, Jer. 1959-1960.

  'Kithbhe Ha-Ramban' ('Nahmanides' Writings'), ed. B. Chavel, Mosad Ha-Rav Kook, Jer., 1964.

Saadiah: *'Emunoth We-Deoth'* ('Beliefs and Opinions'), Arabic text ed. S. Landauer, Leyden, 1880, Heb. text, Constantinople, 1562 and freq. reprinted, Eng. trans. S. Rosenblatt, Yale University Press, 1949 and A. Altmann, East and West Library, Oxford, 1946.

General Works

Agus, J. B.: 'Modern Philosophies of Judaism', Behrman's, New York, 1941.

Ahad Ha-Am: *'Al Parashath Derakhim'*, Berlin, 1921.

Allport, G. W.: 'The Individual and His Religion', Constable, London, 1951.

Altmann, A.: 'The Modern Analysis of Faith' in 'Addresses given at the Ninth Conference of Anglo-Jewish Preachers, May 14th-17th', London, 1951.

Ayer, A. J.: 'Language, Truth and Logic', 2nd. ed., Gollancz, London, 1946.

Bakan, D.: 'Sigmund Freud and the Jewish Mystical Tradition', Van Nostrand, Princeton, N.J., 1958.

Bartley, W. W. III: 'The Retreat to Commitment', Chatto and Windus, London, 1964.

Bertocci, P. A.: 'Introduction to the Philosophy of Religion', Prentice-Hall, New York, 1951.

Bevan, Edwyn: 'Symbolism and Belief', Fontana Library, Collins, London, 1962.

Bonhoeffer, D.: 'Letters and Papers from Prison', SCM Press, 1953.

Bouquet, A. C.: 'Sacred Books of the East', Cassell, London, 1962.

Braithwaite, R. B.: 'An Empiricist's View of the Nature of Religious Belief', The Eddington Memorial Lecture, Cambridge University Press, 1955, also in John Hick: 'The Existence of God', pp. 229-252.

Breisach, E.: 'Introduction to Modern Existentialism', Grove Press, New York, 1962.

Brightman, E. S.: 'The Problem of God', Abingdon Press, New York, 1930.
    'A Philosophy of Religion', Skeffington, London, 1940.

Buber, Martin: 'I and Thou', Eng. trans. by Ronald Gregor Smith, Scribner's, New York, 1937.

Bultmann, Rudolf and Weiser, A.: 'Faith' in Kittel's 'Dictionary of the New Testament', Eng. trans. ed. P. R. Ackroyd, Adam and Charles Black, London, 1961.

Caldecott, A. and Mackintosh, H. R.: 'Selections from the Literature of Theism', T. & T. Clark, 3rd. ed., Edinburgh, 1931.

Charlesworth, M. J.: 'St Anselm's *Proslogion*', Clarendon Press, Oxford, 1965.

Collins, J.: 'God in Modern Philosophy', Routledge, London, 1960.

Copleston, F.: 'Contemporary Philosophy, Studies of Logical Positivism and Existentialism', Burns and Oates, London, 1956.

Cox, Harvey: 'The Secular City', Macmillan, New York, 1965.

Cronbach, A.: 'Psychoanalytic Study of Judaism' in Hebrew Union College Annual, Vol. VIII-IX, 1931-1932.

Davidson, Robert F.: 'Rudolf Otto's Interpretation of Religion', Princeton University Press, 1947.

Diamond, M.: 'Martin Buber, Jewish Existentialist', New York, Oxford University Press, 1960.

Dilley, F. B.: 'Metaphysics and Religious Language' Columbia University Press, New York and London, 1964.

Dobh Baer of Lübavitch: 'Tract on Ecstasy', trans. L. Jacobs, Vallentine, Mitchell, London, 1963.

Driver, S. R.: 'The Book of Genesis' in the Westminster Commentaries, Methuen, 12th ed., London, 1926.

Druyanov, Alter: *'Reshumoth'*, Vol. I, Odessa 1918, Vol. II, Tel-Aviv, no date.

Dupré, L.: 'Kierkegaard as Theologian', Sheed and Ward, London, 1964.

Edwards, P. and Pap. A. ed.: 'A Modern Introduction to Philosophy', The Free Press, Glencoe, Illinois, 1957.

Epstein, I.: 'Social Legislation in the Talmud', *Tnuath Torah Va-Avodah*, London, no date.

Ewing, A. C.: 'Meaninglessness' in 'Mind', 1937.

Feinstein, Mosheh: *'Iggroth Mosheh, Hoshen Mishpat etc.'*. New York, 1962.

Ferré, F.: 'Language, Logic and God', Eyre and Spottiswoode, London, 1962.

Flew, A. and MacIntyre, A.: 'New Essays in Philosophical Theology', SCM Press, London, 1955.

Freud, Sigmund: 'Totem and Taboo', Pelican Books, 1938. 'The Future of an Illusion', Hogarth Press, London, 1934. 'Moses and Monotheism', Hogarth Press, London, 1939.

Friedman, Maurice S.: 'Martin Buber, The Life of Dialogue', and Chicago University Press, 1955.

Glenn, Menahem G.: 'Rabbi Israel Salanter: Religious Ethical Thinker', Bloch, New York, 1953.

Gore, Charles: 'Belief in God', Penguin Books, 1939.

Heichelheim, F. M.: 'Syria' in Tanney Frank's 'An Economic Survey of Ancient Rome', Vol. IV, Baltimore, 1938.

Heinemann, H.: 'Torah and Social Order', *Tnuath Torah Va-Avodah*, London, no date.

Herberg, Will: 'Judaism and Modern Man', Farrer, Straus and Young, New York, 1951.

Heywood Thomas, T.: 'Subjectivity and Paradox', Blackwell, Oxford, 1957.

Hick, John: 'Philosophy of Religion', Prentice-Hall, N.J., 1963 ed. 'The Existence of God', Macmillan, London and New York, 1964. 'Evil and the God of Love', Macmillan, London, 1966.

Hook, S.: ed. 'Religious Experience and Truth', Oliver and Boyd, Edinburgh, 1962.

Howe, I. and Greenberg, E.: 'A Treasury of Yiddish Stories', Andre Deutsch, London, 1955.

Hume, David: 'Dialogues Concerning Natural Religion', ed. Norman Kemp Smith, Edinburgh, 1935, and in 'Hume on Religion', Fontana Books, 1963.

Hurwitz, Yoizel: *'Madregath Ha-Adam'*, Kdem Press, New York, 1947.

Husik, I.: 'A History of Mediaeval Jewish Philosophy', Philadelphia, 1940.

Hutchinson, John A.: 'Faith, Reason and Existence', New York, Oxford University Press, 1956.

Huxley, Aldous: 'The Doors of Perception' and 'Heaven and Hell', Penguin Books, 1959.

Jacobs, Louis: 'We have Reason to Believe', 3rd ed., Vallentine, Mitchell, London, 1965. 'Jewish Values', Vallentine, Mitchell, London, 1960.

'Principles of the Jewish Faith', Vallentine, Mitchell, London, 1964; Basic Books, New York, 1964.

James, William: 'The Will to Believe', Longmans, Green, London, 1897.

Jastrow, Marcus: 'A Dictionary of the Targumim, the Talmud Babli and Yerushalmi and the Midrashic Literature', Shapiro and Vallentine, London, 1926.

Jones, E.: 'Sigmund Freud', III Vol., Hogarth Press, London, 1953-1959.

Jung, C.: 'Modern Man in Search of a Soul', Kegan Paul, London, 1933.

Kadushin, Max: 'The Rabbinic Mind', 2nd ed., Blaisdell, New York, 1962.

Karelitz, A. I.: *'Hazon Ish Al Inyane Emunah, Bittahon We-Od'*, Jer., 1954.

Kant, Immanuel: 'Critique of Pure Reason', trans. J. M. D. Meiklejohn, London, 1897.

Katz, D.: *'Tenuath Ha-Musar'*, Vol. IV, Tel-Aviv, 1957.

Kierkegaard, Søren: 'The Last Years—Journals 1853-55', ed. and trans. Ronald Gregor Smith, Collins, London, 1965.

Laski, Marghanita: 'Ecstasy', Cresset Press, London, 1961.

Levy, Jacob: *'Wörterbuch über die Talmudim und Midraschim'*, Berlin, 1924.

Loewe, Raphael: ed. 'Studies in Rationalism, Judaism and Universalism' (Memorial Volume for Leon Roth), Routledge and Kegan Paul, London, 1966.

Lowrie, W.: 'Kierkegaard', Oxford University Press, 1938.

MacDowell, R. H.: 'Stamped and Inscribed Objects from Seleucia on the Tigris', Ann Arbor, University of Michigan Press, 1935.

MacIntyre, A.: 'Difficulties in Christian Belief', SCM Press, 1959.

Mactaggart, J. E. M.: 'Some Dogmas of Religion', London, 1930.

Malter, H: 'Saadiah Gaon 'His Life and Works', Philadelphia, 1942.

Mascall, E. L.: 'Words and Images', Longmans, Green, London, 1957.

Maslow, A. H.: 'Religions, Values and Peak-Experiences', Ohio State University Press, Columbus, 1964.

Menahem Mendel of Lübavitch: *'Derekh Mitzwothekha'*, Poltava, 1911.

Meynall, H.: 'Sense, Nonsense and Christianity', Sheed and Ward, London and New York, 1964.

Miles, T. R.: 'Religion and the Scientific Outlook', George Allen and Unwin, London, 1959.

Mill, John Stuart: 'Three Essays on Religion', Longmans, Green, London, 1874.

Mitchell, Basil: ed. 'Faith and Logic', George Allen and Unwin, London, 1957.

Montefiore, C. G. and Loewe, H.: 'A Rabbinic Anthology', Macmillan, London, 1938.

Moore, G. F.: 'Judaism', Harvard University Press, 1958.

Moule, C. F. D., and others: 'Faith, Fact and Fantasy', Fontana Books, 1964.

Nahman of Bratzlav: *'Sepher Ha-Middoth'*, Warsaw, 1912. *'Liqqute Moharan'*, 1808-1811.

Otto, Rudolf: 'The Idea of the Holy', Eng. trans. J. W. Harvey, 2nd ed., Oxford University Press, London, 1950.

Paley, William: 'Natural Theology', London, 1802.

Pascal, B.: *'Pensées'*, Modern Library, New York, 1941.

Pauly-Wissowa: *'Real Encyclopädie der Classischen Altertumswissenschaft'*, Stuttgart, 1894-1923.

Pfister, O.: 'Christianity and Fear', George Allen and Unwin, London, 1948.

Philp, H. L.: 'Freud and Religious Belief', Rickcliff, London, 1956.

Price, H. H.: 'Belief "In" and Belief "That" ' in 'Religious Studies', Vol. I, No. 1, Oct. 1965, pp. 5-27.

Rabbinowitz, Z. M.: 'Rabbi Joseph Isaac of Pzhysha' (Heb.), Piotrkow, 1932.

Ramsey, I.: 'Religious Language', SCM Press, 1957.

Reik, T.: 'Ritual', London, 1931. 'Dogma and Compulsion', New York, 1951.

Roberts, David E.: 'Existentialism and Religious Belief', Galaxy Books, New York, 1959.

Robinson, John A. T.: 'Honest to God', SCM Paperback, 1963. 'The New Reformation', SCM Paperback, 1965.

'The Honest to God Debate' with D. L. Edwards, SCM Paperback, 1963.

Roth, Aaron: *'Shomer Emunim'*, Jer., 1964.

Roth, Leon: 'Moralisation and Demoralisation in Jewish Ethics' in *'Judaism'*, Vol. XI, 4 (1962), pp. 291-302.

Schechter, Solomon: 'Aspects of Rabbinic Theology', Schocken Books, New York, 1961.

Schneor Zalman of Liady: *'Tanya'*, Vilna, 1930.

Scholem, G.: 'Major Trends in Jewish Mysticism', 3rd. ed., Thames and Hudson, London, 1955.

Simhah Züssel of Kelm: *'Hokhmah U-Musar'*, Vol. II, Jer., 1964.

Smart, Ninian: 'Philosophers and Religious Truth', SCM Press, 1964.

Spencer Jones, H.: 'Astronomy' in 'The New Outline of Modern Knowledge', Gollancz, London, 1956.

Spinks, G. S.: 'Psychology and Religion', Methuen, 1963.

Steinberg, Milton: 'Anatomy of Faith', ed. Arthur A. Cohen. Harcourt, Brace, New York, 1960.

Tawney, R. H.: 'Religion and the Rise of Capitalism', new ed. Penguin Books, 1961.

Tennant, F. R.: 'Philosophical Theology', Cambridge University Press, 1930.

Tertullian: *'De Carne Christi'*, T. & T. Clark, Edinburgh, 1880.

Tillich, Paul: 'Dynamics of Faith', George Allen and Unwin, London, 1957.

Tishbi, I.: *'Mishnath Ha-Zohar'*, Vol. I, Jer. 1948, Vol. II, Jer., 1961.

Urbach, S. B.: 'Pillars of Jewish Thought' (Heb.), Jer., 1953.

Van Buren, Paul: 'The Secular Meaning of the Gospel', SCM Press, 1963.

Weatherhead, Leslie D.: 'Psychology, Religion and Healing', rev. ed., Hodder and Stoughton, London, 1955.

Weinberg, J. J.: *'Seride Esh'*, Vol. II, Mosad Ha-Rav Kook, Jer., 1962.

Weiss, I. H.: *'Dor Dor We-Doreshaw'*, Berlin, 1924.

Werblowsky, R. J. Zvi: 'Faith, Hope and Trust, A Study in the Concept of Bittahon' in 'Papers of The Institute of

Jewish Studies', London, ed. J. G. Weiss, Magnes Press, Hebrew University, Jer., 1964.

Wisdom, John: 'Gods' in 'Philosophy and Psycho-Analysis', Blackwell, Oxford, 1953.

Wolf, Arnold J.: ed. 'Rediscovering Judaism', Quadrangle Books, Chicago, 1965.

Wolfson, H. A.: 'Notes on Proofs of the Existence of God in Jewish Philosophy' in *Hebrew Union College Annual*, Vol. I, 1924, pp. 575-596.

Zaehner, R. C.: 'Mysticism Sacred and Profane', Clarendon Press, Oxford, 1957.

Zeitlin, Hillel: *'Ha-Tobh We-Ha-Ra'*, Warsaw, 1911.

Zewi Hirsch of Zhydatchov: *'Sur Me-Ra We-Aseh Tobh'*, Kether, no date.

Index

Index

INDEX